PRONOUNCING AMERICAN ENGLISH

Sounds, Stress, and Intonation

Gertrude F. Orion

Queensborough Community College
The City University of New York

HEINLE & HEINLE PUBLISHERS
A Division of Wadsworth, Inc.
Boston, Massachusetts 02116

Development Editor: Jean N. Dale
Text Design: Joyce C. Weston
Cover Design: Wanda Lubelska Design
Text Diagrams and Spot Art: Kathie Kelleher
Text Illustrations: Elisabeth Clark
Compositor: ComCom Division of Haddon Craftsmen, Inc.
Printing: McNaughton & Gunn, Inc.
Audio Tape Program: Phyllis Dolgin

Pronouncing American English: Sounds, Stress, and Intonation

Library of Congress Cataloging-in-Publication Data

Orion, Gertrude F.
    Pronouncing American English.

    1. English language—United States—Pronunciation.
2. English language—Pronunciation by foreign speakers.
3. English language—Text-books for foreign speakers.
I. Title.
PE2815.07 1988 421'.52 86-33223
ISBN 0-8384-2699-9

Printed in the U.S.A.   First Printing: October 1987
63 24412   12 13 14 15 16 17 18 19 20

To the Memory of My Parents

Acknowledgments

I am indebted to a number of individuals who helped in various ways with the preparation of this book: James W. Brown, for his much needed confidence and support; Jean N. Dale, for her valuable assistance in handling the special demands of this project, guiding it from manuscript stage to its present form; John Verrilli, for his careful help with revisions; the reviewers who read various parts of the manuscript and made valuable comments; and, to my students of many years who helped develop and refine the material in this book.

Gertrude F. Orion

Table of Contents

Guide to the Exercises

Introduction

Pronouncing American English: Sounds, Stress, and Intonation, is a pronunciation text for students of English as a second or foreign language. It is suitable for beginning level learners who are developing this skill, as well as intermediate and advanced students who wish to perfect it. Beginning students can learn "correct" pronunciation in the very early stages of speaking, while intermediate and advanced learners can improve their oral proficiency. The materials in this book have been classroom tested over a period of years and have proven to be both effective and enjoyable. They address the problems shared by speakers from various countries of the world who have large categories of speech difficulties in common. This text can be used in a classroom with the teacher modeling the material for the students, or with the tape cassettes in a language laboratory class, or with the tape cassettes by students working alone. A separate Answer Key is available for the convenience of teachers, and for students working independently.

ORGANIZATION OF TEXT

Parts 1 and 2

Pronouncing American English consists of four parts. **Part 1** presents an overview of the sounds of American English. It includes the problems encountered with English spelling as opposed to sounds; the use of a phonetic alphabet; the description of the articulators which help us produce sounds; and the rules governing voiced and voiceless sounds, length of sounds, and combined consonants.

Part 2 is divided into four sections: syllable stress, word stress, content words and function words, and intonation. "Syllable stress" refers to the syllable that is given primary stress in a word, while "word stress" refers to the word that is given stress in an utterance. This terminology proves to be more logical and understandable to students than "word stress" and "sentence stress," since students are taught to think in terms of which syllable is prominent in a word and which word or words are prominent in a phrase or sentence.

Only primary and weak stresses are discussed. Contrasts are made between the primary and weak stresses of syllables in words and the stressing and unstressing of words in phrases or sentences. The rationale is that if students learn this from the very beginning or if they succeed in changing old habits by concentrating on these two stresses, the other stress patterns will fall into place more easily and can be described and detailed extensively, if necessary, when the students are well advanced in their knowledge of the English language.

Syllabification indicating primary stress, in some instances, may not follow established practice. For example, in dictionaries, the words "annoy" and "suppose" are syllabized "an-noy" and "sup-pose," although the doubled letters, "n" and "p" respectively, indicate one sound. The basis for this appears to be that words are divided into syllables arbitrarily, based on historical precedence, and not on a phonetic one. In this text, for simplification purposes, doubled letters are syllabized phonetically and stress in such words is indicated as in "aNNOY," and "suPPOSE." Throughout the exercises, all words of more than one syllable have their primary stress indicated by capital letters.

Although there are several intonation patterns in American English, only two basic ones are covered here: rising intonation and falling intonation. Once again, if the student learns how to use them from the very beginning or succeeds in changing old habits by concentrating on these two intonation patterns, the others will fall into place more easily and can also be detailed extensively at a later date.

Parts 3 and 4

Parts 3 and **4** contain the vowel and consonant units, respectively. These units need not be taken in order but may be assigned according to individual or group need. However, before studying them it is vital that the students cover the materials in Parts 1 and 2 because these sections are the bases for a study of the vowel and consonant sections.

Each unit in **Parts 3** and **4** introduces either one or two sounds and their common and sometimes less common spellings in initial, medial and final positions, wherever applicable. Letters representing the target sound(s) in a given lesson are underlined. A key word for a given sound is included in each unit. Students should be encouraged to memorize this key word, or find one of their own, as a way to self-monitor and self-correct when doing the exercises. In addition, there is an illustration and description of how to produce each target sound. These illustrations and descriptions are teaching aids and are not scientifically exact diagrams or descriptions. They should be referred to when the student cannot produce the sound in a satisfactory manner through auditory stimulation.

The "Contrast" section of each lesson includes auditory discrimination exercises. For a variety of reasons it may be difficult for students to discriminate between particular sounds, especially in the context of a word. Even when they can, it does not necessarily follow that they will be able to produce them acceptably. In these exercises the student first listens and repeats, after the instructor or the tape voice, the target sound in isolation, first "normally," then in an exaggerated manner, then "normally" once again. The sound is then practiced in words. It is important to impress upon the students that we do not normally make sounds in an exaggerated manner but that this is merely a training exercise. Exaggerating the sound allows the student to "hear" it and to "feel" both the place of articulation and the movements of the articulators. It is one way of practicing the target sound and another method of self-monitoring and self-correcting. Also, students should be encouraged to use mirrors to help them see, wherever possible, the movements of those articulators that are easily visible.

In the "Check Your Listening" exercises, if students are listening to the classroom teacher rather than to the tapes, a good technique is for the students not to look at the instructor as the words are said. In this way they receive no visual clues and must rely solely on their auditory perception.

Some students will probably need more practice in auditory discrimination than others. When more is needed the instructor can review the "Contrast" exercises and, for variety, can use additional words from the lesson. It is important that students be successful in this aspect of the instruction before proceeding with the rest of the lesson.

Minimal paired words and sentences, under the heading "Practice the Contrast," are also part of each unit. The purpose of this exercise is to further help the students sharpen their auditory discrimination, heighten their awareness of the differences between sounds, and impress upon them that even small differences in pronunciation can indicate changes in meaning.

An exercise is regularly provided for students in a classroom situation to pair off and practice with each other. This offers them an opportunity to engage in a communicative activity among themselves and, in addition, affords them another form of repetition and practice. These exercises are identified by the symbol $\circlearrowright$.

At least one exercise in each unit of Parts 2, 3, and 4 is devoted specifically to stress and intonation. The sentences and dialogs emphasize affective meanings such as happiness, curiosity, surprise, annoyance, anger, humor, disappointment and many more.

Home assignments are varied and part of each unit; they help reinforce the materials covered. These are identified by the symbol ![]. The student is always directed to practice aloud, whatever the assignment is. These assignments can also be graded.

Theoretical explanations have been kept to a minimum throughout the text. The emphasis instead is on considerable oral practice. Listening and speaking are coordinated in each unit and students are encouraged to listen carefully as well as to speak. A great deal of practice and repetition is included and is desirable for students to get a feel for the rhythm and flow of American English.

The pronunciation described in this book is standard American which is spoken by the majority of educated people in the United States. It is the speech that is most often heard on radio and television.

There will always be some words the students do not know. They should be encouraged to look them up in a dictionary, whenever possible, to expand their vocabulary.

The symbols of the International Phonetic Alphabet are used, with modifications. These were made for purposes of simplification, especially for the vowel sounds; both vowels and diphthongs are classified as vowels.

The symbol ♥ indicates the exercises which have been recorded on cassettes. Pauses are long enough for the more proficient students to repeat the items twice.

The Audio Cassette program and complete Answer Key, which accompany this text, are designed to contribute to the effective use of this program.

To the Student

Acquiring good pronunciation is the most difficult part of learning a new language. As you improve your articulation you have to learn to listen and imitate all over again. You have to learn to make new movements with your tongue, lips, jaw, and other organs of articulation in order to make the new sounds and even old ones in a new way. You are developing a new skill.

We know there are certain movements that are important to the production of any given sound. For example, everyone's handwriting is different. The letter "f" can be written in various ways, *f*, *f*, *f*. However, we know that this letter has to have a certain form, otherwise we will not be able to recognize it and will have difficulty understanding the written word. So it is with pronunciation. If you don't shape the sound with the necessary movements, there may be difficulty in understanding the spoken word.

You may be able to produce some of the sounds by listening and imitating; for other sounds you may need to refer to the illustrations and descriptions given at the beginning of each vowel and consonant unit. In the beginning, it is usually difficult to "hear" yourself. When this happens you might find it beneficial to place the palms of your hands over your ears and then listen to yourself.

One can also compare speaking to playing the piano or singing a song. We can recognize the same piece of music played by two different pianists as well as the same song sung by two different singers. Even though each may play or sing in his own style, there are still certain notes that must be played or sung for us to recognize the tune as being the same. So it is with pronunciation. There are those necessary movements the speaker has to make for the production of any given sound and there are also certain "notes" the speaker must combine in order to give meaning to his or her words.

Some of you may be reluctant to speak because of your "foreign accent." Foreign accents can be very charming as long as the person speaking is able to communicate. So losing your foreign accent or trying to sound like a native American speaker is not the goal for which to reach. Everyone's handwriting is not exactly the same; neither is everyone's pronunciation. What we are aiming for is easily understandable conversational speech.

How do we achieve this? A concert pianist may practice a piece of music for two years, eight hours a day, and an opera singer may work just as long on an operatic role. The same holds true for a person learning to speak a new language. As with any activity you wish to do well, you have to practice, practice, practice, and then practice some more.

Remember that you cannot accomplish good pronunciation overnight. Improvement takes time. Some students may find it more difficult than others and will need more time than others to improve. However, with practice, you can reach your goal.

PART 1

An Overview: Sounds of American English

In the English language there is a difference between sounds and spelling. The influence of English spelling is so strong, however, that many speakers find it difficult to think in terms of sounds. Therefore, it is very important to get into the habit of listening to and thinking of the sounds in words.

There are some letters that represent more than one sound and some sounds that represent more than one letter. Since there is no simple relationship between sound and spelling and since the English language has more sounds than letters, a special *phonetic alphabet* is used. In this alphabet one phonetic symbol represents one sound. It includes some of the letters you already know and adds some new ones to represent additional sounds.

The organs of speech that help us form these sounds are called *articulators.* They include the lips, teeth, tongue, roof of the mouth, nose, jaw, and vocal cords.

The sounds of the language are divided into vowels and consonants. When the vocal cords vibrate, the sound is *voiced.* When the vocal cords do not vibrate, the sound is *voiceless.* All vowels are voiced, but consonants may be either voiced or voiceless. In addition, all vowels and some consonants can be held for a shorter or longer period of time, depending on which sound precedes or follows the sound.

The phonetic alphabet of American English consonant sounds is on pages 5 and 6, vowel sounds, on page 6.

UNIT
1

English Spelling
and English Sounds

1. THE SPELLING SYSTEM

The English spelling system is not easy to learn. It is confusing for both non-native speakers and native American speakers.

The English alphabet has twenty-six letters, but the letters represent more than twenty-six sounds. Some letters represent more than one sound. Some sounds are represented by more than one letter. The following exercises will help you understand some of the differences between English spelling and English sounds.

Listen and Repeat

A. Same Letter, Different Sounds

Each of these seven words has a different sound for the letter "a." Listen and repeat. *Capital letters indicate syllable stress.*

1. h<u>a</u>t	3. <u>a</u>ll	5. <u>a</u>rt	7. OR<u>a</u>nge
2. h<u>a</u>te[1]	4. <u>A</u>Ny	6. <u>a</u>BOVE	

Listen and repeat these three sounds for the letter "s."

1. <u>s</u>ee   2. <u>s</u>ure   3. VI<u>S</u>it

[1]The final "e" in words such as "hate," "ride," and "hope" signals the pronunciation of the preceding vowel. Compare "hat" /hæt/ with "hate" /heyt/. This final "e" signals the sounds /iy/, /ey/, /ay/, /ow/, and /uw/.

3

B. Same Sound, Different Letters

These words all have the same vowel sound, but it is spelled six different ways. Listen and repeat.

1. c<u>a</u>ke	3. st<u>ea</u>k	5. r<u>ai</u>n
2. th<u>ey</u>	4. w<u>eigh</u>	6. m<u>ay</u>

Listen and repeat these words with the consonant sound /f/ spelled four different ways.

1. <u>f</u>ell   2. stu<u>ff</u>   3. <u>ph</u>oto   4. tou<u>gh</u>

2. CHECK YOUR LISTENING

Sometimes a word has more letters than it has sounds. Other times, a word has more sounds than it has letters.

A. More Letters than Sounds

Count the number of letters in each of these words and write it down. Then say each word aloud. Write down the number of sounds you hear. (*Hint:* "th," "ou," and "au" represent one sound each; in these words "gh" is not pronounced.)

1. through   _____ letters   _____ sounds

2. though   _____ letters   _____ sounds

3. caught   _____ letters   _____ sounds

B. More Sounds than Letters

Write down the number of letters in each word. Then say each word aloud and write down the number of sounds. (*Hint:* "x" represents two sounds—/k/ and /s/.)

1. fix   _____ letters   _____ sounds

2. EXtra   _____ letters   _____ sounds

The influence of spelling on speaking is very strong. Many students remember the spelling of a word and then have trouble hearing and saying the correct sounds. Get into the habit of listening to the sounds of words.

---

3. THE PHONETIC ALPHABET

In English there is no simple relationship between spelling and sounds. As a result, people have invented different systems to represent English sounds. These systems use one letter or symbol for each sound. An alphabetic system with one symbol representing one sound is a *phonetic alphabet.*

The phonetic alphabet in this book includes most of the twenty-six letters of the alphabet, along with some new symbols. We write these phonetic letters and symbols between slash marks. For example, the symbols /k/ and /æ/ represent sounds, not letters. The sound /k/ is the first sound in the words "key" and "cat." The sound /æ/ is the second sound in "cat." Phonetically, the word "cat" is written /kæt/.

Remember: One phonetic symbol represents only one sound.

The following charts list the phonetic symbols for all the sounds of American English. The two sets of sounds are the consonants and the vowels. Most of these sounds occur in initial (beginning), medial (middle), and final (end) positions. There are examples for each sound. Memorize these key words. They will help you remember the sound for each phonetic symbol.

🔊 Listen and Repeat

A. Consonants

The symbols in this chart look like letters you already know. Listen and repeat.

Phonetic Symbol	Initial	Medial	Final
/p/	pen	opera	top
/b/	boy	about	rob
/t/	ten	after	sat
/d/	day	candy	mad
/k/	cat	cake	neck
/g/	go	again	egg
/f/	food	before	knife
/v/	voice	never	believe
/s/	see	lesson	bus
/z/	zoo	easy	choose
/m/	me	amount	come

Phonetic Symbol	Initial	Medial	Final
/n/	no	a<u>n</u>imal	soo<u>n</u>
/l/	<u>l</u>ike	a<u>l</u>ive	we<u>ll</u>
/r/	<u>r</u>ed	ve<u>r</u>y	doo<u>r</u>
/w/	<u>w</u>alk	a<u>w</u>ay	[2]
/y/	<u>y</u>es	can<u>y</u>on	[2]
/h/	<u>h</u>ouse	be<u>h</u>ind	[2]

The following symbols are not in the English alphabet. These consonant symbols are more difficult to remember. Listen and repeat.

/θ/	<u>th</u>in	any<u>th</u>ing	ba<u>th</u>
/ð/	<u>th</u>e	fa<u>th</u>er	ba<u>th</u>e
/ʃ/	<u>sh</u>e	ma<u>ch</u>ine	fi<u>sh</u>
/ʒ/	[3]	plea<u>s</u>ure	gara<u>ge</u>
/tʃ/	<u>ch</u>ild	tea<u>ch</u>er	spee<u>ch</u>
/dʒ/	<u>j</u>ob	wa<u>g</u>es	pa<u>ge</u>
/ŋ/	[3]	thi<u>n</u>king	ki<u>ng</u>

B. Vowels

Most American English vowels are combinations of sounds. You may need a lot of practice to say them correctly. Listen and repeat.

Phonetic Symbol	Initial	Medial	Final
/iy/	<u>ea</u>ch	rec<u>ei</u>ve	k<u>ey</u>
/ɪ/	<u>i</u>f	s<u>i</u>t	sunn<u>y</u>
/ey/	<u>a</u>ble	t<u>a</u>ke	p<u>ay</u>
/ɛ/	<u>e</u>gg	br<u>ea</u>d	[2]
/æ/	<u>a</u>pple	c<u>a</u>t	[2]
/uw/	<u>oo</u>ze	sh<u>oo</u>t	d<u>o</u>
/ʊ/	[3]	b<u>oo</u>k	[2]
/ow/	<u>ow</u>n	b<u>oa</u>t	n<u>o</u>
/ɔ/	<u>a</u>ll	b<u>a</u>ll	l<u>aw</u>
/ɔy/	<u>oi</u>l	n<u>oi</u>se	b<u>oy</u>
/a/	<u>a</u>rmy	n<u>o</u>t	M<u>a</u>
/ay/	<u>i</u>ce	b<u>i</u>te	t<u>ie</u>
/aw/	<u>ou</u>t	h<u>ou</u>se	n<u>ow</u>
/ə/	<u>u</u>p	c<u>u</u>t	sod<u>a</u>
/ər/	<u>ear</u>n	g<u>ir</u>l	si<u>r</u>

[2]This sound does not occur in final position.
[3]This sound does not occur in initial position.

⻔ 4. HOME ASSIGNMENT

A. Write down the number of letters and sounds in each word. (The vowel letters "au," "ou," "ei," and "ie" and the consonant letters "th" are each counted as one sound.) Remember to say the words aloud.

Examples:		Letters	Sounds
	a. dumb	4	3
	b. cough	5	3
	1. take	____	____
	2. rough	____	____
	3. hour	____	____
	4. food	____	____
	5. she	____	____
	6. mix	____	____
	7. fight	____	____
	8. bath	____	____
	9. thought	____	____
	10. buy	____	____

B. Match these phonetic symbols with the words in which they appear.

Example:	1.	_c_ /f/	a. house
	2.	____ /iy/	b. child
	3.	____ /h/	c. knife
	4.	____ /ð/	d. come
	5.	____ /ɔ/	e. key
	6.	____ /tʃ/	f. ball
	7.	____ /m/	g. king
	8.	____ /ŋ/	h. the

UNIT	# The Speech Mechanism
2	

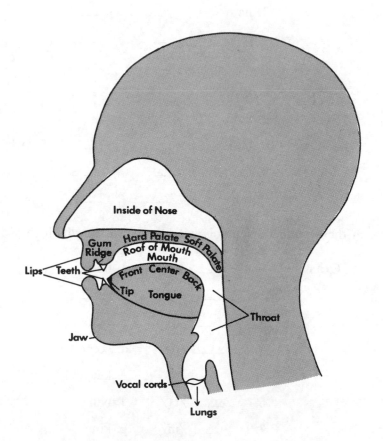

Inside of Nose

Hard Palate — Soft Palate

Gum Ridge

Root of Mouth
Mouth

Lips — Teeth

Front Center Back

Tip Tongue

Throat

Jaw

Vocal cords

Lungs

1. ARTICULATORS

The figure on page 8 shows the parts of the body that help us make sounds. These are called *articulators* or *speech organs.* They include:

lips	tongue	nose
teeth	roof of the mouth	vocal cords
jaw		

These articulators, along with the breath that comes from the lungs, work together to produce sounds. You will practice articulation in more detail in Part 3 (Vowels) and Part 4 (Consonants).

2. IDENTIFY YOUR SPEECH ORGANS

The tongue has four parts: the tip, front, center, and back. The roof of the mouth has three parts: the gum ridge, the hard palate, and the soft palate.

- Place your tongue tip in back of your upper front teeth. Do you feel a hard surface? This is your upper gum ridge.
- Now move your tongue further back. The roof of the mouth is still hard. You are now touching your hard palate.
- Move your tongue still further back. You will begin to feel a soft surface —your soft palate.

Your upper jaw does not move, but your lower jaw moves down and up. Together with your lower lip it opens and closes your mouth. Try opening and closing your mouth. You should feel your lower jaw and lip moving.

3. VOICED AND VOICELESS SOUNDS

- Place two fingers on your throat and say the sound /s/.
- Now say the sound /z/. Do you feel a difference? When you say /z/, you should feel a vibration of the vocal cords. You should not feel any vibration when you say /s/.
- Try it again with the sounds /f/ and /v/. Remember, do not say the name of the letters. Say the sounds for the symbols.

The sounds /z/ and /v/ are *voiced sounds.* Pronounce voiced sounds, and your vocal cords will vibrate. Pronounce *voiceless sounds,* like /s/ and /f/, and your vocal cords will not vibrate.

There are two groups of sounds in English: vowels and consonants.

- All vowels are voiced.
- All consonants are either voiced or voiceless.

It is very important to notice the difference between voiced and voiceless sounds. The difference between them can make a difference in the meaning of a word.

🎧 Listen and Repeat

A. The following chart lists all voiced and voiceless consonants and their key words. Listen and repeat.

CONSONANTS

	Voiced		Voiceless	
Paired	/ b /	boy	/ p /	pen
	/ d /	day	/ t /	ten
	/ g /	go	/ k /	cat
	/ v /	voice	/ f /	food
	/ z /	zoo	/ s /	see
	/ ð /	the	/ θ /	thin
	/ ʒ /	pleasure	/ ʃ /	she
	/ dʒ /	job	/ tʃ /	child
Not Paired	/ l /	like	/ h /	house
	/ r /	red		
	/ w /	walk		
	/ y /	yes		
	/ m /	me		
	/ n /	no		
	/ ŋ /	king		

B. These pairs of words begin with voiced and voiceless sounds. Listen and repeat.

1.	<u>B</u>en	<u>p</u>en	5.	<u>th</u>y	<u>th</u>igh
2.	<u>d</u>o	<u>t</u>oo	6.	<u>z</u>oo	<u>S</u>ue
3.	<u>g</u>old	<u>c</u>old	7.	<u>j</u>eep	<u>ch</u>eap
4.	<u>v</u>ine	<u>f</u>ine			

4. FIVE BASIC VOWELS

The positions of the jaw, lips, and tongue are very important when you pronounce vowels. Say the sound /iy/ as in "s<u>ee</u>." Then say /a/, as in "n<u>o</u>t." Repeat the sounds: /iy. . .a/, /iy. . .a/. You should feel your lips and tongue move and your jaw drop lower, then rise again as you go from one sound to the other. Use a mirror to watch your mouth produce the sounds. Can you feel your vocal cords vibrate?

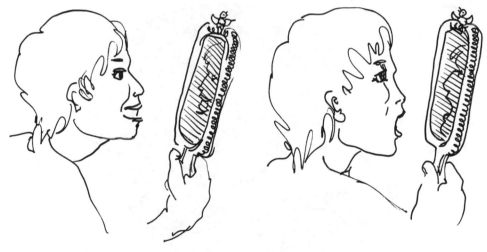

There are five basic vowel sounds in English. They are similar to vowel sounds in other languages. English speakers hold the sounds longer.

/iy/   /ey/   /a/   /ow/   /uw/

🔊 Listen and Repeat

A. Listen and repeat these sounds and words. Concentrate on the position of the tongue, jaw, and lips.

1. /iy/	s<u>ee</u>	/iy/	(front of tongue high, lips spread)
2. /ey/	s<u>ay</u>	/ey/	(front of tongue lower, lips less spread)
3. /a/	n<u>o</u>t	/a/	(front and back of tongue low, lips open wide)
4. /ow/	s<u>o</u>	/ow/	(back of tongue high, lips rounded)
5. /uw/	S<u>ue</u>	/uw/	(back of tongue higher, lips more rounded)

B. These vowel sounds can be illustrated on a triangle. The line of the triangle represents the position of the tongue. The front of the tongue is high for /iy/, the center of the tongue is low for /a/, and the back of the tongue is high for /uw/.

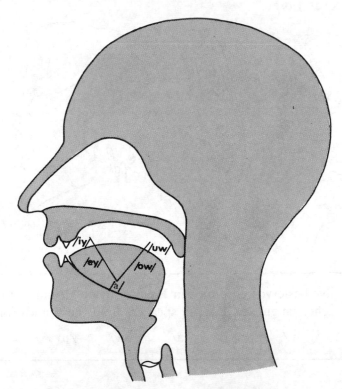

🐎 5. HOME ASSIGNMENT

A. Are the first sounds in these words (represented by the underlined letters) voiced or voiceless? Use the chart on page 10 to help you. Write V (voiced) or VL (voiceless) on the line after each word. Check yourself by placing your fingers on your throat and saying each word. Do you feel any vibration when you make the *first* sound? *Capital letters indicate syllable stress.*

1. <u>b</u>ig	____	7. <u>V</u>ERy	____
2. <u>p</u>ig	____	8. <u>h</u>eLLO	____
3. <u>M</u>ONey	____	9. <u>d</u>ish	____
4. <u>th</u>is	____	10. <u>W</u>Ater	____
5. <u>C</u>ARRy	____	11. <u>t</u>ell	____
6. <u>g</u>irl	____	12. <u>S</u>UGar	____

B. When you say these words, which of the five basic vowel sounds do you hear? Refer to the chart on page 12. Write /iy/, /ey/, /a/, /ow/, or /uw/ on the line after each word.

1. m<u>ay</u>	____	7. n<u>a</u>me	____
2. s<u>oo</u>n	____	8. h<u>o</u>t	____
3. k<u>ey</u>	____	9. w<u>a</u>tch	____
4. g<u>o</u>	____	10. fr<u>o</u>g	____
5. s<u>ou</u>p	____	11. l<u>a</u>te	____
6. s<u>oa</u>p	____	12. w<u>e</u>	____

<table>
<tr><td>UNIT
3</td><td># Long and Short Sounds</td></tr>
</table>

1. LONG VOWELS IN WORDS

English speakers hold vowel sounds longer in some words than in others. Say the words "made" and "mate." Hold the vowel sound /ey/ longer in "made" than in "mate." Say the following pairs of words. The same vowel sound is held longer in the first word than in the second.

1. cab	cap	3. bag	back
2. save	safe	4. prize	price

The longer vowel sounds are followed by the voiced consonant sounds /b, v, g, z/. The shorter vowels are followed by the voiceless consonants /p, f, k, s/.

> Hold a vowel sound longer before a voiced consonant than before a voiceless consonant. Listen for the difference in the length of the vowel sound to help you identify the word.

🎧 Listen and Repeat

In these pairs of words, hold the vowel sound longer in the first word than in the second. Listen and repeat.

1. eyes	ice	4. played	plate	7. leave	leaf
2. save	safe	5. lied	light	8. pig	pick
3. rode	wrote	6. rib	rip	9. cub	cup

2. LONG VOWELS IN SENTENCES

Say the sentences.

- Let's g<u>o</u>.
- Let's g<u>o</u> home.

The vowel sound in "g<u>o</u>" is held longer in the first sentence than in the second. Say the sentences.

- It's the l<u>aw</u>.
- The l<u>aw</u> passed.

The vowel sound in "l<u>aw</u>" is held longer in the first sentence.

> Hold a vowel sound longer when it appears at the end of a sentence.

Listen and Repeat

In these pairs of sentences, the underlined letters stand for a vowel sound. The vowel is held longer in the first sentence than in the second. Listen and repeat.

1. a. We should g<u>o</u>.
   b. We should g<u>o</u> LATer.

2. a. He's going to fl<u>y</u>.
   b. He's going to fl<u>y</u> to TEXas.

3. a. How well can you s<u>ee</u>?
   b. How well can you s<u>ee</u> that sign?

4. a. Please hand me that tr<u>ay</u>.
   b. Please hand me that tr<u>ay</u> from the shelf.

5. a. Where in the world is my sh<u>oe</u>?
   b. Where in the world is my sh<u>oe</u> with the black strap?

3. CONSONANTS AT THE END OF SENTENCES

Say these two sentences:

1. I like the pri<u>z</u>e.

2. I like the pri<u>c</u>e.

Hold the /s/ in "pri<u>c</u>e" longer than the /z/ in "pri<u>z</u>e." This makes it easier for the listener to understand which word was said.

> Hold final voiceless consonant sounds longer than final voiced consonant sounds. Exceptions: voiceless /p, t, k/ and voiced /b, d, g/, which cannot be held.

🎧 Listen and Repeat

A. In these pairs of sentences, the underlined consonant sound is held longer in the second sentence than in the first. Listen and repeat.

1. a. That's li<u>v</u>e.   3. a. It's Mar<u>g</u>e.
   b. That's li<u>f</u>e.   b. It's Mar<u>ch</u>.

2. a. Is it the play<u>s</u>?   4. a. It's my ba<u>dg</u>e.
   b. Is it the pla<u>c</u>e?   b. It's my ba<u>tch</u>.

B. Work with a partner. Say sentence a or b at random. Your partner must identify the correct sentence and repeat it. Can you say and hear the differences in the length of the vowel sounds?

4. COMBINED CONSONANTS

Sometimes a final consonant sound is followed by a word that begins with the same sound. Say this sentence: "My cab broke down." The /b/ at the end of "cab" and the /b/ at the beginning of "broke" are not said separately. The sounds are combined to form one long sound.

Listen and Repeat

The following sentences include combined consonant sounds. Note that the combined consonants are marked by a curved line. Listen and repeat.

1. Keep peace in the house.

2. My friend did it.

3. He did it the first time.

4. The desk came.

5. A big game was played.

6. The thief fled.

7. I have VERy good friends.

8. My boss sent me.

9. It's an ENglish ship.

10. Bathe the child.

11. Come more OFten.

12. I can NEVer go.

13. A doll lay on the floor.

14. Go to the far right.

15. Wear a fresh shirt.

🏃 5. HOME ASSIGNMENT

A. In these pairs of sentences, the underlined letters stand for similar vowel sounds. Which sentence, "a" or "b", has the longer vowel sound? Explain why.

        1a. He r<u>o</u>de it.
           b. He wr<u>o</u>te it.

        2a. She's READy to b<u>uy</u>.
           b. She's READy to b<u>uy</u> the ring.

        3a. We got our pr<u>i</u>ce.
           b. We got our pr<u>i</u>ze.

        4a. The s<u>ur</u>ge began.
           b. The s<u>ear</u>ch began.

        5a. It's time for us to g<u>o</u> to the store.
           b. It's time for us to g<u>o</u>.

B. Compare your answers with a partner. Check the rules about length of vowels in this unit.

PART 2 Stress and Intonation

Every language has a system of sounds, stress, and intonation that gives it a rhythm and melody all its own. You may be able to pronounce each sound of a language correctly, but you must also use correct stress and intonation patterns.

Stress refers to the degree of force or loudness. It indicates the importance of a syllable (a part of a word), and the importance of certain words in phrases and sentences. *Intonation* refers to the various tones of the voice. By using different tones, the speaker gives meaning and expression to the words he says. The tones may be low or high (pitch); they may be rising or falling. Speaking can be compared to singing. Stress provides the rhythm, and intonation provides the melody.

Stress and intonation are made up of more than just two things. They are a combination of many parts. When you are speaking, these parts cannot be separated. But in order to understand them better, you will study them separately. It is important, however, to remember that these parts all go together. In normal conversation one cannot really exist without the other.

<table>
<tr><td>UNIT
4</td><td></td></tr>
</table>

Syllable Stress

1. IDENTIFYING SYLLABLES

A syllable is part of a word that contains one vowel sound; it may also contain one or more consonant sounds. In general, the number of vowel sounds in the word determines the number of syllables.

You can think of syllables as the number of "beats" in a word. For example, say the word "jump" while you tap your desk (or clap your hands) once. "Jump" has one syllable: a vowel sound and three consonant sounds. Now say "magic" while you tap your desk twice, once for each syllable. "Magic" has two vowel sounds. Now tap your desk for each vowel sound in "tomato." How many syllables did you hear? "Tomato" has three syllables and three vowel sounds.

🎧 Listen and Repeat

Practice these words of one, two, and three or more syllables. The letters for the vowel sound in each syllable are underlined. Listen and repeat.

1. One Syllable

   <u>a</u>   <u>a</u>ll   c<u>u</u>p   m<u>a</u>n   c<u>a</u>ke   ch<u>ee</u>se   b<u>e</u>   cr<u>y</u>

2. Two Syllables

   <u>a</u>n-sw<u>er</u>   st<u>u</u>-d<u>e</u>nt   <u>a</u>-fr<u>ai</u>d   d<u>e</u>-gr<u>ee</u>

3. Three or More Syllables

   r<u>a</u>-d<u>i</u>-<u>o</u>   p<u>o</u>-t<u>a</u>-t<u>o</u>   d<u>e</u>-p<u>a</u>rt-m<u>e</u>nt
   d<u>i</u>s-c<u>o</u>v-<u>er</u>-<u>y</u>   v<u>o</u>-c<u>a</u>b-<u>u</u>-l<u>a</u>r-<u>y</u>

🎧 2. CHECK YOUR LISTENING

Listen to each of these words and write down the number of syllables.

1. sister	_____	7. over _____
2. introduction	_____	8. anybody _____
3. this	_____	9. good-bye _____
4. there	_____	10. phone _____
5. professor	_____	11. television _____
6. homework	_____	12. practice _____

3. SYLLABLE STRESS

In every word of two or more syllables, one syllable has more force, is on a higher pitch, and is longer than the others. This pattern is called *syllable stress.* Each word has one *stressed syllable;* the others are *unstressed* or *weak syllables.*

Say the two-syllable word "afraid" while you tap out the syllables. Do you hear the stress in the second syllable? (a-FRAID) Now say "radio." Stress the first syllable: RA-di-o. Say the five-syllable word "vocabulary" and tap out the syllables. Which syllable did you stress? The second syllable is stressed: vo-CAB-u-lar-y.

This pattern of stressed and unstressed syllables is characteristic of American English. In some other languages (Spanish, for example), most syllables receive equal stress. In English this stressing and unstressing creates contrasts between strong and weak syllables, and it results in higher and lower pitches. These contrasts contribute to the rhythm of English.

Making the correct syllable stress in a word creates a rhythm that directly affects the pronunciation of that word and its comprehension. Syllable stress in a word does not change. Each word has its own stress pattern.

Listen and Repeat

A. The following words have one or more syllables. Tap out the rhythm of the words while you say them with the proper stress. *Note: In words of more than one syllable, the stressed syllable is indicated by capital letters. Letters for the vowel sound in each syllable are underlined.*

1. One Syllable
Each word has one beat. Listen and repeat.

   am   make   have   like   slow   do   thought

2. Two Syllables
Each word has two beats, but only one syllable gets the stress.

   TEACH-er   AL-ways   a-LONE   ma-CHINE

3. Three Syllables
Each word has three beats, but only one syllable gets the stress.

   MED-i-cine   dis-COV-er   un-der-STAND

4. Four Syllables
Each word has four beats, but only one syllable gets the stress.

   CAL-cu-la-tor   de-MOC-ra-cy
   math-e-MAT-ics   mis-un-der-STOOD

5. Five and Six Syllables
Each word has either five or six beats, but only one syllable gets the stress.

   vo-CAB-u-lar-y   li-a-BIL-i-ty   ex-am-i-NA-tion
   rev-o-LU-tion-ar-y   bac-ter-i-OL-o-gist

B. Practice syllable stress. Tap out the rhythm of the following words and say them with the correct stress. *Remember that capital letters indicate syllable stress.*

1. Two-Syllable Words

   a. STRESS ON FIRST SYLLABLE
   1. AR-my   6. DEN-tist
   2. AU-to   7. EL-bow
   3. AR-gue   8. FE-male
   4. BA-by   9. PLAS-tic
   5. CAN-dy   10. WIN-dow

   b. STRESS ON SECOND SYLLABLE
   1. cam-PAIGN   6. in-SPECT
   2. gui-TAR   7. in-STEAD
   3. re-MAIN   8. in-STRUCT
   4. in-CLUDE   9. in-VITE
   5. im-PROVE   10. mis-TAKE

2. Three-Syllable Words

   a. STRESS ON FIRST SYLLABLE
   1. AC-ci-dent   4. DAN-ger-ous
   2. AV-e-nue   5. COM-pa-ny
   3. CIT-i-zen

   b. STRESS ON SECOND SYLLABLE
   1. a-NOTH-er   4. me-CHAN-ic
   2. de-POS-it   5. pro-FESS-or
   3. lo-CA-tion

   c. STRESS ON THIRD SYLLABLE
   1. dis-a-PPOINT   4. per-so-NNEL
   2. guar-an-TEE   5. un-a-FRAID
   3. in-tro-DUCE

3. Four-Syllable Words

   a. STRESS ON FIRST SYLLABLE
   1. CER-e-mon-y   4. SAN-i-tar-y
   2. LIT-er-a-ture 5. TEM-po-rar-y
   3. NEC-e-ssar-y

b. STRESS ON SECOND SYLLABLE

1. a-RITH-me-tic
2. e-MER-gen-cy
3. ex-PER-i-ence
4. psy-CHOL-o-gy
5. se-CUR-i-ty

c. STRESS ON THIRD SYLLABLE

1. e-co-NOM-ics
2. con-ver-SA-tion
3. ed-u-CA-tion
4. grad-u-A-tion
5. in-for-MA-tion

4. Five- and Six-Syllable Words

1. i-MME-di-ate-ly
2. re-FRIG-er-a-tor
3. e-lec-TRIC-i-ty
4. in-di-VID-u-al
5. pro-nun-ci-A-tion
6. al-pha-BET-i-cal
7. ge-o-GRAPH-i-cal
8. sat-is-FAC-tor-y
9. en-cy-clo-PE-di-a
10. re-spon-si-BIL-i-ty

4. CHECK YOUR LISTENING

A. Listen to the following list of words. Circle the stressed syllable in each word.

Example: by

1. teacher
2. machine
3. understand
4. guitar
5. company
6. conversation
7. vocabulary
8. education

B. Work with a partner and compare your answers. Say each word while you tap your desk for each beat.

5. VOWELS IN UNSTRESSED SYLLABLES

In many words of two or more syllables, the unstressed vowel sounds are /ə/ as in "<u>u</u>p" and /ɪ/ as in "<u>i</u>t." Because of the large number of unstressed syllables in English, /ə/ is the most common vowel sound in the language.

🎧 **Listen and Repeat**

The following words contain /ə/ or /ɪ/ in the unstressed syllables. Letters for these sounds are marked. Capital letters indicate syllable stress. Listen and repeat.

A. Two-syllable words with the unstressed vowel in the second syllable

1. CHILdren   They're my CHILdren.
2. BAGGage   It's my BAGGage.
3. CARpet   It's my CARpet.
4. FAmous   She's FAmous.
5. HUSband   See her HUSband.
6. POStage   Put on POStage.
7. PRIvate   It's PRIvate.
8. SALad   Make a SALad.
9. STOMach   My STOMach hurts.
10. TICKet   My TICKet is lost.

B. Two-syllable words with the unstressed vowel in the first syllable

1. aSLEEP   He's aSLEEP now.
2. comPARE   Don't comPARE it.
3. coNNECT   Don't coNNECT it.
4. poLITE   Be poLITE.
5. subTRACT   Don't subTRACT.
6. sucCESS   I wish you sucCESS.
7. suPPOSE   I suPPOSE so.
8. eRASE   Don't eRASE it.
9. toDAY   Go toDAY.
10. toNIGHT   Go toNIGHT.

C. Three-syllable words with unstressed vowels

1. anTENNaə̀   My anTENNa.
2. AStrənaut   An AStronaut.
3. emBARRass   Don't emBARRass me.
4. paJAmas   My paJAmas.
5. MARgarine   Use MARgarine.
6. MESSages   ANy MESSages?
7. SENtences   Two SENtences.
8. treMENdous   It's treMENdous.
9. SYLLable   One SYLLable.
10. SYMpathy   My SYMpathy.

6. HOME ASSIGNMENT

A. Say each word aloud several times.

1. Write the number of syllables for each word on the line next to the word.
2. Circle the stressed syllable in each word. You may use a dictionary to check any new words.

	Word	Syllables
Examples:	a. (au)dience	3
	b. pre (scrip) tion	3

	Word	Syllables		Word	Syllables
1.	brother	____	6.	manager	____
2.	remember	____	7.	animal	____
3.	president	____	8.	biology	____
4.	awake	____	9.	agency	____
5.	already	____	10.	occupation	____

B. Work with a partner. Say the words in the list above in random order. Your partner must tell you the number of syllables in the word. After you have both worked through the list, choose other words from this unit to say. Your partner will again tell you the number of syllables in each word.

Word Stress

1. WORD STRESS IN PHRASES AND SENTENCES

In Unit 4 you practiced syllable stress in words. In this unit you will practice *word stress* in phrases and sentences.

Word stress means:

- Stressing the important words in a sentence.
- Saying them with more force than other words.
- Holding them longer and saying them at a higher pitch.

Word stress is very important. It gives meaning to the words you say.

Listen

Listen to the following sentences. They contain both syllable stress and word stress. *Capital letters indicate stressed syllables. The stress mark (´) indicates stressed words.*

1. The CHILdren are in the párk.

2. Our cláss went to the muSEum.

3. I think the tráin is in the STAtion.

4. Most of the STUdents are out of cláss now.

2. PHRASES AND LINKING

Native speakers do not pronounce words one at a time. Instead, they join words together to make a phrase. They say the words in the phrase smoothly, without stopping after each word. This joining of words is called *linking*. Each phrase of linked words has one main idea and one strong word stress.

Listen and Repeat

Each phrase or short sentence in the first column has one stressed word. Each word in the second column has one stressed syllable. Compare them and notice that the phrases and words both have the same number of beats (third column).

Listen and repeat the phrases and words. Listen for stress and the linking of words. *A stress mark (′) indicates word stress and capital letters indicate syllable stress.*

	Phrase or Sentence	Word	Number of Beats
1a.	He's nice.	adVICE	2
b.	On ice.	adVICE	2
2a.	Do it.	DENtist	2
b.	Near it.	DENtist	2
3a.	I don't care.	disaPPEAR	3
b.	On my chair.	disaPPEAR	3
4a.	Don't say it.	meCHANic	3
b.	I like him.	meCHANic	3
5a.	You can take it.	eduCAtion	4
b.	It was made here.	eduCAtion	4

🎧 3. CHECK YOUR LISTENING

You will hear some phrases and short sentences. Each phrase or sentence has one strong word stress. Listen carefully. Mark the word stress with a stress mark.

Example: On the hîll.

1. On the floor.	6. Move it.
2. Up there.	7. On your toes.
3. Did you go?	8. I like it.
4. What time is it?	9. I'm cold.
5. Don't break it.	10. You can't stay here.

🎧 4. WORD STRESS IN SENTENCES

Speakers of English join words together to make a phrase. They also join phrases together to make a sentence. Listen to the following sentences. The connecting lines indicate phrases.

The CHILdren are in the párk.

You can go to the párk and see the CHILdren in the PLAYground.

Notice that there is one stressed word for each phrase. The stressed words are the most important words in the sentence.

Notice the contrast between stressed and unstressed words and between stressed and unstressed syllables. These contrasts are important to the rhythm of spoken English.

---

5. VARIATIONS IN WORD STRESS

There is more than one way to say a sentence. You can stress different words, depending on what you want to say. For example, listen to these two sentences. They look the same, but the word stress is different.

He went to the muSEum YESterday.   (Emphasis is on <u>where</u> he went.)

He went to the muSEum YESterday.   (Emphasis is on <u>when</u> he went.)

Note: one word can be a phrase—usually for emphasis.

> Remember, there is often more than one way to use word stress in a sentence. Stress the words that are most important to your meaning.

6. PAUSES

You should not pause after every phrase in a sentence, but you should pause after long phrases and at the end of a sentence. In written English, commas and periods indicate pauses. Pauses (along with stress) are important for meaning.

Listen

Listen to these pairs of sentences. Notice how their meanings are different.

1a. The SECretary said, "The boss was late."   (Who was late, the boss or the secretary?)
  b. "The SECretary," said the boss, "was late."   (Who was late?)

2a. We're GOing to eat John.

b. We're GOing to eat, John.

Listen and Repeat

Listen and repeat these sentences. Pay attention to word stress, linking of words, and pauses. *Stress marks indicate word stress, and connecting lines indicate phrases.*

1. MaRIE and Paul are at the muSEum.

2. MaRIE and Paul went to the muSEum YESterday.

3. MaRIE, have you seen the PAINTings by PiCASSo?

4. I'm not INterested in GOing.

5. Will you spend the afterNOON with me?

6. We can go for a long walk by the lake.

7. It's a BEAUtiful day to be outDOORS, ISn't it?

8. I've been inSIDE all week, and I need some fresh air and EXercise.

7. CHECK YOUR LISTENING

Listen to each of these sentences twice. First, mark word stress with a stress mark. Then mark phrases with connecting lines. Listen for linking of words. *Capital letters indicate syllable stress.*

Example: We saw his PAINTings in the GALLery.

1. MaRIE and I enJOYED the exHIBit VERy much.

2. We plan to go back next week.

3. Do you want to come with us?

4. We'll be deLIGHTed to have you.

5. The CHILdren are aWAY this week.

6. They're VISiting their GRANDparents.

7. We're enJOYing the free time.

8. But they'll be back in aBOUT two weeks.

8. HOME ASSIGNMENT

A. Write five sentences about your activities this week. Mark the stressed syllable in words with more than one syllable by capitalizing the letters. Mark word stress with a stress mark. Stress the words that are most important to your meaning. Mark phrases with curved lines.

B. Work with a partner. Ask him or her to read your sentences aloud and to explain the meaning of the sentence. Did your stress marks make your meaning clear?

Content Words and Function Words

UNIT 6

1. CONTENT AND FUNCTION

The most important words in a sentence receive the stress. These important words are usually nouns, verbs, adjectives, and adverbs. They are called *content words,* because they express the main idea or content of the phrase or sentence. Less important words are articles, pronouns, prepositions, auxiliary verbs, and conjunctions. They are called *function words.* They connect the content words to form grammatical sentences. *Capital letters indicate syllable stress.*
Here are some examples:

1. Content Words
   Nouns: MaRIE, book, PENcil, chair, BOOKcase
   Verbs: run, teach, speak, reMIND, aPOLogize
   Adjectives: sick, SIMple, green, hot, HAPPy
   Adverbs: REALLy, CERtainly, ALmost, SLOWly, toDAY
2. Function Words
   Articles: a, an, the
   Pronouns: you, your, she, he, our
   Prepositions: for, of, to, at, INto
   Auxiliary Verbs: am, can, have, were, was, had
   Conjunctions: and, as, or, but, it

In Unit 4 you practiced vowel sounds in unstressed syllables. For example, the sound /ə/ as in "<u>u</u>p" often occurs in words of two or more syllables.

/ə/   /ə/ /ə/
FAm<u>ou</u>s   paJAm<u>a</u>s

The same sound also occurs in function words. But it occurs only when the word is unstressed. Thus many function words have two pronunciations: a stressed form and an unstressed form. The unstressed form is called the *reduced form.* This is because the vowel sound is "reduced" or cut down to an unstressed form.

Use the stressed form

- when you say the word by itself.
- when the function word is important to the meaning of the sentence.

🎤 2. STRESSED AND UNSTRESSED FUNCTION WORDS

Listen to these examples of stressed and unstressed function words. Function words in unstressed form have a line through the word.

You cán go ~~to~~ ~~the~~ párk.　("can" is stressed; "to" and "the" are unstressed)　=　You are physically able or have permission to go to the park.

You ~~can~~ gó ~~to~~ ~~the~~ párk.　("can" is now unstressed)　=　The park is one place you can go.

🎤 Listen and Repeat

A. Listen and repeat the following words and sentences. First you will hear the function word alone. This is its stressed form. Then you will hear a sentence with the unstressed form of the word.

	Stressed Form		Unstressed Form	
1. a	/ey/		/ə/	Do you want a good book?
2. an	/æn/		/ən/	Have an ORange.
		or	/ˈn/	
3. and	/ænd/		/ənd/, /ˈnd/	We saw Jack and Jill.
		or	/ˈn/	
4. are	/ar/		/ər/	MARy and June are SISters.
5. as	/æz/		/əz/	You're as sweet as SUGar.
6. beCAUSE	/bɪkɔz/		/bɪkəz/	I like it beCAUSE it's nice.
7. can	/kæn/		/kən/	I can do it.
8. for	/fɔr/		/fər/	Is this for me?

9. fr<u>o</u>m	/fram/		/frəm/	This is ~~from~~ my BROTHer.
10. h<u>a</u>d	/hæd/		/həd/	He ~~had~~ been there.
11. h<u>a</u>s	/hæz/		/həz/	~~Has~~ it rained LATEly?
		or	/əz/	
12. h<u>a</u>ve	/hæv/		/həv/	We should ~~have~~ WAITed
		or	/əv/	LONGer.
13. <u>o</u>f	/av/		/əv/	I'm THINKing ~~of~~ you.
14. <u>o</u>r	/ɔr/		/ər/	I want three ~~or~~ four.
15. th<u>a</u>t	/ðæt/		/ðət/	It's the one ~~that~~ got aWAY.
16. th<u>a</u>n	/ðæn/		/ðən/	It's NICer ~~than~~ yours.
17. t<u>o</u>	/tuw/		/tə/	Go ~~to~~ school.
18. w<u>a</u>s	/waz/		/wəz/	It ~~was~~ good.

B. You will hear the same sentence twice. The first time, the sentence will include the unstressed form of a function word. The second time, the sentence will include the stressed form. Notice the change in the meaning of the sentence. *Capital letters indicate syllable stress.* Listen and repeat.

1a. /ˈn/   We saw Jack ~~and~~ Jill.   (We saw both Jack and Jill.)

b. /ænd/   We saw Jack and´ Jill.   (Jill was there too, but we didn't expect to see her.)

2a. /ər/   MARy ~~and~~ June ~~are~~ SISters.   (They are sisters. Simple information.)

b. /ar/   MARy ~~and~~ June are´ SISters.   (They are sisters, but we thought they weren't.)

3a. /wəz/   It ~~was~~ good.   (It was good. Simple statement of opinion.)

b. /waz/   It was´ good.   (It was good, but I was surprised about it.)

4a. /kən/   I ~~can~~ do it.   (I am able to do it. Simple statement of fact.)

b. /kæn/   I can´ do it.   (Of course I can do it. Did you think I couldn't?)

5a. /həd/   He h̶a̶d̶ been there.   (He was there at an earlier time.)

  b. /hǽd/   He hád been there.   (It was a surprise to learn that

he was there at an earlier time.)

The meaning could be an

accusation. (You told me he

hadn't been there, but that

wasn't true.)

🎧 3. CHECK YOUR LISTENING

You will hear each of the following sentences twice. Draw a line through unstressed function words. Put a stress mark above stressed function words.

1. I think Tom and Lee went home.

2. The PARty was fun.

3. You can pass the test.

4. We have been here all day.

5. Yes, we are COMing home now.

🎧 4. FUNCTION WORDS IN PHRASES AND SENTENCES

In the following exercises you will practice the reduced form of function words. Link the function word with the other words of the phrase and say the phrase with a smooth rhythm. *Remember, capital letters indicate syllable stress, and stress marks indicate word stress.*

A. Articles: <u>a</u>, <u>an</u>, <u>the</u>

1. Pronounce the word "a" as /ə/ before words beginning with a consonant. Listen and repeat.

  1. a drínk   Have a drínk.

  2. a NÚMber   Take a NÚMber.

  3. a MÓVie   See a MÓVie.

  4. a good MÓVie   See a good MÓVie.

2. Pronounce the word "an" as /ən/ before words beginning with a vowel sound. Listen and repeat.

1. ~~an~~ AÚto   Buy ~~an~~ AÚto.
2. ~~an~~ égg   Boil ~~an~~ égg.
3. ~~an~~ OFFice   He has ~~an~~ OFFice.
4. ~~an~~ old mán   He's ~~an~~ old mán.

3. Pronounce the word "the" as /ðə/ before words beginning with consonants. Listen and repeat.

1. ~~the~~ máp   Get ~~the~~ máp.
2. ~~the~~ cláss   Take ~~the~~ cláss.
3. ~~the~~ bóy   Meet ~~the~~ bóy.

4. Pronounce the word "the" as /ðiy/ before words beginning with a vowel sound. Listen and repeat.

1. ~~the~~ ORder   Take ~~the~~ ORder.
2. ~~the~~ ENtrance   Near ~~the~~ ENtrance.
3. ~~the~~ OPPosite door It's ~~the~~ OPPosite door.

B. Pronouns: <u>you</u>, <u>your</u>

1. You is often reduced to /yə/ in normal speech. Reduce "you" to /yə/ and say it quickly, as part of the phrase. Do not reduce "you" at the end of a sentence. Listen and repeat.

1. What time are ~~you~~ COMing?
2. I saw ~~you~~ DANCing.
3. Was it REALLy you?
4. He's COUNTing on you.

2. Reduce "your" to /yər/. Listen and repeat.

1. Here's ~~your~~ hát.
2. He took ~~your~~ pláce.
3. Tell ~~your~~ bóss.

C. Prepositions: <u>of</u>, <u>to</u>, <u>at</u>, <u>for</u>

1. Reduce "of" to /əv/. Listen and repeat.

    1. Tired of WORKing?

    2. That's most of it.

    3. I'll take some of them.

2. Reduce "to" to /tə/. Do not reduce it at the end of a sentence. Listen and repeat.

    1. I'd like to see it.

    2. Talk to me.

    3. What is he LIStening to?

    4. Which show is he GOing to?

3. Reduce "at" to /ət/. Do not reduce it at the end of a sentence. Listen and repeat.

    1. I'm at school.

    2. Come at once.

    3. What is he LOOKing at?

4. Reduce "for" to /fər/. Do not reduce it at the end of a sentence. Listen and repeat.

    1. Get it for me.

    2. Ask for change.

    3. What did she do that for?

    4. What's his bill for?

D. Auxiliary Verbs: <u>am</u>, <u>was</u>, <u>can</u>

1. Reduce "am" to /əm/. Do not reduce it at the end of a sentence. Listen and repeat.

    1. Where ~~am~~ I GÓing?

    2. ~~Am~~ I FÍNished?

    3. I thínk I am.

    4. I knów I am.

2. Reduce "was" to /wəz/. Do not reduce it at the end of a sentence. Listen and repeat.

    1. I ~~was~~ ríght.

    2. ~~Was~~ it RÁINing?

    3. Yes, it wás.

    4. They shówed me where it was.

3. Reduce "can" to /kən/. Do not reduce it at the end of a sentence. Listen and repeat.

    1. He ~~can~~ réad.

    2. ~~Can~~ they tálk?

    3. I thínk I can.

    4. He'll come when he cán.

E. Conjunctions: <u>and</u>, <u>as</u>, <u>or</u>

1. Reduce "and" to /ən/ or /'n/ Listen and repeat.

    1. Come ~~and~~ sée me.

    2. They're SÍSter ~~and~~ BRÓTHer.

    3. I'd like BÁcon ~~and~~ eggs.

2. Reduce "as" to /əz/. Listen and repeat.

   1. He's as old as Ánn.

   2. It's as white as snów.

   3. Good as góld.

3. Reduce "or" to /ər/. Listen and repeat.

   1. Take it or leáve it.

   2. I'll take one or twó.

   3. It's now or NÉVer.

5. HOME ASSIGNMENT

A. 1. Read each sentence aloud several times. You may use a dictionary to help you with new words.
   2. Mark the stressed words in each sentence. Use a stress mark (´).
   3. Draw a line through the function words that are reduced. Place the symbol /ə/ above the letters that represent this sound. (You may want to use /'n/ for "and.")
   4. After you finish, read the sentence aloud again.

   Example: AFter I mét my MOTHer and FÁther, I wént
   to the LIbrary to STUDy for my tést.

1. My BROTHer is as old as you.

2. Was your GIRLfriend at home?

3. MARgaret is STUDying to be a SECretary.

4. SOONer or LATer the work will have to be done.

5. He was tired of DOing the same thing all day.

6. My SISter can read ENglish, but not VERy well.

7. She goes to school DURing the day and works at night.

8. I'll go with you to the COLLege BOOKstore.

9. Sam ORdered ham and eggs for BREAKfast.

10. I like to eat bread and BUTTer with my meals.

11. My friends and I ate lunch in the cafeTERia.

12. Lee is STUDying to be an eLECtrical engiNEER.

B. Work with a partner. Read your sentences aloud while you and your partner look at your sentences. Explain why you stressed the words in your sentences. What did you want to emphasize in your meaning? Is your meaning clear to your partner? Now work with your partner's sentences. Compare the two lists. Notice how the stress marks change the meaning.

Intonation

1. RISING AND FALLING INTONATION

Stress and intonation give rhythm and melody to our speech. Intonation creates the melody. When we speak, our voices rise and fall, like notes in a musical scale. Intonation also expresses feelings: happiness, curiosity, surprise, annoyance, and so on.

> English has two basic intonation patterns: *rising* and *falling*. With rising intonation, the *pitch* (musical tone) of your voice goes up. With falling intonation, it goes down.

🎧 **Listen**

Listen to these two words.

HeLLO?

No.

"Hello" has rising intonation. The speaker is asking a question on the phone: "Who's there?" "No" has falling intonation. The speaker is answering a question.

🎧 Listen and Repeat

Note that:

* *capital letters indicate syllable stress,*
* *a stress mark (ˊ) indicates word stress,*
* *arrows (◡◞ ◝◞) indicate rising and falling intonation.*

Falling Intonation

A. Use falling intonation with statements and commands. Listen and repeat.

1. Nó.   5. It's SNÓWing.
2. Dó it.   6. He's my TEÁCHer.
3. Do it nów.   7. The man is CRÁzy.
4. Come hére.   8. I don't líke it.

B. Use falling intonation with *WH-questions.* WH-questions begin with such words as *when, what, where, why,* and *how, who, whose* and *which.* Listen and repeat.

1. Who's CÓMing?   5. What's the DÍFFerence?
2. Where ís it?   6. How much does it cóst?
3. Why are you GÓing?   7. When did it HÁPPen?
4. Which one ís it?   8. Whose bóok is it?

Rising Intonation

A. Use rising intonation when you ask *yes-no questions.* Yes-no questions require "yes" or "no" for an answer. Listen and repeat.

1. Do you líke it?   5. Are you PLÁYing?
2. Are you GÓing?   6. Is he my TEÁCHer?
3. Do I háve to?   7. Is it SNÓWing?
4. Is the man CRÁzy?   8. Did you dó it?

B. Use rising intonation for items in a list. Use it mid-sentence when you offer choices. But in both cases, use falling intonation for the last item. Listen and repeat.

1. He went to ENgland, France, Spain, and RUSSia.

2. The CHILdren want pens, PENcils, PAper, and glue.

3. Do you want WAter or SOda?

4. You can come with us, or you can stay home.

5. BeFORE I left, I had to take out the GARbage and feed the cat.

2. INTONATION AND STRESS

Intonation and stress work together to express meaning. Usually, the last word or next to the last word in the sentence is stressed. Listen to these sentences:

The man is CRAzy.

I don't like it.

The speaker's voice rises with the stress and falls at the end of the sentence. This rising-falling pattern is very common in American English.

● Listen and Repeat

Remember that

- *capital letters indicate syllable stress,*
- *a stress mark (') indicates word stress,*
- *arrows (⌒ ⌒) indicate rising and falling intonation.*

A. Stress and intonation give these sentences different meanings. Listen and repeat.

	Sentence	Meaning
1a.	I like my jób.	Normal statement of fact.
b.	I like my jób.	You may not like yours, but I like mine.
c.	I líke my job.	I didn't say I didn't like it!
d.	Í like my job.	I don't know about you, but I do.
e.	Í like my jób?	What gave you that idea?
2a.	I told him I was GOing.	Normal statement of fact.
b.	I told him I wás GOing.	Definitely!
c.	I told him Í was GOing.	I was, not Jane.
d.	I told hím I was GOing.	Him, not John.
e.	I tóld him I was GOing.	I warned him.
f.	Í told him I was going.	I did, no one else.
g.	Í told him I was GOing?	Who told you that?

B. You can say each of these words in different ways. Listen and repeat these pairs. The first word has falling intonation and the second one has rising intonation.

1a. Yes.	3a. Oh.	5a. HeLLO.
b. Yes?	b. Oh?	b. HeLLO?
2a. No.	4a. OK.	
b. No?	b. OK?	

🔊 3. CHECK YOUR LISTENING

Listen to each of the following sentences twice. The first time, mark the stressed words. The second time, mark the rising or falling intonation with arrows.

Example: Are you COMing to the PARty, or are you GOing

to the MOvie?

1. Please get APPles, ORanges, and baNANas.

2. I like my new aPARTment.

3. Are you GOing home?

4. How much is it?

5. Where is the PAper?

6. Would you like APPle pie or CHOColate cake?

7. I know most of the PEOple.

8. Please come here!

4. HOME ASSIGNMENT

A. Each of these sentences has a different meaning. Read the sentences and their meanings. Then mark the sentences for stress and intonation. Use a stress mark (´) for stressed words and arrows (⌣ ⌐) for rising and falling intonation. (Capital letters indicate syllable stress.)

Sentence	Meaning
Examples:	Jóhn loves me.	John does, not Paul.

John loves me. Me, not you.

John loves me? Is it really true?

Sentence	Meaning
1a. I speak ENglish.	I do, but he doesn't.
b. I speak ENglish.	But I don't read it.
c. I speak ENglish.	Not another language.
2a. Go to your room.	Normal command.
b. Go to your room.	To yours, not to hers.
c. Go to your room?	Why are you saying that?
3a. Who wants to go?	Who?
b. Who wants to go?	Who really wants to?
c. Who wants to go?	Normal question.
4a. Don't go there.	Do not.
b. Don't go there.	Any place but there.
c. Don't go there?	Why not?

B. Bring your assignment to class. Work with a partner. Read your marked sentences at random. Your partner must tell you the meaning. He or she may use any paraphrase that clearly explains the meaning.

Vowel Sounds

The vowel sounds of American English are:

/iy/	s<u>ee</u>	/uw/	d<u>o</u>	/ə/	<u>u</u>p
/ɪ/	s<u>i</u>t	/ʊ/	b<u>oo</u>k	/ər/	s<u>ir</u>
/ey/	p<u>ay</u>	/ow/	n<u>o</u>	/ay/	b<u>uy</u>
/ɛ/	m<u>e</u>t	/ɔ/	<u>a</u>ll	/aw/	n<u>ow</u>
/æ/	c<u>a</u>t	/a/	n<u>o</u>t	/ɔy/	b<u>oy</u>

You will practice all these sounds. There are three major things to consider when producing vowel sounds:

1. Which part of the tongue helps to shape the sound? Is it the tip, front, center, or back? Say /uw/ as in "f<u>oo</u>l." It's the back part of the tongue. Say /iy/ as in "s<u>ee</u>." It's the front part.
2. What is the height of the tongue in the mouth? Is it held high, low, or in the center of the mouth? The back part of the tongue is held high for the sound /uw/ as in "f<u>oo</u>l." The front part of the tongue is held high for /iy/ as in "s<u>ee</u>."
3. What is the position of the lips? Are they rounded, spread, or wide open? They are rounded for the sound /uw/ as in "f<u>oo</u>l" and spread for the sound /iy/ as in "s<u>ee</u>." They are wide open for the sound /a/ as in "F<u>A</u>ther."

<table>
<tr><td>

UNIT
8

</td><td>

/iy/ as in <u>see</u>
/ɪ/ as in <u>sit</u>

</td></tr>
</table>

1. PRODUCING /iy/

Examples: <u>ea</u>t, <u>ea</u>st, reC<u>EI</u>VE, beL<u>IE</u>VE, P<u>EO</u>ple, sw<u>ee</u>t, b<u>e</u>,
 sk<u>i</u>, k<u>ey</u>

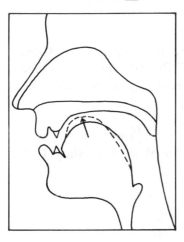

- Hold the front part of your tongue high in your mouth, close to the roof.
- Press the sides of your tongue against the upper back teeth. The muscles of your tongue should be tense.
- Spread your lips.
- As you say the sound, move the front part of your tongue forward and up.
- Place your thumb underneath your chin to feel the tense muscles.

2. PRODUCING /ɪ/

Examples: h<u>i</u>t, l<u>i</u>p, h<u>i</u>m, b<u>ee</u>n, b<u>ui</u>ld, W<u>O</u>Men, S<u>Y</u>Stem

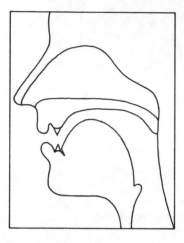

- Hold the front part of your tongue high in your mouth, but lower than for /iy/.
- Place the sides of your tongue against the upper back teeth, but *do not press.* The muscles of your tongue should *not* be tense.
- The lips are a little less spread than for /iy/.
- The tongue does not move as you say the sound.
- Place your thumb underneath your chin. You should feel no tense muscles; the muscles are *relaxed.*

3. CONTRAST: /iy/ AND /ɪ/

A. Many students of English as a second language do not hear the difference between /iy/ as in "s<u>ee</u>," and /ɪ/ as in "s<u>i</u>t." Practice these two sounds, first normally, then with exaggeration, then normally. Listen and repeat.

1.	/iy/	/iy. . . ./	/iy/
2.	/ɪ/	/ɪ. . . ./	/ɪ/

B. Now practice these sounds in words. Notice the phonetic spelling. Listen and repeat each word twice.

1.	kn<u>ee</u>	/niy/	kn<u>ee</u>
2.	b<u>e</u>	/biy/	b<u>e</u>
3.	b<u>ea</u>t	/biyt/	b<u>ea</u>t
4.	<u>ea</u>t	/iyt/	<u>ea</u>t
5.	<u>i</u>t	/ɪt/	<u>i</u>t
6.	<u>i</u>ll	/ɪl/	<u>i</u>ll
7.	h<u>i</u>m	/hɪm/	h<u>i</u>m
8.	b<u>i</u>g	/bɪg/	b<u>i</u>g

🎧 4. CHECK YOUR LISTENING

You will hear words with the sounds /iy/ and /ɪ/. First, cover the words in the following list. Then listen to each word. Concentrate on the sound, not the spelling. Which vowel sound do you hear? Write a check mark in the correct column.

	/iy/ as in "s<u>ee</u>"	/ɪ/ as in "s<u>i</u>t"
1. tr<u>ee</u>	_____	_____
2. m<u>ea</u>n	_____	_____
3. sick	_____	_____
4. d<u>i</u>d	_____	_____
5. sh<u>ee</u>p	_____	_____
6. sh<u>i</u>p	_____	_____
7. h<u>e</u>	_____	_____
8. thr<u>ee</u>	_____	_____
9. th<u>i</u>n	_____	_____
10. h<u>i</u>s	_____	_____

🎧 5. PRACTICE THE CONTRAST: /iy/ AS IN "S<u>EE</u>" WITH /ɪ/ AS IN "S<u>I</u>T"

A. Practice these contrasting sounds. Listen and repeat each word pair. *Capital letters indicate syllable stress.*

	/iy/	/ɪ/		/iy/	/ɪ/
1.	<u>ea</u>t	<u>i</u>t	11.	s<u>ee</u>k	s<u>i</u>ck
2.	<u>ea</u>ch	<u>i</u>tch	12.	p<u>ea</u>k	p<u>i</u>ck
3.	r<u>ea</u>ch	r<u>i</u>ch	13.	l<u>ea</u>k	l<u>i</u>ck
4.	s<u>ea</u>t	s<u>i</u>t	14.	h<u>ea</u>p	h<u>i</u>p
5.	f<u>ee</u>t	f<u>i</u>t	15.	t<u>ea</u>m	T<u>i</u>m
6.	b<u>ea</u>t	b<u>i</u>t	16.	s<u>ee</u>n	s<u>i</u>n
7.	h<u>ea</u>t	h<u>i</u>t	17.	r<u>ea</u>d	r<u>i</u>d
8.	l<u>ea</u>st	l<u>i</u>st	18.	h<u>ea</u>l	h<u>i</u>ll
9.	d<u>ee</u>p	d<u>i</u>p	19.	st<u>ea</u>l	st<u>i</u>ll
10.	l<u>ea</u>p	l<u>i</u>p	20.	CAEsar's	SC<u>I</u>SSors

B. Now practice the contrasting sounds in sentence pairs. The first sentence of each pair has the sound /iy/ and the second has the sound /ɪ/. Notice the change in meaning. Visual clues can help. Make a simple drawing in each blank box. *Capital letters indicate syllable stress.*

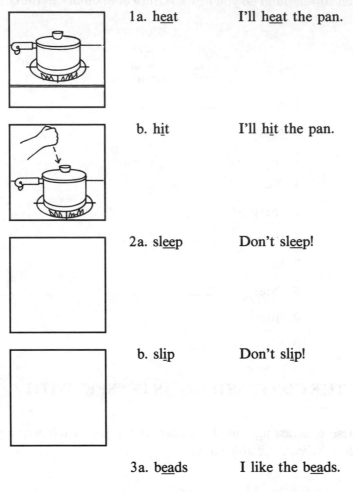

1a. heat   I'll heat the pan.

b. hit   I'll hit the pan.

2a. sleep   Don't sleep!

b. slip   Don't slip!

3a. beads   I like the beads.

b. bids   I like the bids.

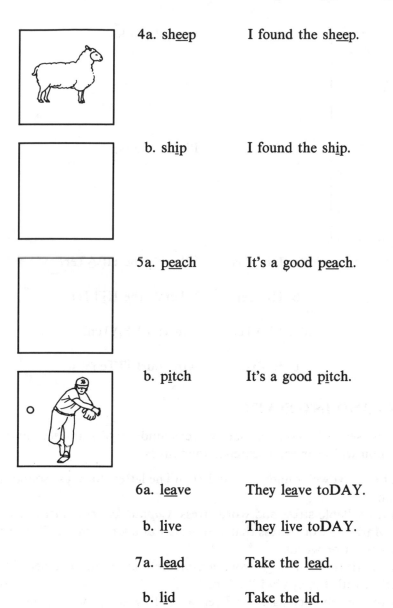

4a. sh<u>ee</u>p   I found the sh<u>ee</u>p.

b. sh<u>i</u>p   I found the sh<u>i</u>p.

5a. p<u>ea</u>ch   It's a good p<u>ea</u>ch.

b. p<u>i</u>tch   It's a good p<u>i</u>tch.

6a. l<u>ea</u>ve   They l<u>ea</u>ve toDAY.

b. l<u>i</u>ve   They l<u>i</u>ve toDAY.

7a. l<u>ea</u>d   Take the l<u>ea</u>d.

b. l<u>i</u>d   Take the l<u>i</u>d.

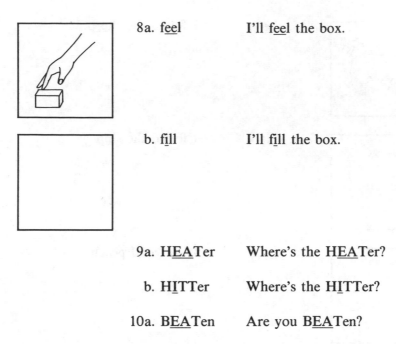

8a. f<u>ee</u>l   I'll f<u>ee</u>l the box.

b. f<u>i</u>ll   I'll f<u>i</u>ll the box.

9a. H<u>EA</u>Ter   Where's the H<u>EA</u>Ter?

b. H<u>I</u>TTer   Where's the H<u>I</u>TTer?

10a. B<u>EA</u>Ten   Are you B<u>EA</u>Ten?

b. B<u>I</u>TTen   Are you B<u>I</u>TTen?

🔘 6. STRESS AND INTONATION

Each of these sentences contains both vowel sounds, /iy/ as in "s<u>ee</u>" and /ɪ/ as in "s<u>i</u>t." You will hear each sentence four times:

1. Listen for the vowel sounds /iy/ and /ɪ/. (The letters for these sounds are underlined.)
2. Listen for syllable stress and word stress. *Capital letters indicate syllable stress.* Mark the word stress that you hear. Put a stress mark (´) over the stressed word or words.
3. Listen for rising or falling intonation at the end of the sentence. Mark intonation with the symbol "⤴" or "⤵."
4. Listen to the sentence again and repeat it. Pay attention to pauses and linking of words.

Examples: a. Sp<u>ea</u>k to h<u>i</u>m.

b. Are they M<u>EE</u>Ting for D<u>I</u>NNer?

1. <u>Ea</u>t <u>i</u>t.	6. R<u>ea</u>ch for the b<u>i</u>ll.
2. I f<u>ee</u>l <u>i</u>ll.	7. ComPL<u>E</u>TE the l<u>i</u>st.
3. Sh<u>e</u>'s s<u>i</u>ck.	8. Can you s<u>ee</u> the D<u>I</u>FFerence?
4. H<u>e</u>'s s<u>i</u>ck.	9. Are they TAKing gr<u>ee</u>n p<u>i</u>lls?
5. They h<u>ea</u>l the s<u>i</u>ck.	10. When can you l<u>ea</u>ve the K<u>I</u>TCHen?

🎧 7. DIALOG

You will hear a dialog with words that contain the sounds /iy/ as in "s<u>ee</u>" and /ɪ/ as in "s<u>i</u>t." Listen to the dialog five times:

1. Concentrate on the meaning. Discuss any new vocabulary with your teacher and classmates.
2. Listen for the vowel sounds /iy/ and /ɪ/. (The letters for these sounds are underlined.)
3. Listen for syllable stress and word stress. *Capital letters indicate syllable stress.* Put a stress mark (ʹ) over the stressed word or words.
4. Listen for rising or falling intonation at the end of each sentence. Mark intonation with the symbol (⤴) or (⤵).
5. Listen to each sentence of the dialog again and repeat it. Pay attention to pauses and linking of words.

The first sentence is marked for you.

(Jim and Jean are at a party.)

Jim: Do you see that man with the pink shirt? Is he a TEACHer?

Jean: Yes, he is.

Jim: Does he teach BUSiness?

Jean: No, he's a speech TEACHer.

Jim: And that WOman in the green dress. Who's she?

Jean: She's his SISter. . . . Do you know the man WEARing jeans?

Jim: Yes, he's a MINister. His name is Breen.

Jean: I know him, too. Did he come with his wife?

Jim: I think so. There she is.

Jean: He has a SEcret.

Jim: Oh? What's his SEcret?

Jean: I heard him WHISper SOMEthing aBOUT keys.

↻ **8.** ROLE PLAY

Practice the dialog with a partner. Help each other with correct sounds, stress, and intonation.

🛌 **9.** HOME ASSIGNMENT

A. Write /iy/ as in "s<u>ee</u>" or /ɪ/ as in "s<u>i</u>t" for the underlined sound in each word. Say each word aloud several times. Use a dictionary to help you with any new words.

Examples: a. dr<u>i</u>ll   <u>/ɪ/</u>
                 b. m<u>ee</u>t   /iy/

1. b<u>i</u>ll	____	11. f<u>i</u>sh	____
2. r<u>i</u>p	____	12. p<u>i</u>nch	____
3. h<u>i</u>m	____	13. V<u>I</u>sion	____
4. b<u>ea</u>ns	____	14. sw<u>ee</u>t	____
5. d<u>i</u>sh	____	15. k<u>i</u>ll	____
6. ch<u>ea</u>p	____	16. b<u>ui</u>ld	____
7. d<u>i</u>d	____	17. M<u>I</u>Ster	____
8. th<u>i</u>nk	____	18. S<u>Y</u>Rup	____
9. m<u>ea</u>l	____	19. M<u>I</u>RRor	____
10. m<u>ea</u>n	____	20. <u>i</u>nSTEAD	____

B. Write /iy/ as in "see" or /ɪ/ as in "sit" inside the slash marks above the underlined letters. Say each phrase aloud several times. You may need to refer to a dictionary.

            /iy/   /iy/   /iy/ /ɪ/
Examples: a. e<u>a</u>t the b<u>ee</u>f   b. k<u>ee</u>p <u>i</u>t

1. cr<u>ea</u>m ch<u>ee</u>se

2. <u>i</u>t's ch<u>ea</u>p

3. b<u>i</u>g sh<u>ee</u>ts

4. h<u>ea</u>t the m<u>i</u>lk

5. sl<u>ee</u>p on the P<u>I</u>LLow

6. p<u>i</u>nk L<u>I</u>Pst<u>i</u>ck

7. s<u>ee</u> my <u>i</u>nSTRUCtor

8. p<u>i</u>ck <u>i</u>t up

9. s<u>i</u>t st<u>i</u>ll

10. CHOCol<u>a</u>te ch<u>i</u>p <u>i</u>ce cr<u>ea</u>m

<table>
<tr><td>

UNIT
9

</td><td>

/ey/ as in <u>pay</u>
/ɛ/ as in <u>met</u>

</td></tr>
</table>

1. PRODUCING /ey/

Examples: <u>ai</u>m, <u>eigh</u>t, t<u>a</u>ke¹ w<u>ai</u>t, v<u>ai</u>n, br<u>ea</u>k, s<u>ay</u>, th<u>ey</u>

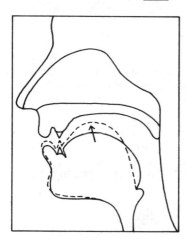

- Hold the front part of your tongue high in your mouth, but lower than for /iy/ and /ɪ/.
- Press the sides of your tongue against the upper back teeth. The muscles of your tongue should be tense.
- Lower your jaw and open your lips more than for /iy/ and /ɪ/.
- As you say the sound, raise your jaw slightly and move the front part of your tongue forward and up.
- Place your thumb underneath your chin to feel the tense muscles.

---

¹The final "e" in words such as "take," "date," and "age" signals the /ey/ pronunciation for the letter "a." Compare "hat" /hæt/ with "hate" /heyt/.

2. PRODUCING /ɛ/

Examples: end, ANy, men, says, said, bread

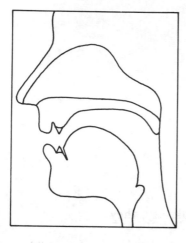

- Hold your tongue in the same position as for /ey/, but a little lower in your mouth.
- Place the sides of your tongue against the upper back teeth, but *do not press.* The muscles of your tongue should *not* be tense.
- Open your lips slightly more than for /ey/.
- Your jaw and tongue do not move as you say this sound.
- Place your thumb underneath your chin. You should feel no tense muscles; the muscles are *relaxed.*

3. CONTRAST: /ey/ AND /ɛ/

A. Students may confuse the sound /ey/ as in "pay" with the sound /ɛ/ as in "met." Practice these two sounds, first normally, then with exaggeration, then normally. Listen and repeat.

1. /ey/	/ey. . . ./	/ey/
2. /ɛ/	/ɛ. . . ./	/ɛ/

B. Now practice these sounds in words. Notice the phonetic spelling. Listen and repeat each word twice.

1.	eight	/eyt/	eight
2.	say	/sey/	say
3.	hate	/heyt/	hate
4.	egg	/ɛg/	egg
5.	guess	/gɛs/	guess
6.	neck	/nɛk/	neck
7.	date	/deyt/	date
8.	red	/rɛd/	red

🔊 4. CHECK YOUR LISTENING

You will hear words with the sounds /ey/ and /ɛ/. First, cover the words in the following list. Then listen to each word. Concentrate on the sound, not the spelling. Which vowel sound do you hear? Write a check mark in the correct column.

	/ey/ as in "p<u>ay</u>"	/ɛ/ as in "m<u>e</u>t"
1. <u>a</u>ge	___	___
2. <u>e</u>dge	___	___
3. m<u>e</u>t	___	___
4. m<u>ai</u>n	___	___
5. p<u>e</u>n	___	___
6. l<u>e</u>t	___	___
7. w<u>ai</u>t	___	___
8. th<u>ey</u>	___	___
9. wh<u>e</u>n	___	___
10. steak	___	___

🔊 5. PRACTICE THE CONTRAST: /ɛ/ AS IN "M<u>E</u>T" WITH /ey/ AS IN "P<u>A</u>Y"

A. Practice these contrasting sounds. Listen and repeat each word pair. *Capital letters indicate syllable stress.*

	/ɛ/	/ey/		/ɛ/	/ey/
1.	B<u>e</u>ss	b<u>a</u>se	6.	g<u>e</u>t	g<u>a</u>te
2.	ch<u>e</u>ss	ch<u>a</u>se	7.	f<u>e</u>d	f<u>a</u>de
3.	m<u>e</u>t	m<u>a</u>te	8.	r<u>e</u>d	r<u>ai</u>d
4.	w<u>e</u>t	w<u>ai</u>t	9.	bl<u>e</u>d	bl<u>a</u>de
5.	w<u>e</u>st	w<u>a</u>ste	10.	l<u>e</u>d	l<u>ai</u>d

	/ɛ/	/ey/			/ɛ/	/ey/
11.	let	late		16.	yell	Yale²
12.	LETTer	LATer		17.	den	Dane
13.	bell	bail²		18.	men	main
14.	tell	tail²		19.	sent	saint
15.	fell	fail²		20.	rest	raced

B. Now practice the contrasting sounds in sentence pairs. The first sentence of each pair has the sound /ɛ/ and the second has the sound /ey/. Notice the change in meaning. Visual clues can help. Make a simple drawing in each blank box. *Capital letters indicate syllable stress.*

	1a. edge	It's the edge.
	b. age	It's the age.
	2a. Ed	Did you find Ed?
	b. aid	Did you find aid?
	3a. less	Use less.
	b. lace	Use lace.
	4a. bet	Who has the bet?
	b. bait	Who has the bait?

²Adding the sound /ə/ as in the word "up" before some final /l/ sounds may help you produce the vowel sound better. For example, "bail" /beyªl/, "tail" /teyªl/.

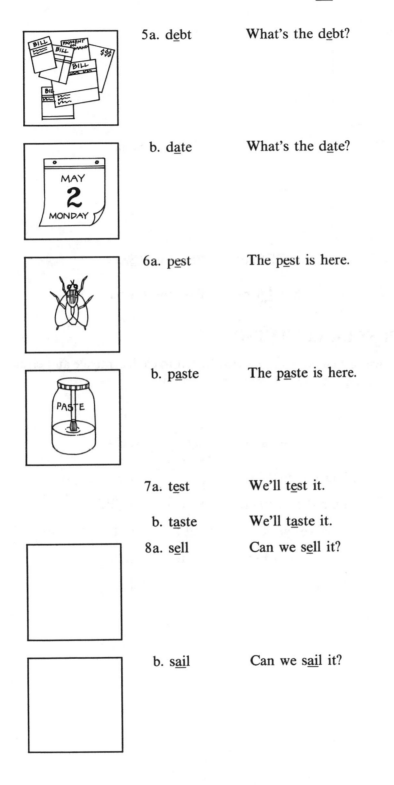

5a. d<u>e</u>bt   What's the d<u>e</u>bt?

b. d<u>a</u>te   What's the d<u>a</u>te?

6a. p<u>e</u>st   The p<u>e</u>st is here.

b. p<u>a</u>ste   The p<u>a</u>ste is here.

7a. t<u>e</u>st   We'll t<u>e</u>st it.

b. t<u>a</u>ste   We'll t<u>a</u>ste it.

8a. s<u>e</u>ll   Can we s<u>e</u>ll it?

b. s<u>ai</u>l   Can we s<u>ai</u>l it?

9a. pen   He has a p<u>e</u>n.

b. pain   He has a p<u>ai</u>n.

10a. P<u>E</u>PPer   Pass the P<u>E</u>PPer.

b. P<u>A</u>per   Pass the P<u>A</u>per.

🔊 6. CHECK YOUR LISTENING

Cover the list of sentences on the left. Listen to each sentence and circle the correct word in one of the columns on the right.

Example:		/ey/	/ɛ/
	What's the date?	d<u>a</u>te	d<u>e</u>bt
1.	Did you find <u>E</u>d?	<u>ai</u>d	<u>E</u>d
2.	Pass the P<u>E</u>PPer.	P<u>A</u>per	P<u>E</u>PPer
3.	Can we s<u>ai</u>l it?	s<u>ai</u>l	s<u>e</u>ll
4.	The p<u>a</u>ste is here.	p<u>a</u>ste	p<u>e</u>st
5.	Use l<u>e</u>ss.	l<u>a</u>ce	l<u>e</u>ss

🎤 7. STRESS AND INTONATION

Each of these sentences contains both vowel sounds, /ey/ as in "p<u>ay</u>" and /ɛ/ as in "m<u>e</u>t." You will hear each sentence four times:

1. Listen for the vowel sounds /ey/ and /ɛ/. (The letters for these sounds are underlined.)
2. Listen for syllable stress and word stress. (Capital letters indicate syllable stress.) Mark the word stress that you hear. Put a stress mark (ˊ) over the stressed word or words.
3. Listen for rising or falling intonation at the end of the sentence. Mark intonation with the symbol "↗" or "↘."
4. Listen to the sentence again and repeat it. Pay attention to pauses and linking of words.

Examples: a. I was WAITing for the WEATHer to clear.

b. Did you wait for the WEATHer to clear?

1. M<u>ai</u>l the L<u>E</u>TTer.

2. I f<u>ai</u>led my t<u>e</u>st.

3. P<u>ay</u> the r<u>e</u>nt.

4. Do you pl<u>ay</u> T<u>E</u>NNis?

5. The tr<u>ai</u>n is b<u>e</u>st.

6. I T<u>A</u>STed the br<u>ea</u>d.

7. Does Sp<u>ai</u>n have good WEATHer?

8. Does she have a p<u>ai</u>n in her l<u>e</u>g?

9. Does he have a p<u>ai</u>n in his h<u>ea</u>d?

10. Do you have a p<u>ai</u>n in your ch<u>e</u>st?

8. DIALOG

You will hear a dialog with words that contain the sounds /ey/ as in "p<u>ay</u>" and /ɛ/ as in "m<u>e</u>t." Listen to the dialog five times:

1. Concentrate on the meaning. Discuss any new vocabulary with your teacher and classmates.
2. Listen for the vowel sounds /ey/ and /ɛ/. (The letters for these sounds are underlined.)
3. Listen for syllable stress and word stress. (Capital letters indicate syllable stress.) Mark the word stress that you hear. Put a stress mark (´) over the stressed word or words.
4. Listen for rising or falling intonation at the end of each sentence. Mark intonation with the symbol "⤴" or "⤵."
5. Listen to each sentence of the dialog again and repeat it. Pay attention to pauses and linking of words.

The first sentence is marked for you.

James: He<u>L</u>LÓ, R<u>A</u>chél. Did you t<u>a</u>ke the ch<u>é</u>m t<u>é</u>st?

R<u>A</u>chel: No, I COULDn't m<u>a</u>ke it.

James: How come you COULDn't m<u>a</u>ke it?

R<u>A</u>chel: I w<u>e</u>nt to see a BROADw<u>ay</u> pl<u>ay</u>.

James: InST<u>EA</u>D of T<u>A</u>King the t<u>e</u>st?

R<u>A</u>chel: Y<u>es</u>, I REALLy WANTed to see the pl<u>ay</u>.

James: What's the n<u>a</u>me of the pl<u>ay</u>?

R<u>A</u>chel: "MEASure for MEASure," by WILLiam SHAKEspeare.

James: Oh. Wh<u>en</u> will you t<u>a</u>ke the M<u>A</u>KE-up t<u>e</u>st?

R<u>A</u>chel: PROBably in <u>A</u>pril or M<u>ay</u>.

9. ROLE PLAY

Practice the dialog with a partner. Help each other with correct sounds, stress, and intonation.

🔊 10. HOME ASSIGNMENT

A. Say each word aloud several times. You can use a dictionary to check the pronunciation and meaning of new words. Then write /ey/ as in "p<u>ay</u>" or /ɛ/ as in "m<u>e</u>t" for the underlined letters in each word.

Examples: a. br<u>ea</u>th   /ɛ/
              b. j<u>ai</u>l   /ey/

1. ch<u>e</u>ss	_____	11. R<u>AI</u>Lroad	_____
2. ST<u>A</u>tion	_____	12. <u>E</u>Xit	_____
3. tr<u>ay</u>	_____	13. str<u>aigh</u>t	_____
4. V<u>E</u>Ry	_____	14. M<u>EA</u>Sure	_____
5. B<u>U</u>Ry	_____	15. n<u>ai</u>l	_____
6. pr<u>e</u>ss	_____	16. reM<u>E</u>Mber	_____
7. sh<u>a</u>pe	_____	17. c<u>e</u>nt	_____
8. d<u>e</u>sk	_____	18. str<u>a</u>nge	_____
9. pl<u>a</u>ce	_____	19. thr<u>ea</u>d	_____
10. sc<u>a</u>le	_____	20. sk<u>a</u>te	_____

B. Say each phrase aloud several times. You may need to use a dictionary. Then write either /ey/ as in "p<u>ay</u>" or /ɛ/ as in "m<u>e</u>t" inside the slash marks above the underlined letters.

              /ɛ/   /ɛ/   /ɛ/   /ey/
Examples: a. s<u>e</u>lls the b<u>e</u>st   b. m<u>e</u>t his m<u>a</u>te

1. s<u>e</u>nt by m<u>ai</u>l
2. gr<u>ay</u>-haired L<u>A</u>dy
3. aFR<u>AI</u>D to t<u>e</u>ll
4. tr<u>ai</u>n or pl<u>a</u>ne
5. <u>e</u>nd of ST<u>A</u>tion
6. t<u>a</u>stes B<u>E</u>TTer
7. <u>EIGH</u>teen m<u>e</u>n
8. <u>A</u>Ny d<u>ay</u>
9. th<u>ey</u> p<u>ai</u>d
10. <u>E</u>Xtra <u>e</u>ggs

<table>
<tr><td>UNIT
10</td><td></td></tr>
</table>

/æ/ as in c<u>a</u>t

1. PRODUCING /æ/

Examples: <u>a</u>m, <u>a</u>t, <u>A</u>Nswer, b<u>a</u>d, b<u>a</u>nk, l<u>au</u>gh, b<u>a</u>t

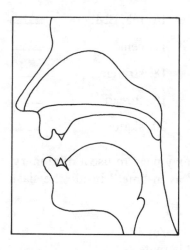

- Hold the front and back parts of your tongue low in your mouth.
- Touch the lower front teeth lightly with the tip of the tongue.
- Lower your jaw and open your lips wide.
- The muscles in your tongue should not be tense.

2. CONTRAST: /æ/ AND /ε/

A. Students may confuse the sound /æ/ as in "c<u>a</u>t" with the sound /ε/ as in "m<u>e</u>t." Practice these two sounds, first normally, then with exaggeration, then normally. Listen and repeat.

1. /æ/   /æ. . . ./   /æ/
2. /ε/   /ε . . . ./   /ε/

B. Now practice these sounds in words. Notice the phonetic spelling. Listen and repeat each word twice.

1.	c<u>a</u>t	/kæt/	c<u>a</u>t
2.	<u>a</u>nd	/ænd/	<u>a</u>nd
3.	m<u>a</u>n	/mæn/	m<u>a</u>n
4.	g<u>a</u>s	/gæs/	g<u>a</u>s
5.	gu<u>e</u>ss	/gɛs/	gu<u>e</u>ss
6.	b<u>e</u>t	/bɛt/	b<u>e</u>t
7.	<u>a</u>dd	/æd/	<u>a</u>dd
8.	bl<u>a</u>ck	/blæk/	bl<u>a</u>ck

🎧 3. CHECK YOUR LISTENING

You will hear words with the sounds /æ/ and /ɛ/. First, cover the words in the following list. Then listen to each word. Concentrate on the sound, not the spelling. Which vowel sound do you hear? Write a check mark in the correct column.

	/æ/ as in "c<u>a</u>t"	/ɛ/ as in "m<u>e</u>t"
1. b<u>a</u>t	_____	_____
2. b<u>e</u>st	_____	_____
3. l<u>a</u>nd	_____	_____
4. b<u>e</u>t	_____	_____
5. <u>a</u>sk	_____	_____
6. <u>e</u>nd	_____	_____
7. m<u>e</u>n	_____	_____
8. s<u>a</u>d	_____	_____
9. h<u>ea</u>d	_____	_____
10. m<u>a</u>n	_____	_____

4. PRACTICE THE CONTRAST: /ɛ/ AS IN "M**E**T" WITH /æ/ AS IN "C**A**T"

A. Practice these contrasting sounds. Listen and repeat each word pair.

	/ɛ/	/æ/			/ɛ/	/æ/
1.	met	mat	6.		bed	bad
2.	set	sat	7.		end	and
3.	Ed	add	8.		bend	band
4.	said	sad	9.		head	had
5.	dead	Dad	10.		beg	bag

B. Now practice the contrasting sounds in sentence pairs. The first sentence of each pair has the sound /ɛ/ and the second has the sound /æ/. Listen and repeat. Notice the change in meaning. Visual clues can help. Make a simple drawing in each blank box. *Capital letters indicate syllable stress.*

1a. bet   I have a bet.

b. bat   I have a bat.

2a. pen   He has a pen.

b. pan   He has a pan.

3a. p<u>e</u>st   The p<u>e</u>st is gone.

b. p<u>a</u>st   The p<u>a</u>st is gone.

4a. m<u>e</u>n   The m<u>e</u>n came.

b. m<u>a</u>n   The m<u>a</u>n came.

5a. <u>A</u>Ny   Did you see <u>A</u>Ny?

b. <u>A</u>NNie   Did you see <u>A</u>NNie?

6a. l<u>e</u>ft   She l<u>e</u>ft.

b. l<u>au</u>ghed   She l<u>au</u>ghed.

7a. p<u>e</u>t   Don't p<u>e</u>t the dog.

b. p<u>a</u>t   Don't p<u>a</u>t the dog.

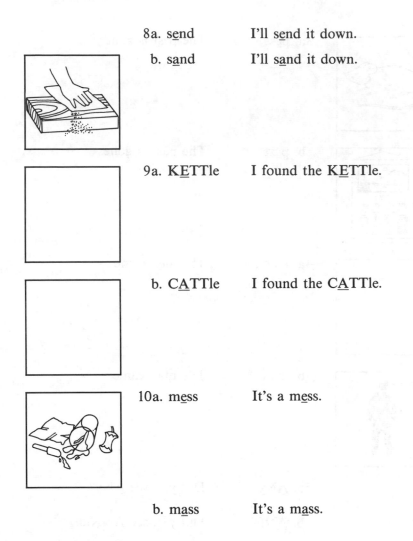

8a. s<u>e</u>nd   I'll s<u>e</u>nd it down.

  b. s<u>a</u>nd   I'll s<u>a</u>nd it down.

9a. K<u>E</u>TTle   I found the K<u>E</u>TTle.

  b. C<u>A</u>TTle   I found the C<u>A</u>TTle.

10a. m<u>e</u>ss   It's a m<u>e</u>ss.

   b. m<u>a</u>ss   It's a m<u>a</u>ss.

5. CHECK YOUR LISTENING

Work with a partner. Read a sentence from 4B to your partner. Can your partner define the sentence? He or she must be truthful.

Your partner will: • Say: I know what _____ means.
                            It means _____. (definition or paraphrase)
                            or
  • Act out what the word means.
                            or
  • Make a simple drawing.

Or your partner will ask: What does _____ mean? You must define the sentence, act it out, or make a drawing.

Example: Student 1:   Don't pet the dog.
                    Student 2:   What does "pet" mean?
                                  or
                                  I know what "pet" means.
                                  Possible responses:

- It means rubbing the dog's head.
- Act out: Rubbing an imaginary dog's head,
- Make a simple drawing.

Or student 1 will define the word,
act it out, or make a simple drawing.

You may each choose two or three sentences. Try to choose sentences with words that your partner may not know. Say the sentence clearly. Concentrate on the sound /æ/ or /ɛ/.

🔊 6. STRESS AND INTONATION

Each of these sentences contains both vowel sounds /ɛ/ as in "m<u>e</u>t" and /æ/ as in "c<u>a</u>t." You will hear each sentence four times:

1. Listen for the vowel sounds /ɛ/ and /æ/. (The letters for these sounds are underlined.)
2. Listen for syllable stress and word stress. *Capital letters indicate syllable stress.* Mark the word stress that you hear. Put a stress mark (´) over the stressed word or words.
3. Listen for rising or falling intonation at the end of the sentence. Mark intonation with the symbol "⌐↗" or "⌐↘."
4. Listen to the sentence again and repeat it. Pay attention to pauses and linking of words.

Examples: a. He met Jack.

b. Did he say he met Jack?

1. He said it was a fact.

2. Send him back.

3. Get some APPles.

4. How MANy CLASSes are there?

5. Sell the gas.

6. Were the men ANgry?

7. Was the EVidence satisFACtory?

8. It was set for JANuary.

9. Is the WEATHer bad?

10. They met beFORE it HAPPened.

♥ 7. DIALOG

You will hear a dialog with words that contain the sounds /æ/ as in "cat" and /ɛ/ as in "met." Listen to the dialog five times:

1. Concentrate on the meaning. Discuss any new vocabulary with your teacher and classmates.
2. Listen for the vowel sounds /æ/ and /ɛ/. (The letters for these sounds are underlined.)
3. Listen for syllable stress and word stress. *Capital letters indicate syllable stress.* Mark the word stress that you hear. Put a stress mark (´) over the stressed word or words.
4. Listen for rising or falling intonation at the end of each sentence. Mark intonation with the symbol "⤴" or "⤵."
5. Listen to each sentence of the dialog again and repeat it. Pay attention to pauses and linking of words.

The first sentence is marked for you.

Jack: What's the MATTer, ALice? You look so unHAPPy.

ALice: I had a bad exPERience YESterday.

Jack: What HAPPened?

ALice: I went to Saks Fifth AVenue and left my bag in the DRESSing room.

Jack: Your bag? Did you get it back?

ALice: No, it was alREADy gone when I went back for it.

Jack: You must feel TERRible.

ALice: Yes, as a MATTer of fact, I'm VERy upSET.

Jack: Did you have ANything VALuable in your bag?

ALice: Yes, I did. I had chem notes, GLASSes, a train pass, TRAVeler's checks, and TWENty DOLLars.

Jack: That's too bad. Well, at least you'll get your MONey back for your TRAVeler's checks.

⟳ 8. ROLE PLAY

Practice the dialog with a partner. Help each other with correct sounds, stress, and intonation.

☚ 9. HOME ASSIGNMENT

The words listed below have these sounds:

/iy/ as in "s<u>ee</u>"   /ɪ/ as in "s<u>i</u>t"   /æ/ as in "c<u>a</u>t"
/ey/ as in "p<u>ay</u>"   /ɛ/ as in "m<u>e</u>t"

First, say the word aloud. Then write the word in the column that corresponds to the sound of the *underlined* letter or letters. For example, the word "s<u>ee</u>" goes in the /iy/ column; the word "s<u>i</u>t" in the /ɪ/ column; the word "p<u>ay</u>" in the /ey/ column, and so on.

1. ch<u>ee</u>se
2. T<u>EA</u>CHer
3. W<u>IN</u>dow
4. tr<u>i</u>p
5. s<u>ai</u>d
6. m<u>a</u>tch
7. C<u>AN</u>dle
8. m<u>a</u>de
9. w<u>eigh</u>
10. R<u>A</u>dio
11. <u>EL</u>bow
12. <u>a</u>xe
13. s<u>ay</u>s
14. L<u>I</u>Quor
15. sh<u>a</u>ve
16. wh<u>i</u>ch
17. <u>EN</u>vy
18. ch<u>ea</u>t
19. S<u>EA</u>son
20. maCH<u>I</u>NE
21. B<u>U</u>Siness
22. aW<u>A</u>KE
23. ch<u>a</u>nce
24. t<u>a</u>x
25. <u>eigh</u>t
26. ch<u>e</u>ss
27. beL<u>IE</u>VE
28. C<u>A</u>Lendar
29. H<u>I</u>Story
30. m<u>ea</u>nt

/iy/	/ɪ/	/ey/	/ɛ/	/æ/
s<u>ee</u>	s<u>i</u>t	p<u>ay</u>	m<u>e</u>t	c<u>a</u>t

/a/ as in <u>not</u>

UNIT
11

1. PRODUCING /a/

Examples: <u>a</u>h, <u>O</u>CCupy, c<u>a</u>lm, l<u>a</u>rge, h<u>o</u>t, C<u>O</u>LLege, M<u>a</u>

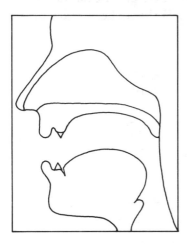

- Hold the front and back parts of your tongue low in your mouth, lower than for any other sound.
- Touch the lower front teeth lightly with the tip of the tongue.
- Lower your jaw and open your lips wide.
- Say "ahhh." Imagine that a doctor wants to look at your throat.

🎧 2. CONTRAST: /a/, /æ/, AND /ɛ/

A. Students may confuse the sound /a/ as in "n<u>o</u>t" with the sound /æ/ as in "c<u>a</u>t" or /ɛ/ as in "m<u>e</u>t." Practice these sounds, first normally, then with exaggeration, then normally. Listen and repeat.

1. /a/	/a. . . . ./	/a/
2. /æ/	/æ . . . ./	/æ/
3. /ɛ/	/ɛ. . . . ./	/ɛ/

B. Now practice these sounds in words. Notice the phonetic spelling. Listen and repeat each word twice.

1. arm	/arm/	arm
2. not	/nat/	not
3. clock	/klak/	clock
4. am	/æm/	am
5. laugh	/læf/	laugh
6. map	/mæp/	map
7. met	/mɛt/	met
8. sell	/sɛl/	sell
9. less	/lɛs/	less

3. CHECK YOUR LISTENING

You will hear words with the sounds /a/, /æ/, and /ɛ/. First, cover the words in the following list. Then listen to each word. Concentrate on the sound, not the spelling. Which vowel sound do you hear? Write a check mark in the correct column.

	/a/ as in "not"	/æ/ as in "cat"	/ɛ/ as in "met"
1. mop	_____	_____	_____
2. leg	_____	_____	_____
3. land	_____	_____	_____
4. calm	_____	_____	_____
5. odd	_____	_____	_____
6. end	_____	_____	_____
7. said	_____	_____	_____
8. sad	_____	_____	_____
9. on	_____	_____	_____
10. map	_____	_____	_____

4. PRACTICE THE CONTRAST: /a/ AS IN "N<u>O</u>T," /æ/ AS IN "C<u>A</u>T," /ɛ/ AS IN "M<u>E</u>T"

A. Practice these contrasting sounds. Listen and repeat each group of three words. *Capital letters indicate syllable stress.*

	/a/	/æ/	/ɛ/
1.	p<u>o</u>t	p<u>a</u>t	p<u>e</u>t
2.	<u>o</u>dd	<u>a</u>dd	<u>E</u>d
3.	b<u>o</u>nd	b<u>a</u>nd	b<u>e</u>nd
4.	<u>o</u>n	<u>a</u>n	"N"
5.	D<u>o</u>n	D<u>a</u>n	d<u>e</u>n
6.	S<u>o</u>l	S<u>a</u>l	s<u>e</u>ll
7.	l<u>o</u>g	l<u>a</u>g	l<u>e</u>g
8.	r<u>o</u>ck	r<u>a</u>ck	wr<u>e</u>ck
9.	<u>o</u>x	<u>a</u>xe	"X"
10.	F<u>O</u>LLow	F<u>A</u>LLow	F<u>E</u>LLow

B. Now practice the contrasting sounds in sentence pairs. The first sentence of each pair has the sound /a/ and the second has the sound /æ/. Listen and repeat. Notice the change in meaning. Visual clues can help. Make a simple drawing in each blank box. *Capital letters indicate syllable stress.*

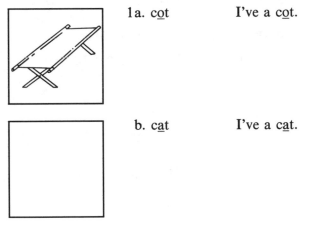

1a. c<u>o</u>t   I've a c<u>o</u>t.

b. c<u>a</u>t   I've a c<u>a</u>t.

2a. b<u>o</u>x   I see their b<u>o</u>x.

b. b<u>a</u>cks   I see their b<u>a</u>cks.

3a. p<u>o</u>t   She gave me a p<u>o</u>t.

 b. p<u>a</u>t   She gave me a p<u>a</u>t.

4a. m<u>o</u>p   I need a new m<u>o</u>p.

 b. m<u>a</u>p   I need a new m<u>a</u>p.

5a. S<u>o</u>l   She came with S<u>o</u>l.

 b. S<u>a</u>l   She came with S<u>a</u>l.

6a. c<u>o</u>p   The c<u>o</u>p is here.

 b. c<u>a</u>p   The c<u>a</u>p is here.

7a. m<u>o</u>sque   The m<u>o</u>sque is new.

 b. m<u>a</u>sk   The m<u>a</u>sk is new.

8a. sock   I've a hole in my sock.

b. sack   I've a hole in my sack.

9a. ox   He has an ox.

b. axe   He has an axe.

10a. POCKet   It's in my POCKet.

b. PACKet   It's in my PACKet.

C. The first sentence of each pair has the sound /a/ and the second has the sound /ɛ/. Listen and repeat. Notice the change in meaning. Visual clues can help. Make a simple drawing in each blank box.

1a. pot   I bought a pot.

b. pet   I bought a pet.

2a. John   Give it to John.

b. Jen   Give it to Jen.

3a. r<u>o</u>ck   I saw the r<u>o</u>ck.

b. wr<u>e</u>ck   I saw the wr<u>e</u>ck.

4a. d<u>o</u>t   The d<u>o</u>t is mine.

b. d<u>e</u>bt   The d<u>e</u>bt is mine.

5a. g<u>o</u>t   I g<u>o</u>t it!

b. g<u>e</u>t   I g<u>e</u>t it!

6a. st<u>o</u>p   Where's the st<u>o</u>p?

b. st<u>e</u>p   Where's the st<u>e</u>p?

7a. <u>o</u>dd   ISn't that <u>o</u>dd?

b. <u>E</u>d   ISn't that <u>E</u>d?

8a. bl<u>o</u>nd   He likes the bl<u>o</u>nd.

b. bl<u>e</u>nd   He likes the bl<u>e</u>nd.

○ 5. CHECK YOUR LISTENING

Work with a partner. Read a sentence from 4B or 4C to your partner. Can your partner define the sentence? He or she must be truthful.

Your partner will: • Say: I know what _____ means.
                          It means _____. (definition or paraphrase)
                          or
                       • Act out what the word means.
                          or
                       • Make a simple drawing.

Or your partner will ask: What does _____ mean? Then you must define the sentence, act it out, or make a drawing.

♠ 6. STRESS AND INTONATION

The words in the following list all begin with the letter "o." In these words, "o" represents the sound /a/ as in "n<u>o</u>t." Each word is followed by a sentence. You will hear each word and sentence four times:

1. Listen for the vowel sound /a/. (The letter for this sound is underlined.)
2. Listen for syllable stress and word stress. *Capital letters indicate syllable stress.* Mark the word stress that you hear. Put a stress mark (´) over the stressed word or words.
3. Listen for rising or falling intonation at the end of the sentence. Mark intonation with the symbol "⌐" or "⌐."
4. Listen to the word and sentence again and repeat it. Pay attention to pauses and linking of words.

The first sentence is marked for you.

1. <u>O</u>Bject   The <u>O</u>Bject of the game is to win.

2. <u>O</u>Bligated   I'm <u>O</u>Bligated to him.

3. <u>o</u>dd   It looks <u>o</u>dd, DOESn't it?

4. <u>O</u>Ctopus   It looks like an <u>O</u>Ctopus.

5. <u>O</u>Bvious   The dent in the car was quite <u>O</u>Bvious.

6. <u>o</u>ccuPAtion   What's your <u>o</u>ccuPAtion?

7. <u>O</u>cTOber   She'll VISit him in <u>O</u>cTOber.

8. <u>OB</u>stinate   Don't be <u>OB</u>stinate, do it!

9. <u>OC</u>Cupy   My SISter will <u>OC</u>Cupy the house.

10. <u>OB</u>stacle   The <u>OB</u>stacle course was DIFFicult.

🔆 7. DIALOGS

You will hear eight short dialogs with three sentences each. The first sentence contains words with /a/ as in "n<u>o</u>t," the second contains words with /æ/ as in "c<u>a</u>t," and the third has words with /ɛ/ as in "m<u>e</u>t." Listen to each dialog five times:

1. Concentrate on the meaning. Discuss any new vocabulary with your teacher and classmates.
2. Listen for the vowel sounds /a/, /æ/, and /ɛ/. (The letters for these sounds are underlined.)
3. Listen for syllable stress and word stress. (Capital letters indicate syllable stress.) Mark the word stress that you hear. Put a stress mark (ʹ) over the stressed word or words.
4. Listen for rising or falling intonation at the end of each sentence. Mark intonation with the symbol "↗" or "↘."
5. Listen to each sentence of the dialog again and repeat it. Pay attention to pauses and linking of words.

The first sentence is marked for you.

Mark: Is the c<u>a</u>rd in the gl<u>o</u>ve comP<u>A</u>RTment of the c<u>a</u>r?

SALLy: No, it's in the b<u>a</u>ck of the bl<u>a</u>ck C<u>A</u>Binet. L<u>e</u>t me g<u>e</u>t it for you.

ARthur: <u>A</u>re there two c<u>a</u>rs in your gaR<u>A</u>GE?

P<u>A</u>trick: I hope so; the bl<u>a</u>ck C<u>A</u>dill<u>a</u>c beLONGS to S<u>A</u>LLy. The r<u>e</u>d Ch<u>e</u>vroLET beLONGS to <u>E</u>d.

Mr. P<u>a</u>rk: Did the <u>A</u>Rtist C<u>O</u>py the carTOON?

Ms. T<u>A</u>NNer: No, he deM<u>A</u>NDed MONey in adV<u>A</u>NCE.

Mr. P<u>a</u>rk: W<u>e</u>ll, wh<u>e</u>n I g<u>e</u>t the time, I'll do it myS<u>E</u>LF.

MARcy: Does he play r<u>o</u>ck MUsic on his guiT<u>A</u>R?

<u>A</u>nn: I don't think he c<u>a</u>n; <u>a</u>sk him.

MARcy: No, I just m<u>e</u>t him YESterday.

B<u>o</u>b: What do we w<u>a</u>nt to eat?

R<u>a</u>lph: <u>A</u>sk the m<u>a</u>n for a h<u>a</u>m SALad SANDwich.

B<u>o</u>b: W<u>e</u>ll, I'd like some <u>e</u>ggs for BREAKfast.

Charles: <u>A</u>re you SHOPPing at the MARKet toMORRow?

<u>A</u>Lice: I'm GOing to buy some baN<u>A</u>Nas <u>a</u>nd h<u>a</u>lf a GALLon of APPle CIder.

Charles: W<u>e</u>ll, don't forGET to g<u>e</u>t the STRAWberries, JELLy, br<u>ea</u>d, LEMons, and PRETzcls.

J<u>o</u>hn: Did you s<u>o</u>lve the PROBlem? The one we h<u>a</u>d in m<u>a</u>th cl<u>a</u>ss?

<u>E</u>d: Y<u>e</u>s, l<u>e</u>t's g<u>e</u>t aNOTHer one.

D<u>o</u>n: Why is the c<u>a</u>r in the BODy sh<u>o</u>p?

<u>A</u>Ndy: It was DAMaged in the ACcident.

D<u>o</u>n: Will we g<u>e</u>t it by WEDNESday?

8. ROLE PLAY

Practice the short dialogs above with a partner. Help each other with sounds, stress, and intonation.

🔊 9. HOME ASSIGNMENT

A. Circle the word that has the same vowel sound as the word in the model column. Reminder: Say all the words aloud.

Example: Model

	h<u>a</u>t	s<u>o</u>ck	m<u>e</u>t	(bl<u>a</u>ck)
1.	c<u>a</u>n	c<u>e</u>nt	c<u>a</u>t	c<u>a</u>lm
2.	d<u>ea</u>d	l<u>au</u>gh	l<u>a</u>rge	h<u>ea</u>d
3.	w<u>e</u>t	wh<u>a</u>t	wh<u>e</u>n	w<u>as</u>
4.	m<u>a</u>th	m<u>e</u>n	m<u>e</u>ss	m<u>a</u>ss
5.	P<u>E</u>Ncil	P<u>AR</u>ty	p<u>a</u>st	p<u>e</u>st
6.	<u>A</u>Ny	<u>a</u>rt	pl<u>a</u>n	fr<u>ie</u>nd
7.	s<u>ai</u>d	s<u>a</u>d	R<u>EA</u>Dy	c<u>a</u>lm
8.	s<u>e</u>ll	s<u>o</u>lve	h<u>e</u>lp	S<u>A</u>Turday
9.	w<u>a</u>sh	C<u>O</u>LLar	wr<u>e</u>ck	c<u>a</u>tch
10.	h<u>a</u>ve	h<u>ea</u>d	h<u>ea</u>rt	h<u>a</u>nd
11.	H<u>O</u>Nest	C<u>O</u>LLege	h<u>a</u>m	h<u>e</u>ll
12.	<u>A</u>PPle	s<u>ay</u>s	m<u>a</u>tch	<u>a</u>rm

B. Make up six short sentences with six different words selected from the column marked "Model." Underline the word in your sentence.

Example: The <u>hat</u> her mother wore to the wedding looked beautiful.

/ay/ as in <u>buy</u>

1. PRODUCING /ay/

Examples: <u>i</u>ce, <u>eye</u>, n<u>i</u>ce, h<u>eight</u>, g<u>ui</u>de,[1] rh<u>y</u>me, m<u>y</u>, d<u>ie</u>

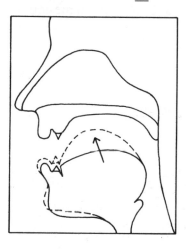

- Hold the front and back parts of your tongue low in your mouth, as for /a/ as in "n<u>o</u>t."
- Touch the lower front teeth lightly with the tip of the tongue.
- Lower your jaw and open your lips wide.
- Begin by saying "ahhh." Then raise your jaw and the front part of your tongue at the same time to complete the sound.

2. CONTRAST: /ay/ AND /æ/

A. Students may confuse the sound /ay/ as in "b<u>uy</u>" with the sound /æ/ as in "c<u>a</u>t." Practice these two sounds, first normally, then with exaggeration, then normally. Listen and repeat.

1. /ay/	/ay. . . ./	/ay/
2. /æ/	/æ . . . ./	/æ/

[1]The final "e" in words such as "g<u>ui</u>de," "rh<u>y</u>me," and "h<u>i</u>de" signals the /ay/ pronunciation for the first vowel sound. Compare "h<u>i</u>d" /h<u>ı</u>d/ with "h<u>i</u>de" /hayd/. But in words such as "<u>i</u>ce," the final "e" marks the "c" as /s/.

B. Now practice these sounds in words. Notice the phonetic spelling. Listen and repeat each word twice.

1. ice	/ays/	ice
2. die	/day/	die
3. hide	/hayd/	hide
4. back	/bæk/	back
5. had	/hæd/	had
6. sand	/sænd/	sand
7. fine	/fayn/	fine
8. fly	/flay/	fly

3. CHECK YOUR LISTENING

You will hear words with the sounds /ay/ and /æ/. First, cover the words in the following list. Then listen to each word. Concentrate on the sound, not the spelling. Which vowel sound do you hear? Write a check mark in the correct column.

	/ay/ as in "buy"	/æ/ as in "cat"
1. fly	____	____
2. sigh	____	____
3. mine	____	____
4. hat	____	____
5. man	____	____
6. height	____	____
7. wife	____	____
8. crash	____	____
9. side	____	____
10. sand	____	____

🎧 4. PRACTICE THE CONTRAST: /ay/ AS IN "B<u>UY</u>" WITH /æ/ AS IN "C<u>A</u>T"

A. Practice these contrasting sounds. Listen and repeat each word pair.

	/ay/	/æ/		/ay/	/æ/
1.	r<u>igh</u>t	r<u>a</u>t	8.	m<u>igh</u>t	m<u>a</u>t
2.	h<u>i</u>de	h<u>a</u>d	9.	f<u>igh</u>t	f<u>a</u>t
3.	s<u>i</u>de	s<u>a</u>d	10.	m<u>i</u>ce	m<u>a</u>ss
4.	d<u>ie</u>d	D<u>a</u>d	11.	m<u>i</u>ne	m<u>a</u>n
5.	b<u>i</u>ke	b<u>a</u>ck	12.	f<u>i</u>ne	f<u>a</u>n
6.	h<u>eigh</u>t	h<u>a</u>t	13.	l<u>i</u>ke	l<u>a</u>ck
7.	b<u>i</u>te	b<u>a</u>t	14.	l<u>ie</u>d	l<u>a</u>d

B. Now practice the contrasting sounds in sentence pairs. The first sentence of each pair has the sound /ay/ and the second has the sound /æ/. Listen and repeat. Notice the change in meaning. Visual clues can help. Make a simple drawing in each blank box. *Capital letters indicate syllable stress.*

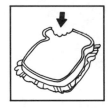

1a. b<u>i</u>te   It was a big b<u>i</u>te.

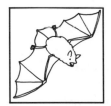

b. b<u>a</u>t   It was a big b<u>a</u>t.

2a. h<u>i</u>de   They ALways h<u>i</u>de it.

b. h<u>a</u>d   They ALways h<u>a</u>d it.

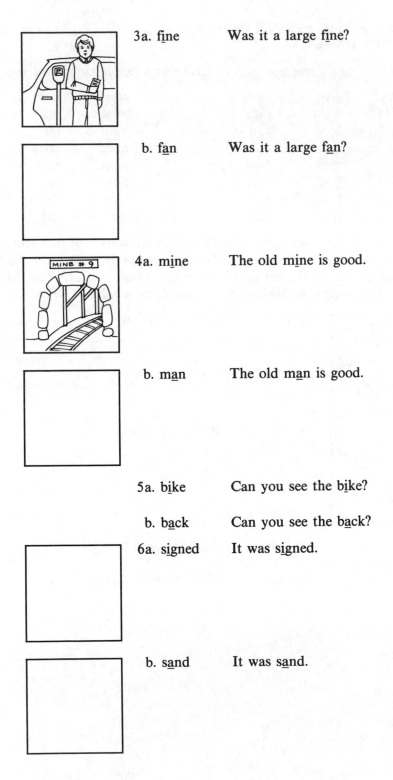

3a. f<u>i</u>ne   Was it a large f<u>i</u>ne?

b. f<u>a</u>n   Was it a large f<u>a</u>n?

4a. m<u>i</u>ne   The old m<u>i</u>ne is good.

b. m<u>a</u>n   The old m<u>a</u>n is good.

5a. b<u>i</u>ke   Can you see the b<u>i</u>ke?

b. b<u>a</u>ck   Can you see the b<u>a</u>ck?

6a. s<u>i</u>gned   It was s<u>i</u>gned.

b. s<u>a</u>nd   It was s<u>a</u>nd.

☊ 5. CHECK YOUR LISTENING

Work with a partner. Read a sentence from Exercise 4B to your partner. Can your partner define the sentence? He or she must be truthful.

Your partner will: • Say: I know what _____ means.
It means _____. (definition or paraphrase)
or
• Act out what the word means.
or
• Make a simple drawing.

Or your partner will ask: What does _____ mean? Then you must define the sentence, act it out, or make a drawing.

🎧 6. STRESS AND INTONATION

You will hear each sentence four times:

1. Listen for the vowel sound /ay/ as in "b<u>uy</u>." (The letters for this sound are underlined.)
2. Listen for syllable stress and word stress. (Capital letters indicate syllable stress.) Mark the word stress that you hear. Put a stress mark (´) over the stressed word or words.
3. Listen for rising or falling intonation at the end of the sentence. Mark intonation with the symbol "➚" or "➘."
4. Listen to the sentence again and repeat it. Pay attention to pauses and linking of words.

Examples: a. I'd like to eat r<u>i</u>ce toN<u>I</u>GHT.

b. Did he say he WANTed to tr<u>y</u> the french fr<u>ie</u>s?

1. You're qu<u>i</u>te r<u>i</u>ght to do that.

2. The br<u>i</u>de cr<u>i</u>ed as she walked down the <u>ai</u>sle.

3. <u>I</u> was deL<u>I</u>GHTed with the r<u>i</u>pe P<u>I</u>NEapple.

4. The <u>I</u>Sland of <u>I</u>CEland is qu<u>i</u>te n<u>i</u>ce.

5. FL<u>Y</u>ing to CH<u>I</u>na is exC<u>I</u>Ting.

6. Wh<u>y</u> did the wh<u>i</u>te dog b<u>i</u>te <u>I</u>da?

7. Did you see the H<u>I</u>GHway s<u>i</u>gn?

8. When did you reMIND him to get the ice?
9. The bright lights were SHINing.
10. Did the suPPLIES aRRIVE on time?

7. DIALOG

You will hear a dialog with words that contain the sound /ay/ as in "buy." Listen to the dialog five times:

1. Concentrate on the meaning. Discuss any new vocabulary with your teacher and classmates.
2. Listen for the vowel sound /ay/. (The letters for this sound are underlined.)
3. Listen for syllable stress and word stress. *Capital letters indicate syllable stress.* Mark the word stress that you hear. Put a stress mark (′) over the stressed word or words.
4. Listen for rising or falling intonation at the end of each sentence. Mark intonation with the symbol "↗" or "↘."
5. Listen to each sentence of the dialog again and repeat it. Pay attention to pauses and linking of words.

The first sentence is marked for you.

Mr. Pyle:	Are you SEEing Míke toNÍGHT? ↗
Ivy:	Yes. He has a new MOtorcycle.
Mr. Pyle:	Did he let you ride it?
Ivy:	Yes, I tried it. And I liked it.
Mr. Pyle:	Weren't you FRIGHTened?
Ivy:	Sure, but I still liked it.
Mr. Pyle:	Would you like to buy a MOtorcycle?
Ivy:	No, I don't think so. I think I'll buy a bike.
Mr. Pyle:	A bike?
Ivy:	Yes. RIDing on Mike's MOtorcycle was nice, but I'd RATHer have a bike. And it's CHEAPer.

↻ 8. ROLE PLAY

Practice the dialog with a partner. Help each other with correct sounds, stress, and intonation.

⛷ 9. HOME ASSIGNMENT

The following poem is an old rhyme that contains a riddle.

1. Read it aloud. You can use a dictionary to help you with the pronunciation of new words.
2. Draw a single line under all words that have the sound /ay/ as in "b<u>uy</u>."
3. Draw a double line under all words with the sound /æ/ as in "c<u>a</u>t."
4. Mark stressed words with a stress mark (´).
5. Read the rhyme aloud one more time.

Example: <u>I</u> met a m<u>a</u>n with SEVen w<u>i</u>ves.

As I Was GOing to St. Ives[2]

As I was GOing to St. Ives,

I met a man with SEVen wives,

Each wife had SEVen sacks,

Each sack had SEVen cats.

Each cat had SEVen kits[3],

Kits, cats, sacks, and wives,

How MANy were GOing to St. Ives?

Can you answer the last question of the rhyme?

[2]St. Ives: a town in England.
[3]kit: an old word for "kitten."

/aw/ as in <u>now</u>

1. PRODUCING /aw/

Examples: <u>ou</u>ch, <u>ou</u>t, cl<u>ou</u>d, h<u>ou</u>se, t<u>ow</u>n, v<u>ow</u>el, h<u>ow</u>, c<u>ow</u>

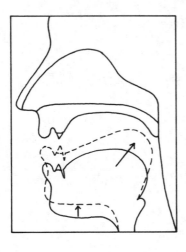

- Hold the front and back parts of your tongue low in your mouth, as for /a/ as in "n<u>o</u>t."
- Touch the lower front teeth lightly with the tip of the tongue.
- Lower your jaw and open your lips wide.
- Begin by saying "ahhh." Then raise your jaw and round your lips. Move the back part of your tongue toward the roof (soft palate) of your mouth to complete the sound.

2. CONTRAST: /aw/ AND /a/

A. Students do not usually have a problem pronouncing the sound /aw/ as in "n<u>ow</u>." However, they may confuse it with /a/ as in "n<u>o</u>t." Practice these two sounds, first normally, then with exaggeration, then normally. Listen and repeat.

1. /aw/   /aw. . . ./   /aw/
2. /a/   /a. . . . ./   /a/

B. Now practice these sounds in words. Notice the phonetic spelling. Listen and repeat each word twice.

1. <u>ou</u>t	/awt/	<u>ou</u>t
2. p<u>ou</u>nd	/pawnd/	p<u>ou</u>nd
3. d<u>ou</u>bt	/dawt/	d<u>ou</u>bt
4. p<u>o</u>nd	/pand/	p<u>o</u>nd
5. d<u>o</u>t	/dat/	d<u>o</u>t
6. f<u>a</u>r	/far/	f<u>a</u>r
7. h<u>ow</u>	/haw/	h<u>ow</u>
8. br<u>ow</u>n	/brawn/	br<u>ow</u>n

☀ **3.** CHECK YOUR LISTENING

You will hear words with the sounds /aw/ and /a/. First, cover the words in the following list. Then listen to each word. Concentrate on the sound, not the spelling. Which vowel sound do you hear? Write a check mark in the correct column.

	/aw/ as in "<u>now</u>"	/a/ as in "n<u>o</u>t"
1. t<u>ow</u>n	_____	_____
2. <u>a</u>h	_____	_____
3. h<u>ou</u>r	_____	_____
4. <u>a</u>re	_____	_____
5. T<u>o</u>m	_____	_____
6. cl<u>ou</u>d	_____	_____
7. <u>ou</u>ch	_____	_____
8. g<u>o</u>t	_____	_____
9. d<u>ow</u>n	_____	_____
10. sh<u>ou</u>t	_____	_____

💡 4. PRACTICE THE CONTRAST: /aw/ AS IN "N<u>OW</u>" WITH /a/ AS IN "N<u>O</u>T"

A. Practice these contrasting sounds. Listen and repeat each word pair.

	/aw/	/a/
1.	<u>ow</u>	<u>a</u>h
2.	p<u>ou</u>nd	p<u>o</u>nd
3.	t<u>ow</u>n	T<u>o</u>m
4.	d<u>ou</u>bt	d<u>o</u>t
5.	sh<u>ou</u>t	sh<u>o</u>t
6.	sp<u>ou</u>t	sp<u>o</u>t
7.	d<u>ow</u>n	D<u>o</u>n
8.	f<u>ou</u>nd	f<u>o</u>nd
9.	br<u>ow</u>ns	br<u>o</u>nze
10.	sc<u>ou</u>ts	Sc<u>o</u>ts

B. Now practice the contrasting sounds in sentence pairs. The first sentence of each pair has the sound /aw/ and the second has the sound /a/. Listen and repeat. Notice the change in meaning. Visual clues can help. Make a simple drawing in each blank box.

1a. <u>ow</u>   Did she say "<u>Ow</u>?"

b. <u>a</u>h   Did she say "<u>A</u>h?"

2a. sh<u>ou</u>t   I heard a sh<u>ou</u>t.

b. sh<u>o</u>t   I heard a sh<u>o</u>t.

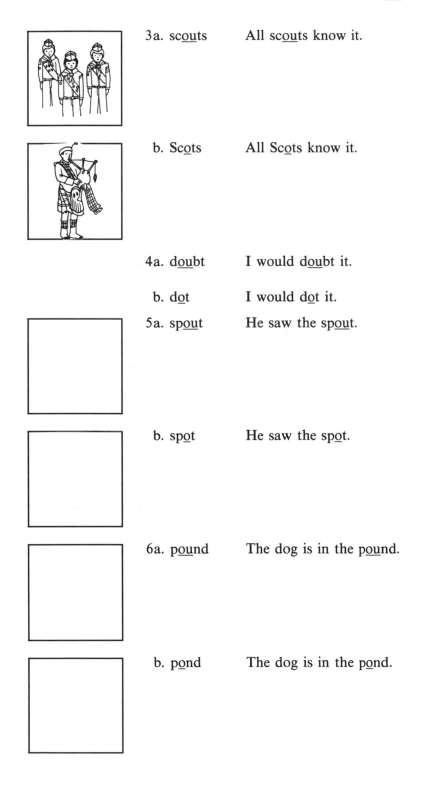

3a. sc<u>ou</u>ts   All sc<u>ou</u>ts know it.

b. Sc<u>o</u>ts   All Sc<u>o</u>ts know it.

4a. d<u>ou</u>bt   I would d<u>ou</u>bt it.

b. d<u>o</u>t   I would d<u>o</u>t it.

5a. sp<u>ou</u>t   He saw the sp<u>ou</u>t.

b. sp<u>o</u>t   He saw the sp<u>o</u>t.

6a. p<u>ou</u>nd   The dog is in the p<u>ou</u>nd.

b. p<u>o</u>nd   The dog is in the p<u>o</u>nd.

7a. d<u>ow</u>n   Did you call d<u>ow</u>n?

b. D<u>o</u>n   Did you call D<u>o</u>n?

8a. f<u>ou</u>nd   I said "f<u>ou</u>nd."

b. f<u>o</u>nd   I said "f<u>o</u>nd."

9a. t<u>ow</u>n   I went to t<u>ow</u>n.

b. T<u>o</u>m   I went to T<u>o</u>m.

10a. br<u>ow</u>ns   I like them in br<u>ow</u>ns.

b. br<u>o</u>nze   I like them in br<u>o</u>nze.

↻ 5. CHECK YOUR LISTENING

Work with a partner. Read a sentence from 4B to your partner. Can your partner define the sentence? He or she must be truthful.

Your partner will: • Say: I know what _____ means.
It means _____. (definition or paraphrase)
or
• Act out what the word means.
or
• Make a simple drawing.

Or your partner will ask: What does _____ mean? Then you must define the sentence, act it out, or make a drawing.

🎧 6. STRESS AND INTONATION

Each of these sentences contains both vowel sounds, /a/ as in "n<u>o</u>t" and /aw/ as in "n<u>ow</u>." You will hear each word and sentence four times:

1. Listen for the vowel sounds /a/ and /aw/. (The letters for these sounds are underlined.)
2. Listen for syllable stress and word stress. *Capital letters indicate syllable stress.* Mark the word stress that you hear. Put a stress mark (ʹ) over the stressed word or words.
3. Listen for rising or falling intonation at the end of the sentence. Mark intonation with the symbol "⟋" or "⟍."
4. Listen to the sentence again and repeat it. Pay attention to pauses and linking of words.

The first sentence is marked for you.

1. The cl<u>o</u>ck broke d<u>own</u>.
2. The j<u>o</u>b is in aNOTHer COUNty.
3. It's aPPR<u>O</u>Ximately one <u>ou</u>nce.
4. Is it PR<u>O</u>Per to aNN<u>OU</u>NCE it?
5. The SERgeant sat <u>o</u>n the c<u>ou</u>ch.
6. Did the <u>A</u>Rchitect sh<u>ou</u>t at the OWNer?
7. Is it P<u>O</u>SSible to take a SH<u>OW</u>er?
8. The aL<u>A</u>RM went off at an EARly h<u>ou</u>r.
9. The H<u>O</u>Spital is aR<u>OU</u>ND the CORner.
10. The MONey MARket aCC<u>OU</u>NT is new.

🎧 7. DIALOG

You will hear a dialog with words that contain the sounds /aw/ as in "n<u>ow</u>" and /a/ as in "n<u>o</u>t." Listen to the dialog five times:

1. Concentrate on the meaning. Discuss any new vocabulary with your teacher and classmates.
2. Listen for the vowel sounds /aw/ and /a/. The letters for these sounds are underlined.
3. Listen for syllable stress and word stress. *Capital letters indicate syllable stress.* Mark the word stress that you hear. Put a stress mark (ʹ) over the stressed word or words.

4. Listen for rising or falling intonation at the end of each sentence. Mark intonation with the symbol "⤴" or "⤵."

5. Listen to each sentence of the dialog again and repeat it. Pay attention to pauses and linking of words.

The first sentence is marked for you.

Tom is on the phone. We hear only one side of this dialog.

Tom: I heard a sh<u>o</u>t COMing from t<u>ow</u>n!

J<u>o</u>hn: _____

Tom: EVeryone in the h<u>ou</u>se was SHOUTing at D<u>o</u>n!

       But he DIDn't go d<u>ow</u>n there, and I DIDn't EIther.

J<u>o</u>hn: _____

Tom: I don't see any sense in BEing aR<u>OU</u>ND TROUBle.

J<u>o</u>hn: _____

Tom: D<u>o</u>n said, "I d<u>ou</u>bt that ANyone was hurt.

       But the H<u>O</u>Spital is just aR<u>OU</u>ND the CORner. That's LUCKy."

J<u>o</u>hn: _____

Tom: He's PRETTy c<u>a</u>lm, don't you think?

J<u>o</u>hn: _____

Tom: Well, things have been BETTer. I have to go <u>ou</u>t n<u>ow</u>. So long!

J<u>o</u>hn: _____

↻ 8. ROLE PLAY

Work with a partner. Make up John's lines for the telephone conversation. Practice the dialog. Help each other with correct sounds, stress, and intonation.

🐎 9. HOME ASSIGNMENT

1. Read the following old rhyme aloud. You can use a dictionary to help you with the pronunciation of new words.
2. Draw a line under all words that have the sound /aw/ as in "n<u>ow</u>." (Hint: There are thirteen different words. Words that are repeated should be counted once only.)
3. Mark stressed words with a stress mark (´).
4. Read the poem aloud one more time.

The first sentence is marked for you.

The <u>ówl</u> looked d<u>ówn</u> with his great <u>round</u> éyes

At the low clouds and the dark skies,

"A good night for SCOUTing[1]," says he,

"With NEVer a sound I'll go PROWLing aROUND.[2]

A mouse or two may be found on the ground

Or a fat little bird in a tree."

So down he flew from the old church TOWer,

The mouse and the BIRDie crouch[3] and COWer,[4]

Back he flies in half an hour,

"A VERy good SUPPer," says he.

[1]scouting: exploring.
[2]prowling around: searching here and there.
[3]crouch: bend down.
[4]cower: crouch in fear.

UNIT
14

/ə/ as in <u>up</u>

1. PRODUCING /ə/

Examples: <u>u</u>s, <u>U</u>Mpire, S<u>U</u>Nday, bl<u>oo</u>d, TR<u>OU</u>Ble, <u>a</u>BOUT,
<u>o</u>PPOSE, b<u>a</u>NAN<u>a</u>, PRECI<u>ou</u>s, COm<u>a</u>

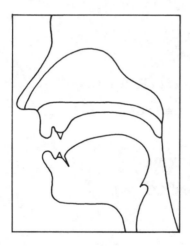

- Hold the front part of your tongue low in your mouth.
- Touch the lower front teeth lightly with the tip of the tongue.
- Lower your jaw and open your lips slightly.
- Raise the center part of your tongue toward the roof (hard palate) of your mouth.
- Native speakers often use this sound when they are hesitating. It is usually written "uh."

🎧 2. CONTRAST: /ə/, /a/, /æ/, AND /ɛ/

A. Students may confuse the sound /ə/ as in "<u>up</u>" with other sounds. These sounds include /a/ as in "n<u>o</u>t," /æ/ as in "c<u>a</u>t," and /ɛ/ as in "m<u>e</u>t." Practice these sounds, first normally, then with exaggeration, then normally. Listen and repeat.

1. /ə/	/ə. . . . ./	/ə/
2. /a/	/a. . . . ./	/a/
3. /æ/	/æ . . . ./	/æ/
4. /ɛ/	/ɛ. . . . ./	/ɛ/

B. Now practice these sounds in words. Notice the phonetic spelling. Listen and repeat each word twice.

1.	up	/əp/	up
2.	love	/ləv/	love
3.	cut	/kət/	cut
4.	not	/nat/	not
5.	clock	/klak/	clock
6.	mob	/mab/	mob
7.	cat	/kæt/	cat
8.	have	/hæv/	have
9.	bag	/bæg/	bag
10.	met	/mɛt/	met
11.	dead	/dɛd/	dead
12.	end	/ɛnd/	end

3. CHECK YOUR LISTENING

You will hear words with the sounds /ə/, /a/, /æ/, and /ɛ/. First, cover the words in the following list. Then listen to each word. Concentrate on the sound, not the spelling. Which vowel sound do you hear? Write a check mark in the correct column.

	/ə/ as in "up"	/a/ as in "not"	/æ/ as in "cat"	/ɛ/ as in "met"
1. cup	____	____	____	____
2. sun	____	____	____	____
3. can	____	____	____	____
4. set	____	____	____	____
5. shop	____	____	____	____
6. leg	____	____	____	____
7. pot	____	____	____	____
8. gum	____	____	____	____
9. sad	____	____	____	____
10. lunch	____	____	____	____

⚇ 4. PRACTICE THE CONTRAST: /ə/ AS IN "U̱P" WITH /æ/ AS IN "CA̱T"

A. Practice these contrasting sounds. Listen and repeat each word pair.

	/ə/	/æ/			/ə/	/æ/
1.	luck	lack		6.	stuck	stack
2.	suck	sack		7.	mud	mad
3.	some	Sam		8.	ton	tan
4.	fun	fan		9.	dumb	dam
5.	but	bat		10.	much	match

B. Now practice the contrasting sounds in sentence pairs. The first sentence of each pair has the sound /ə/ and the second has the sound /æ/. Listen and repeat. Notice the change in meaning. Visual clues can help. Make a simple drawing in each blank box. *Capital letters indicate syllable stress.*

1a. cup   I found the cup.

  b. cap   I found the cap.

2a. cut   I've a small cut.

  b. cat   I've a small cat.

3a. trucks   The trucks are here.

  b. tracks   The tracks are here.

4a. h<u>u</u>t   I found the h<u>u</u>t.

b. h<u>a</u>t   I found the h<u>a</u>t.

5a. b<u>u</u>g   Here's the b<u>u</u>g!

b. b<u>a</u>g   Here's the b<u>a</u>g!

6a. <u>U</u>Ncle   Did you see my <u>U</u>Ncle?

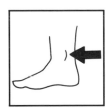

b. <u>A</u>Nkle   Did you see my <u>A</u>Nkle?

5. PRACTICE THE CONTRAST: /ə/ AS IN "<u>U</u>P" WITH /ɛ/ AS IN "M<u>E</u>T"

A. Practice these contrasting sounds. Listen and repeat each word pair.

	/ə/	/ɛ/		/ə/	/ɛ/
1.	b<u>u</u>t	b<u>e</u>t	5.	fl<u>oo</u>d	fl<u>e</u>d
2.	t<u>o</u>n	t<u>e</u>n	6.	b<u>u</u>g	b<u>e</u>g
3.	d<u>o</u>ne	d<u>e</u>n	7.	m<u>u</u>st	m<u>e</u>ssed
4.	bl<u>oo</u>d	bl<u>e</u>d	8.	b<u>u</u>nch	b<u>e</u>nch

B. Now practice the contrasting sounds in sentence pairs. The first sentence of each pair has the sound /ə/ and the second has the sound /ɛ/. Listen and repeat. Notice the change in meaning. Visual clues can help. Make a simple drawing in each blank box. *Capital letters indicate syllable stress.*

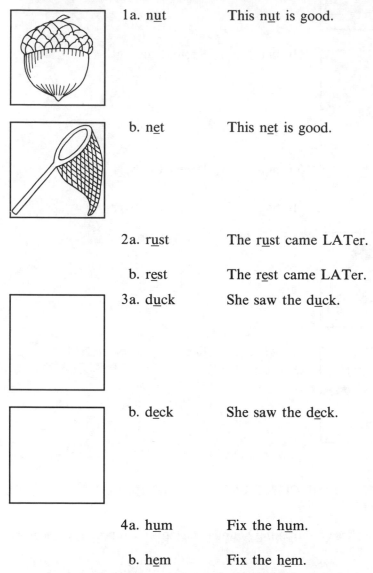

1a. n<u>u</u>t   This n<u>u</u>t is good.

b. n<u>e</u>t   This n<u>e</u>t is good.

2a. r<u>u</u>st   The r<u>u</u>st came LATer.

b. r<u>e</u>st   The r<u>e</u>st came LATer.

3a. d<u>u</u>ck   She saw the d<u>u</u>ck.

b. d<u>e</u>ck   She saw the d<u>e</u>ck.

4a. h<u>u</u>m   Fix the h<u>u</u>m.

b. h<u>e</u>m   Fix the h<u>e</u>m.

5a. b<u>u</u>st   He will b<u>u</u>st it.

 b. b<u>e</u>st   He will b<u>e</u>st it.

6a. MO<u>O</u>Ney   Do you have M<u>O</u>Ney READy?

 b. M<u>A</u>Ny   Do you have M<u>A</u>Ny READy?

6. PRACTICE THE CONTRAST: /ə/ AS IN "<u>UP</u>" WITH /a/ AS IN "N<u>O</u>T"

A. Practice these contrasting sounds. Listen and repeat each word pair.

	/ə/	/a/			/ə/	/a/
1.	c<u>u</u>p	c<u>o</u>p		5.	d<u>u</u>ck	d<u>o</u>ck
2.	sh<u>u</u>t	sh<u>o</u>t		6.	d<u>u</u>ll	d<u>o</u>ll
3.	r<u>u</u>b	r<u>o</u>b		7.	b<u>u</u>m	b<u>o</u>mb
4.	f<u>u</u>nd	f<u>o</u>nd		8.	st<u>u</u>ck	st<u>o</u>ck

B. Now practice the contrasting sounds in sentence pairs. The first sentence of each pair has the sound /ə/ and the second has the sound /a/. Listen and repeat. Notice the change in meaning. Visual clues can help. Make a simple drawing in each blank box.

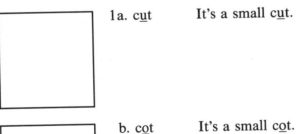

1a. c<u>u</u>t   It's a small c<u>u</u>t.

 b. c<u>o</u>t   It's a small c<u>o</u>t.

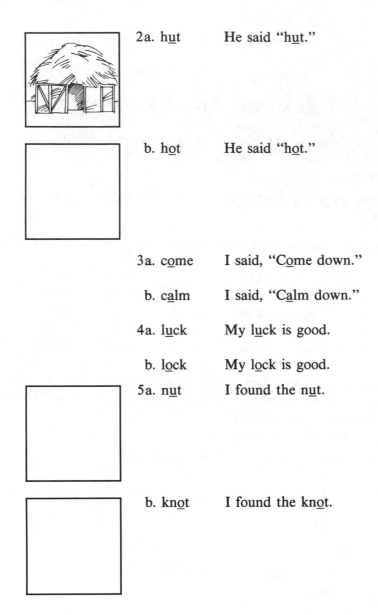

2a. h<u>u</u>t   He said "h<u>u</u>t."

b. h<u>o</u>t   He said "h<u>o</u>t."

3a. c<u>o</u>me   I said, "C<u>o</u>me down."

b. c<u>a</u>lm   I said, "C<u>a</u>lm down."

4a. l<u>u</u>ck   My l<u>u</u>ck is good.

b. l<u>o</u>ck   My l<u>o</u>ck is good.

5a. n<u>u</u>t   I found the n<u>u</u>t.

b. kn<u>o</u>t   I found the kn<u>o</u>t.

 6a. d<u>u</u>ck   The d<u>u</u>ck is white.

 b. d<u>o</u>ck   The d<u>o</u>ck is white.

⟳ 7. CHECK YOUR LISTENING

Work with a partner. Read a sentence from 4B, 5B, or 6B to your partner. Can your partner define the sentence? He or she must be truthful.

Your partner will: • Say: I know what _____ means.
                          It means _____. (definition or paraphrase)
                          or
                         • Act out what the word means.
                          or
                         • Make a simple drawing.

Or your partner will ask: What does _____ mean? Then you must define the sentence, act it out, or make a drawing.

🎧 8. /ə/ IN UNSTRESSED SYLLABLES

A. Words Beginning with "a"
Some two syllable words begin with the sound /ə/ as in "<u>up</u>" in the unstressed syllable. This sound is represented by the letter "a." Listen and repeat these words and sentences. *Capital letters indicate syllable stress.*

       1a. sleep   Go to sleep.
         b. aSLEEP   He's aSLEEP.

       2a. side   It's on my side.
         b. aSIDE   Put it aSIDE.

       3a. way   It's in the way.
         b. aWAY   Put it aWAY.

4a. dress   It's a nice dress.
  b. aDDRESS   Will you aDDRESS it?

5a. go   Let's go.
  b. aGO   It was long aGO.

6a. like   He's like you.
  b. aLIKE   They're both aLIKE.

B. Words Ending with "ous"
Some words end with the sounds /əs/ in an unstressed syllable. These sounds are represented by the letters "ous." Listen and repeat these words and sentences. *Capital letters indicate syllable stress.*

1. CAUtious   He's CAUtious.
2. CONscious   Was he CONscious?
3. conTINuous   It's conTINuous.
4. COURteous   She's COURteous.
5. CURious   I'm CURious.
6. DANgerous   That's DANgerous.
7. eNORmous   It was eNORmous.
8. FAmous   They're FAmous.
9. HUmorous   It's HUmorous.
10. JEALous   He's a JEALous man.

C. Dropping /ə/ in Unstressed Syllables
In some words, /ə/ occurs as an unstressed syllable between two consonant sounds. Many speakers, in informal speech, do not pronounce the /ə/ in such words. Listen and repeat these examples. *Capital letters indicate syllable stress.*

1. acciDENtally	13. FAMily	25. reCOVery
2. BACHelor	14. GALLery	26. REFerence
3. BAKery	15. GENeral	27. SALary
4. BEVerage	16. GROcery	28. satisFACtory
5. CAMera	17. HIStory	29. SEVeral
6. CHOColate	18. INterested	30. SLIPPery
7. COMfortable[1]	19. LABoratory	31. TEMperature
8. DIFFerent	20. LIBeral	32. TRAVeler
9. disCOVery	21. MEMory	33. VEGetable
10. eleMENtary	22. MYStery	34. VETeran
11. EVery	23. OPera	35. WONdering
12. FACtory	24. PRIVilege	

[1]The sound /r/ in this word is also omitted.

🎧 9. STRESS AND INTONATION

Each of these phrases and sentences contains the vowel sound /ə/ as in "up." You will hear each phrase and sentence four times:

1. Listen for the vowel sound /ə/. (The letters for this sound are underlined.)
2. Listen for syllable stress and word stress. *Capital letters indicate syllable stress.* Mark the word stress that you hear. Put a stress mark (ʹ) over the stressed word or words.
3. Listen for rising or falling intonation at the end of the sentence. Mark intonation with the symbol "⤴" or "⤵."
4. Listen to the phrase and sentence again and repeat it. Pay attention to pauses and linking of words.

The first phrase and sentence are marked for you.

1a. some fún

  b. Let's have some fún.

2a. aRRIVE HUNgry

  b. I'll aRRIVE HUNgry.

3a. STUDy on MONday

  b. Why don't you STUDy on MONday?

4a. DOUBle my MONey

  b. Can you DOUBle my MONey?

5a. lunch on SUNday

  b. Let's have lunch on SUNday.

6a. come up

  b. Will you come up with me?

7a. DIet SOda

  b. Do you drink DIet SOda?

8a. CINNamon buns

  b. I ate CINNamon buns.

9a. aBOUT the aMOUNT

b. Let's talk aBOUT the aMOUNT.

10a. FUNNy-LOOKing MONkey

b. He's a FUNNy-LOOKing MONkey.

💡 10. DIALOG

You will hear a dialog with words that contain the sound /ə/ as in "up." Listen to the dialog five times:

1. Concentrate on the meaning. Discuss any new vocabulary with your teacher and classmates.
2. Listen for the vowel sound /ə/. (Letters for this sound are underlined.)
3. Listen for syllable stress and word stress. *Capital letters indicate syllable stress.* Mark the word stress that you hear. Put a stress mark (´) over the stressed word or words.
4. Listen for rising or falling intonation at the end of each sentence. Mark intonation with the symbol "⤴" or "⤵."
5. Listen to each sentence of the dialog again and repeat it. Pay attention to pauses and linking of words.

The first sentence is marked for you. Notice that unstressed /ə/ is marked for function words, like "to." "To" is pronounced /tə/ in conversational speech (see Unit 6.)

DOUGlas: What are your plans for the WEEKend?

DANiel: Uh, I don't know. I'll PROBably be aSLEEP half of SATurday.

I'll be DREAMing aBOUT a date with a FAMous MOVie star.

DOUGlas: Well, I'm GOing to STUDy on SUNday. How aBOUT a MOVie SATurday night?

DANiel: Uh, well, I might have a date.

DOUGlas: Oh, come on aLONG with me. We'll have a good time.

MAYbe I can find dates for both of us.

DANiel: I'm broke. Do you have ANy MONey?

DOUGlas: ENOUGH to lend you a few DOLLars. OK?

DANiel: OK. You've got a deal!

☉ 11. ROLE PLAY

Practice the dialog with a partner. Help each other with correct sounds, stress, and intonation.

🐎 12. HOME ASSIGNMENT

The vowel sound /ə/ as in "<u>up</u>" is spelled different ways in the following list of words. Sometimes it is stressed and sometimes it is unstressed. Draw a line through the letters representing /ə/ in unstressed syllables. Put a stress mark above the letters for the /ə/ sounds that are stressed.

Examples: a. comma (unstressed)

b. toúch (stressed)

1. us	11. does
2. alarm	12. punish
3. announce	13. tough
4. ugly	14. Canada
5. complete	15. discuss
6. won	16. data
7. justice	17. mustang
8. island	18. complain
9. support	19. cousin
10. coma	20. dynasty

/ər/ as in <u>sir</u>

1. PRODUCING /ər/

Examples: <u>ur</u>ge, <u>EAR</u>ly, ch<u>ur</u>ch, h<u>ear</u>d, shi<u>r</u>t, w<u>or</u>m, P<u>ER</u>son, JO<u>UR</u>Nal, PLEAS<u>ure</u>, h<u>er</u>, SUG<u>ar</u>, WA<u>ter</u>

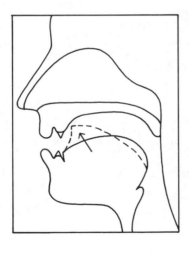

- This sound is a combination of /ə/ and /r/. The result is a single sound that can be represented by the letters "er."
- Hold the front part of your tongue low in your mouth.
- Touch the lower front teeth lightly with the tip of the tongue.
- Lower your jaw and open your lips slightly.
- As you begin to say the sound raise the center part of your tongue toward the roof (hard palate) of your mouth.
- Move the tongue tip up, toward the upper gum ridge, but do not touch it.
- The muscles in your tongue should be tense.

2. CONTRAST: /ər/ AND /ar/

A. Students may confuse the sound /ər/ as in "s<u>ir</u>" with /ar/ as in "f<u>ar</u>." Practice these sounds, first normally, then with exaggeration, then normally. Listen and repeat.

        1. /ər/   /ər. . . ./   /ər/
        2. /ar/   /ar. . . ./   /ar/

B. Now practice these sounds in words. Notice the phonetic spelling. Listen and repeat each word twice.

1.	earn	/ərn/	earn
2.	bird	/bərd/	bird
3.	sir	/sər/	sir
4.	art	/art/	art
5.	hard	/hard/	hard
6.	far	/far/	far

☍ 3. CHECK YOUR LISTENING

You will hear words with the sounds /ər/ and /ar/. First, cover the words in the following list. Then listen to each word. Concentrate on the sound, not the spelling. Which vowel sound do you hear? Write a check mark in the correct column.

	/ər/ as in "sir"	/ar/ as in "far"
1. turn	_____	_____
2. heard	_____	_____
3. bar	_____	_____
4. hard	_____	_____
5. farm	_____	_____
6. shirt	_____	_____
7. tar	_____	_____
8. burn	_____	_____
9. verb	_____	_____
10. card	_____	_____

🔊 4. PRACTICE THE CONTRAST: /ər/ AS IN "S<u>IR</u>," /ar/ AS IN "F<u>AR</u>," AND /ə/ AS IN "<u>U</u>P"

A. Practice the contrasting sounds /ər/ and /ar/ in sentence pairs. The first sentence of each pair has the sound /ər/ and the second has the sound /ar/. Listen and repeat. Notice the change in meaning. Visual clues can help. Make a simple drawing in each blank box. *Capital letters indicate syllable stress.*

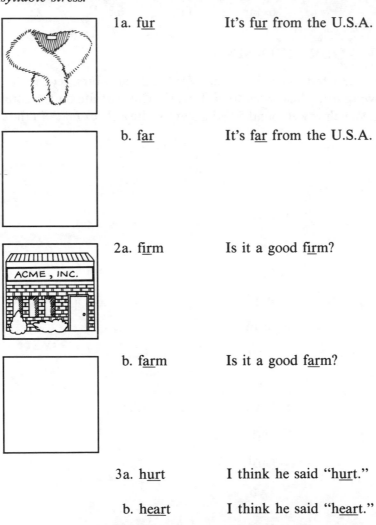

1a. f<u>ur</u>   It's f<u>ur</u> from the U.S.A.

b. f<u>ar</u>   It's f<u>ar</u> from the U.S.A.

2a. f<u>ir</u>m   Is it a good f<u>ir</u>m?

b. f<u>ar</u>m   Is it a good f<u>ar</u>m?

3a. h<u>ur</u>t   I think he said "h<u>ur</u>t."

b. h<u>ear</u>t   I think he said "h<u>ear</u>t."

4a. h<u>ear</u>d   Was it h<u>ear</u>d?

b. h<u>ar</u>d   Was it h<u>ar</u>d?

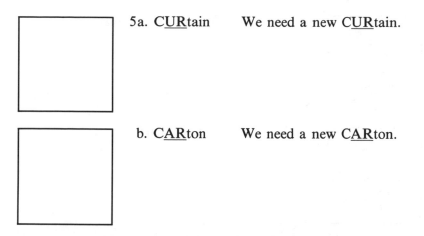

5a. CURtain   We need a new CURtain.

b. CARton   We need a new CARton.

B. Now practice the contrasting sounds /ər/ and /ə/. The first sentence of each pair has the sound /ər/ and the second has the sound /ə/. Listen and repeat. Notice the change in meaning. Visual clues can help. Make a simple drawing in each blank box.

1a. turn   It's my turn.

b. ton   It's my ton.

2a. shirt   I said "shirt."

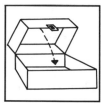

b. shut   I said "shut."

3a. h<u>ur</u>t   We see you're h<u>ur</u>t.

b. h<u>u</u>t   We see your h<u>u</u>t.

4a. b<u>ur</u>n   The b<u>ur</u>n is here.

b. b<u>u</u>n   The b<u>u</u>n is here.

5a. s<u>ear</u>ch   Is it "s<u>ear</u>ch?"

b. s<u>u</u>ch   Is it "s<u>u</u>ch?"

↻ 5. CHECK YOUR LISTENING

Work with a partner. Read a sentence from 4A or 4B to your partner. Can your partner define the sentence? He or she must be truthful.

Your partner will: • Say: I know what _____ means.
It means _____. (definition or paraphrase)
or
• Act out what the word means.
or
• Make a simple drawing.

Or your partner will ask: What does _____ mean? Then you must define the sentence, act it out, or make a drawing.

🎤 6. SPELLING OF /ər/

The sound /ər/ as in "<u>sir</u>" is represented by seven different spellings. Examples of each spelling are listed below. The sound /ər/ occurs in both stressed and unstressed syllables. Listen and repeat each word and sentence. *Capital letters indicate syllable stress.*

A. "ir" Spelling

1. th<u>ir</u>d — It's the th<u>ir</u>d one.
2. CIR<u></u>cle — I have a CIR<u></u>cle of friends.
3. g<u>ir</u>l — That g<u>ir</u>l is tall.
4. DIR<u></u>ty — The floor is DIR<u></u>ty.
5. sk<u>ir</u>t — She bought a sk<u>ir</u>t.

B. "ear" Spelling

1. <u>ear</u>th — The <u>ear</u>th is round.
2. <u>ear</u>n — I <u>ear</u>n MON<u></u>ey.
3. EAR<u></u>nest — He said it in EAR<u></u>nest.
4. p<u>ear</u>ls — The p<u>ear</u>ls are BEAU<u></u>tiful.
5. l<u>ear</u>n — Can we learn it?

C. "or" Spelling

1. w<u>or</u>k — We all w<u>or</u>k.
2. w<u>or</u>d — Look up the w<u>or</u>d.
3. w<u>or</u>se — It's w<u>or</u>se.
4. w<u>or</u>ld — Let's see the w<u>or</u>ld!
5. aTTOR<u></u>ney — Is he my aTTOR<u></u>ney?

D. "ur" Spelling

1. UR<u></u>gent — Is it UR<u></u>gent?
2. p<u>ur</u>se — I lost my p<u>ur</u>se.
3. PUR<u></u>pose — What's the PUR<u></u>pose?
4. SUR<u></u>face — Where's the SUR<u></u>face?
5. reTURN — May I reTURN a book?

E. "er" Spelling

1. s<u>er</u>ve — Serve the meat.
2. n<u>er</u>ve — He has a lot of n<u>er</u>ve.
3. CER<u></u>tain — It's a CER<u></u>tain song.
4. deTER<u></u>mine — He'll deTER<u></u>mine it.
5. reSER<u></u>VE — May I reSER<u></u>VE a book?

F. "ar" Spelling

1. DOLL<u>ar</u>	Can you spare a DOLL<u>ar</u>?
2. COLL<u>ar</u>	Is your COLL<u>ar</u> white?
3. SUG<u>ar</u>	SUG<u>ar</u> is sweet.
4. GRAMM<u>ar</u>	Is it GRAMM<u>ar</u>?
5. COW<u>ard</u>	Is he a COW<u>ard</u>?

G. "our" Spelling

1. J<u>OUR</u>nal	I have a J<u>OUR</u>nal.
2. J<u>OUR</u>ney	He took a J<u>OUR</u>ney.
3. aDJ<u>OURN</u>	He'll aDJ<u>OURN</u> the case.
4. C<u>OUR</u>age	She has C<u>OUR</u>age.
5. GLAM<u>our</u>	She has GLAM<u>our</u>.

🔊 7. STRESS AND INTONATION

Each of these sentences contains the sound /ər/ as in "s<u>ir</u>." You will hear each sentence four times:

1. Listen for the sound /ər/. (The letters for this sound are underlined.)
2. Listen for syllable stress and word stress. *Capital letters indicate syllable stress.* Mark the word stress that you hear. Put a stress mark (´) over the stressed word or words.
3. Listen for rising or falling intonation at the end of the sentence. Mark intonation with the symbol "⤴" or "⤵."
4. Listen to the sentence again and repeat it. Pay attention to pauses and linking of words.

The first sentence is marked for you.

1. Is this an eMÉRgency? It CÉRtainly ís!
2. The n<u>ur</u>se h<u>ur</u>t h<u>er</u> head.
3. ReF<u>ER</u> h<u>er</u> to the b<u>ur</u>n Unit.
4. She got h<u>ur</u>t when h<u>er</u> p<u>ur</u>se was snatched.
5. All the g<u>ir</u>ls bought sh<u>ir</u>ts.
6. They preF<u>ER</u> to wear sk<u>ir</u>ts to w<u>or</u>k.
7. Ask the P<u>ER</u>son in p<u>er</u>soNNEL.

8. Have you h<u>ear</u>d the b<u>ir</u>ds sing?

9. I'm CER<u></u>tain to get up <u>EAR</u>ly.

10. "The <u>EAR</u>ly b<u>ir</u>d will catch the w<u>or</u>m," they say.

🎧 8. DIALOG

You will hear a dialog with words that contain the sound /ər/ as in "s<u>ir</u>." Listen to the dialog five times:

1. Concentrate on the meaning. Discuss any new vocabulary with your teacher and classmates.
2. Listen for the sound /ər/. (The letters for this sound are underlined.)
3. Listen for syllable stress and word stress. (Capital letters indicate syllable stress.) Mark the word stress that you hear. Put a stress mark (´) over the stressed word or words.
4. Listen for rising or falling intonation at the end of each sentence. Mark intonation with the symbol "⤴" or "⤵."
5. Listen to each sentence of the dialog again and repeat it. Pay attention to pauses and linking of words.

The first sentence is marked for you.

ANa: W<u>ere</u> you EV<u>er</u> h<u>ur</u>t in an ACcident?

REIko: Yes, once. I h<u>ur</u>t my head, and I got a b<u>ur</u>n on my leg.

ANa: W<u>ere</u> you TAKen to the eM<u>ER</u>gency deP<u>AR</u>Tment?

REIko: Oh, yes, sure. Some g<u>ir</u>ls helped me get there. And then it was the N<u>UR</u>Ses' t<u>ur</u>n. They CER<u></u>tainly w<u>ere</u> conC<u>ER</u>NED. But I s<u>ur</u>VIVED—quite NICEly.

ANa: W<u>ere</u> you in the HOSpital f<u>or</u> a long time?

REIko: I thought it was an eT<u>ER</u>nity, but I went home <u>EAR</u>ly the next MO<u>R</u>ning. I can't say it was the w<u>or</u>st exP<u>ER</u>ience I've EV<u>er</u> had. How aBOUT you?

⟳ 9. ROLE PLAY

Practice the dialog with a partner. Help each other with correct sounds, stress, and intonation.

🐴 10. HOME ASSIGNMENT

1. Read the following story aloud. You can use a dictionary to help you with the meaning and pronunciation of new words.
2. Underline all words that contain the sounds /ər/ as in "si̲r." *(Hint: There are seventeen different words.)*
3. Mark stressed words with a stress mark (´).

The first sentence is marked for you.

Last THURSday, while I was STANDing on the CORner of Third AVenue and ThirTEENTH Street, I felt a BURNing senSAtion in the palm of my hand. I DIDn't know what had HAPPened. SUDDenly I REalized that I had been stung by a bee. My palm beGAN to hurt and swell up. My friend urged me to go to a DOCtor. Since it was SUNday, I knew that no DOCtor would be in, so I deCIDed to go to the eMERgency room of UniVERsity HOSpital. MANy PEOple were beFORE me and I had to wait my turn. AFter I had WAITed a long time, an INtern FInally looked at my hand. But by that time the pain had gone aWAY and the SWELLing had gone down. I went home WONdering why I EVer BOTHered GOing to the eMERgency room!

/ɔy/ as in <u>boy</u>

1. PRODUCING /ɔy/

Examples: <u>oi</u>l, <u>OY</u>Ster, c<u>oi</u>n, s<u>oi</u>l, R<u>OY</u>al, en<u>JOY</u>, t<u>oy</u>

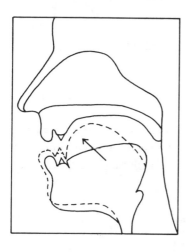

- Hold the front part of your tongue low in your mouth. The back part is raised toward the roof (soft palate) of the mouth.
- Touch the lower front teeth lightly with the tip of the tongue.
- Round your lips.
- Begin the sound, then raise your jaw slightly.
- Move the front part of your tongue forward and up and move your lips back slightly.

2. PRACTICING THE SOUND

A. Students usually have no problem pronouncing the sound /ɔy/ as in "b<u>oy</u>." Practice the sound, first normally, then with exaggeration, then normally. Listen and repeat.

/ɔy/   /ɔy. . . . ./   /ɔy/

B. Now practice the sound in words. Notice the phonetic spelling. Listen and repeat each word twice.

1. oil	/ɔyl/	oil
2. boil	/bɔyl/	boil
3. toy	/tɔy/	toy
4. noise	/nɔyz/	noise

C. Practice the contrasting sounds /ɔy/ and /ay/. The first word in each pair has the sound /ɔy/ as in "boy" and the second has the sound /ay/ as in "buy." Listen and repeat.

1a. toy	/tɔy/	toy
b. tie	/tay/	tie
2a. oil	/ɔyl/	oil
b. aisle	/ayl/	aisle
3a. toil	/tɔyl/	toil
b. tile	/tayl/	tile
4a. points	/pɔynts/	points
b. pints	/paynts/	pints

☀ 3. CHECK YOUR LISTENING

You will hear words with the sounds /ɔy/ and /ay/. First, cover the words in the following list. Then listen to each word. Concentrate on the sound, not the spelling. Which vowel sound do you hear? Write a check mark in the correct column.

	/ɔy/ as in "boy"	/ay/ as in "buy"
1. file	_____	_____
2. noise	_____	_____
3. boil	_____	_____
4. tie	_____	_____
5. boy	_____	_____

	/ɔy/ as in "b<u>oy</u>"	/ay/ as in "b<u>uy</u>"
6. m<u>i</u>ce	_____	_____
7. v<u>oi</u>ce	_____	_____
8. v<u>i</u>ce	_____	_____
9. c<u>oi</u>n	_____	_____
10. <u>oi</u>l	_____	_____

4. PRACTICE THE CONTRAST: /ɔy/ AS IN "B<u>OY</u>" WITH /ay/ AS IN "B<u>UY</u>"

Now practice the contrasting sounds /ɔy/ as in "b<u>oy</u>" and /ay/ as in "b<u>uy</u>" in sentence pairs. The first sentence in each pair has the sound /ɔy/ and the second has the sound /ay/. Listen and repeat. Notice the change in meaning. Visual clues can help. Make a simple drawing in each blank box.

1a. t<u>oy</u>   That's a nice t<u>oy</u>.

b. t<u>ie</u>   That's a nice t<u>ie</u>.

2a. p<u>oi</u>nts   How MANy p<u>oi</u>nts did you get?

b. p<u>i</u>nts   How MANy p<u>i</u>nts did you get?

 3a. <u>oi</u>l   Don't slip in the <u>oi</u>l.

 b. <u>ai</u>sle¹   Don't slip in the <u>ai</u>sle.

4a. t<u>oi</u>l   Did you say "t<u>oi</u>l?"

b. t<u>i</u>le   Did you say "t<u>i</u>le?"

5a. f<u>oi</u>l   It's a f<u>oi</u>l card.

b. f<u>i</u>le   It's a f<u>i</u>le card.

☉ 5. CHECK YOUR LISTENING

Work with a partner. Read a sentence from 4 to your partner. Can your partner define the sentence? He or she must be truthful.

Your partner will: • Say: I know what _____ means.
                       It means _____. (definition or paraphrase)
                       or
                     • Act out what the word means.
                       or
                     • Make a simple drawing.

Or your partner will ask: What does _____ mean? Then you must define the sentence, act it out, or make a drawing.

¹Note that the "s" in aisle is not pronounced.

🎤 6. STRESS AND INTONATION

Each of these sentences contains the vowel sound /ɔy/ as in "b<u>oy</u>." You will hear each word and sentence four times:

1. Listen for the vowel sound /ɔy/. (The letters for this sound are underlined.)
2. Listen for syllable stress and word stress. *Capital letters indicate syllable stress.* Mark the word stress that you hear. Put a stress mark (′) over the stressed word or words.
3. Listen for rising or falling intonation at the end of the sentence. Mark intonation with the symbol "⟋" or "⟍."
4. Listen to the sentence again and repeat it. Pay attention to pauses and linking of words.

The first sentence is marked for you.

1. Does R<u>oý</u> pláy with his t<u>oýs</u>?
2. Don't sp<u>oi</u>l the <u>oi</u>l.
3. His v<u>oi</u>ce was full of j<u>oy</u>.
4. The b<u>oy</u>s found the c<u>oi</u>n in the s<u>oi</u>l.
5. The men on the ship CON<u>voy</u> re<u>JOI</u>CED.
6. Do I have a ch<u>oi</u>ce aBOUT WEARing the CORdur<u>oy</u> pants?
7. The N<u>OI</u>Sy crowd was L<u>OY</u>al to the R<u>OY</u>al COUPle.
8. Please p<u>oi</u>nt to the emPL<u>OY</u>ment OFFice.
9. Do you like <u>OY</u>sters b<u>oi</u>led or br<u>oi</u>led?
10. She a<u>VOI</u>Ded the B<u>OY</u>cott.

🎤 7. DIALOG

You will hear a dialog with words that contain the sounds /ɔy/ as in "b<u>oy</u>" and /ay/ as in "b<u>uy</u>." Listen to the dialog five times:

1. Concentrate on the meaning. Discuss any new vocabulary with your teacher and classmates.
2. Listen for the vowel sounds /ɔy/ and /ay/. (The letters for these sounds are underlined.)

3. Listen for syllable stress and word stress. (Capital letters indicate syllable stress.) Mark the word stress that you hear. Put a stress mark (´) over the stressed word or words.
4. Listen for rising or falling intonation at the end of each sentence. Mark intonation with the symbol "⌐↗" or "⌐↘."
5. Listen to each sentence of the dialog again and repeat it. Pay attention to pauses and linking of words.

The first sentence is marked for you.

Joyce: MIchael, have you read ANy of SHAKEspeare's plays yet?

MIchael: No, I HAVEn't.

Joyce: Well, I have to read MacBETH. I had no choice.

MIchael: Oh, boy! ISn't the LANguage VERy DIFFicult? How can you enJOY READing it?

Joyce: I'm just GETTing STARTed. I found a few lines that I'd like you to hear.

MIchael: Sure! Go aHEAD. In a loud clear voice!

Joyce: There are WITCHes STANDing aROUND a B<u>OI</u>Ling pot.

DOUBle, DOUBle, t<u>oi</u>l and TROUBle;

F<u>i</u>re burn and CAULdron² BUBBle . . .

For a charm³ of POWerful TROUBle,

L<u>i</u>ke a HELL-broth⁴ b<u>oi</u>l and BUBBle.

MIchael   Hey, are you FR<u>IGH</u>Tened?

Joyce: TERRif<u>i</u>ed!

8. ROLE PLAY

Practice the dialog with a partner. Help each other with correct sounds, stress, and intonation. Read Shakespeare's lines dramatically.

9. HOME ASSIGNMENT

A. Write eight sentences with as many words as you can with the sound /ɔy/ as in "b<u>oy</u>." Mark them for stress and intonation. Practice saying the sentences.

B. Bring your sentences to class. Ask a partner to read them aloud. Use the stress and intonation as you marked them. Is your meaning clear?

²cauldron: large cooking pot.
³charm: magic power.
⁴hell-broth: a liquid from hell—evil.

UNIT 17 — /ɔ/ as in <u>all</u>

1. PRODUCING /ɔ/

Examples: <u>AL</u>so, <u>OR</u>gan, <u>AW</u>ful, c<u>o</u>st, wr<u>o</u>ng, p<u>au</u>se, th<u>ou</u>ght, l<u>aw</u>

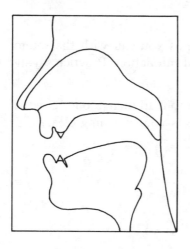

- This is the first part of the sound /ɔy/ as in "b<u>oy</u>."
- Hold the front part of your tongue low in your mouth, with the tip lightly touching the lower front teeth.
- Raise the back of your tongue towards the roof (soft palate) of your mouth.
- Round your lips.

2. CONTRAST: /ɔ/, /ə/, /a/, AND /ɔy/

A. Students may sometimes confuse the sound /ɔ/ as in "<u>a</u>ll" with other sounds. These sounds include /ə/ as in "<u>u</u>p," /a/ as in "n<u>o</u>t," and /ɔy/ as in "b<u>oy</u>." Practice these sounds, first normally, then with exaggeration, then normally. Listen and repeat.

1. /ɔ/	/ɔ. . . . ./	/ɔ/
2. /ə/	/ə. . . . ./	/ə/
3. /a/	/a. . . . ./	/a/
4. /ɔy/	/ɔy . . . ./	/ɔy/

136

B. Now practice these sounds in words. Notice the phonetic spelling. Listen and repeat each word twice.

1. ought	/ɔt/	ought
2. law	/lɔ/	law
3. boy	/bɔy/	boy
4. voice	/vɔys/	voice
5. fun	/fən/	fun
6. none	/nən/	none
7. far	/far/	far
8. not	/nat/	not
9. or	/ɔr/	or
10. saw	/sɔ/	saw

3. CHECK YOUR LISTENING

You will hear words with the sounds /ɔ/, /ɔy/, /ə/, and /a/. First, cover the words in the following list. Then listen to each word. Concentrate on the sound, not the spelling. Which vowel sound do you hear? Write a check mark in the correct column.

	/ɔ/ as in "all"	/ɔy/ as in "boy"	/ə/ as in "up"	/a/ as in "not"
1. ball	_____	_____	_____	_____
2. boil	_____	_____	_____	_____
3. lawn	_____	_____	_____	_____
4. cut	_____	_____	_____	_____
5. must	_____	_____	_____	_____
6. calm	_____	_____	_____	_____
7. come	_____	_____	_____	_____
8. jaw	_____	_____	_____	_____
9. tall	_____	_____	_____	_____
10. voice	_____	_____	_____	_____

💡 4. PRACTICE THE CONTRAST: /ɔy/ AS IN "B<u>OY</u>" WITH /ɔ/ AS IN "<u>A</u>LL"

A. Practice these contrasting sounds. Listen and repeat each word pair.

	/ɔy/	/ɔ/			/ɔy/	/ɔ/
1.	<u>oi</u>l	<u>a</u>ll		4.	s<u>oi</u>l	S<u>au</u>l
2.	b<u>oi</u>l	b<u>a</u>ll		5.	R<u>oy</u>	r<u>aw</u>
3.	t<u>oi</u>l	t<u>a</u>ll		6.	j<u>oy</u>	j<u>aw</u>

B. Now practice the contrasting sounds in sentence pairs. The first sentence of each pair has the sound /ɔy/ and the second has the sound /ɔ/. Listen and repeat. Notice the change in meaning. Visual clues can help. Make a simple drawing in each blank box.

    1a. <u>oi</u>l   Is that <u>oi</u>l?

     b. <u>a</u>ll   Is that <u>a</u>ll?

    2a. b<u>oi</u>l   He has a b<u>oi</u>l.

     b. b<u>a</u>ll   He has a b<u>a</u>ll.

    3a. t<u>oi</u>l   The word is "t<u>oi</u>l."

     b. t<u>a</u>ll   The word is "t<u>a</u>ll."

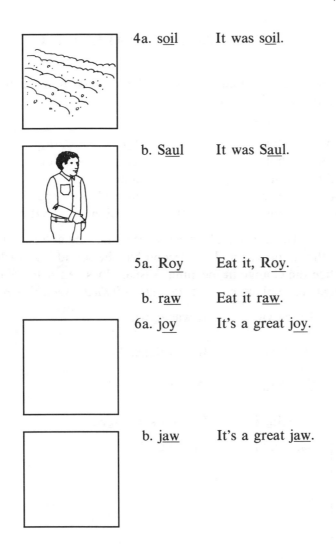

4a. s<u>oi</u>l   It was s<u>oi</u>l.

b. S<u>au</u>l   It was S<u>au</u>l.

5a. R<u>oy</u>   Eat it, R<u>oy</u>.

b. r<u>aw</u>   Eat it r<u>aw</u>.

6a. j<u>oy</u>   It's a great j<u>oy</u>.

b. j<u>aw</u>   It's a great j<u>aw</u>.

5. PRACTICE THE CONTRAST: /ɔ/ AS IN "ALL" WITH /ə/ AS IN "UP"

A. Practice these contrasting sounds. Listen and repeat each word pair. *Capital letters indicate syllable stress.*

	/ɔ/	/ə/		/ɔ/	/ə/
1.	dawn	done	6.	dog	dug
2.	bought	but	7.	long	lung
3.	caught	cut	8.	gone	gun
4.	cough	cuff	9.	crossed	crust
5.	boss	bus	10.	CALLer	COLor

B. Now practice the contrasting sounds in sentence pairs. The first sentence of each pair has the sound /ɔ/ and the second has the sound /ə/. Listen and repeat. Notice the change in meaning. Visual clues can help. Make a simple drawing in each blank box. *Capital letters indicate syllable stress.*

1a. dawn   It was dawn.

b. done   It was done.

2a. chalk   Do you see chalk?

b. Chuck   Do you see Chuck?

3a. caught   They caught it.

b. cut   They cut it.

4a. b<u>o</u>ss   This is my b<u>o</u>ss.

b. b<u>u</u>s   This is my b<u>u</u>s.

5a. c<u>ough</u>   I have a c<u>ough</u>.

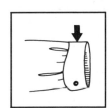

b. c<u>u</u>ff   I have a c<u>u</u>ff.

6a. C<u>A</u>LLer   We see the C<u>A</u>LLer.

b. C<u>O</u>Lor   We see the C<u>O</u>Lor.

6. PRACTICE THE CONTRAST: /ɔ/ AS IN "<u>A</u>LL" WITH /a/ AS IN "N<u>O</u>T"

A. Practice these contrasting sounds. Listen and repeat each word pair. *Capital letters indicate syllable stress.*

	/ɔ/	/a/		/ɔ/	/a/
1.	p<u>aw</u>	P<u>a</u>	6.	p<u>o</u>rt	p<u>a</u>rt
2.	t<u>augh</u>t	t<u>o</u>t	7.	p<u>o</u>rk	p<u>a</u>rk
3.	c<u>augh</u>t	c<u>o</u>t	8.	c<u>o</u>urt	c<u>a</u>rt
4.	f<u>o</u>r	f<u>a</u>r	9.	c<u>o</u>rd	c<u>a</u>rd
5.	b<u>o</u>rn	b<u>a</u>rn	10.	F<u>O</u>Rmer	F<u>A</u>Rmer

B. Now practice the contrasting sounds in sentence pairs. The first sentence of each pair has the sound /ɔ/ and the second has the sound /a/. Listen and repeat. Notice the change in meaning. Visual clues can help. Make a simple drawing in each blank box. *Capital letters indicate syllable stress.*

1a. paw   I like his paw.

  b. Pa   I like his Pa.

2a. store   I see a store.

  b. star   I see a star.

3a. port   That port is good.

  b. part   That part is good.

4a. court   It's a court.

  b. cart   It's a cart.

5a. cord   He has the cord.

  b. card   He has the card.

6a. FORmer   The FORmer is from TEXas.

b. FARmer   The FARmer is from TEXas.

🔁 7. CHECK YOUR LISTENING

Work with a partner. Read a sentence from 4B, 5B or 6B to your partner. Can your partner define the sentence? He or she must be truthful.

Your partner will: • Say: I know what _____ means.
It means _____. (definition or paraphrase)
or
• Act out what the word means.
or
• Make a simple drawing.

Or your partner will ask: What does _____ mean? Then you must define the sentence, act it out, or make a drawing.

💡 8. STRESS AND INTONATION

Each of these sentences contains the vowel sound /ɔ/ as in "<u>all</u>." You will hear each sentence four times:

1. Listen for the vowel sound /ɔ/. (The letters for this sound are underlined.)
2. Listen for syllable stress and word stress. *Capital letters indicate syllable stress.* Mark the word stress that you hear. Put a stress mark (´) over the stressed word or words.
3. Listen for rising or falling intonation at the end of the sentence. Mark intonation with the symbol "⤴" or "⤵."
4. Listen to the sentence again and repeat it. Pay attention to pauses and linking of words.

The first sentence is marked for you.

1. Don't w<u>a</u>lk on the l<u>aw</u>n.

2. Did he <u>OR</u>ganize the c<u>o</u>rpoRAtion?

3. The d<u>o</u>g c<u>au</u>ght his p<u>aw</u> in the d<u>oo</u>r.

4. Why did the <u>AU</u>dience aPPL<u>AU</u>D?

5. She t<u>o</u>re it up beF<u>ORE</u> I s<u>aw</u> it.

6. Do you live aCROSS the h<u>a</u>ll from me?

7. Were <u>a</u>ll the <u>AU</u>tos reC<u>A</u>LLED?

8. He spent a F<u>OR</u>tune on his D<u>AUGH</u>ter.

9. Why did you y<u>aw</u>n <u>a</u>ll through the t<u>a</u>lk?

10. We live on the N<u>or</u>th sh<u>or</u>e of L<u>o</u>ng ISland.[1]

🔊 9. DIALOG

You will hear a dialog with words that contain the sounds /ə/ as in "<u>u</u>p," /ɔy/ as in "b<u>oy</u>," /ɔ/ as in "<u>a</u>ll," and /a/ as in "n<u>o</u>t." Listen to the dialog five times:

1. Concentrate on the meaning. Discuss any new vocabulary with your teacher and classmates.
2. Listen for the vowel sounds /ɔy/, /ɔ/, /ə/ and /a/. (The letters for these sounds are underlined.)
3. Listen for syllable stress and word stress. *Capital letters indicate syllable stress.* Mark the word stress that you hear. Put a stress mark (′) over the stressed word or words.
4. Listen for rising or falling intonation at the end of each sentence. Mark intonation with the symbol "➚" or "➘."
5. Listen to each sentence of the dialog again and repeat it. Pay attention to pauses and linking of words.

The first sentence is marked for you. Notice that unstressed /ə/ is marked for function words, like "to." "To" is pronounced /tə/ in conversational speech. (See Unit 6.)

[1]Note that the "s" in "island" is not pronounced.

CrisTIna̲: Hi. Wha̲t a̲re yóu GOing to̲ do to̲MÓRRow?

TOshio: BAbysit, beLIEVE it o̲r no̲t! My NEIGHbors have three LITTle boys and a̲ do̲g. And they're a̲ll mine fo̲r a̲ day.

CrisTIna̲: How did yo̲u get ca̲ught in a̲ situAtio̲n like that?

TOshio: Oh, I WANTe̲d to̲ do it. They've been VERy nice to̲ me. They ca̲ll OFten to̲ see how I am. And they OFten inVITE me to̲ lunch, too.

CrisTIna̲: Well, how do yo̲u plan to̲ keep those boys BUSy and out o̲f TROUBle?

TOshio: We'll play so̲me games, I guess. And we'll teach the̲ do̲g so̲me tricks. How to̲ sit u̲p, and how to̲ shake hands with his pa̲w. We'll a̲ll have lo̲ts o̲f fu̲n.

CrisTIna̲: Well, no̲ne o̲f that fo̲r me! Bu̲t ca̲ll me when yo̲u get home. I'll co̲me a̲nd LISten to̲ a̲ll yo̲ur STORies.

↻ 10. ROLE PLAY

A. Practice the dialog with a partner. Help each other with sounds, stress, and intonation.

B. Continue the dialog. Make up the stories about Toshio's day with the three little boys and the dog. Write out the sentences. Perform the second part of the dialog for other members of your class.

11. HOME ASSIGNMENT

A. Unscramble the letters to make words with the sound /ɔ/ as in "<u>a</u>ll." Write the words in the spaces provided. Then say the words aloud.

	Examples:	a. remo	<u>more</u>
		b. fgthuo	<u>fought</u>

1. wand   _____

2. gtohu   _____

3. lalh   _____

4. lalm   _____

5. eoshr   _____

6. gnlo   _____

7. rood   _____

8. alwl   _____

9. kalt   _____

10. drebor   _____

B. Each of the following sentences is missing a word that rhymes with another word in the sentence. Both words have the sound /ɔ/ as in "<u>a</u>ll." Choose a word from the list above to complete the sentence. The first letter of the missing word is given.

> **Examples:**   a. He t<u>o</u>re it <u>m ore</u>.
> b. He th<u>ou</u>ght he <u>f ought</u>.

1. There's <u>OR</u>der on the <u>b</u>_____.

2. It's on the fl<u>oo</u>r near the <u>d</u>_____.

3. It's <u>a</u>ll on the <u>w</u>_____.

4. The f<u>ou</u>r went to the <u>s</u>_____.

5. His b<u>a</u>ll is in the <u>h</u>_____.

6. See the l<u>aw</u>n at <u>d</u>_____.

7. P<u>au</u>l shopped at the <u>m</u>_____.

8. Let's w<u>a</u>lk and <u>t</u>_____.

9. The s<u>o</u>ng is <u>l</u>_____.

10. He b<u>ou</u>ght what he <u>o</u>_____.

/ow/ as in no

1. PRODUCING /ow/

Examples: <u>o</u>h, <u>O</u>pen, h<u>o</u>me,[1] b<u>oa</u>t, s<u>ou</u>l, s<u>ew</u>, CAR<u>go</u>

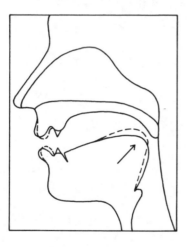

- Hold the front part of your tongue low in your mouth, with the tip lightly touching the lower front teeth.
- As you begin to say the sound raise the back of your tongue towards the roof (soft palate) of your mouth.
- Round your lips and push them forward a little.
- The opening of your mouth is smaller than for the sound /ɔ/ as in "<u>a</u>ll."

2. CONTRAST: /ow/, /ɔ/, /a/, AND /ə/

A. Students may confuse the sound /ow/ as in "n<u>o</u>" with other sounds. These sounds include /ɔ/ as in "<u>a</u>ll," /a/ as in "n<u>o</u>t," and /ə/ as in "<u>u</u>p." Practice these sounds, first normally, then with exaggeration, then normally. Listen and repeat.

1.	/ow/	/ow. . . ./	/ow/
2.	/ɔ/	/ɔ. . . ./	/ɔ/
3.	/a/	/a. . . ./	/a/
4.	/ə/	/ə. . . ./	/ə/

[1]The final "e" in words such as "home" and "note" signals the /ow/ pronunciation for the letter "o." Compare "not" /nat/ with "note" /nowt/.

B. Now practice these sounds in words. Notice the phonetic spelling. Listen and repeat each word twice.

1.	<u>o</u>h	/ow/	<u>o</u>h
2.	s<u>ew</u>	/sow/	s<u>ew</u>
3.	l<u>aw</u>	/lɔ/	l<u>aw</u>
4.	t<u>a</u>lk	/tɔk/	t<u>a</u>lk
5.	c<u>a</u>lm	/kam/	c<u>a</u>lm
6.	n<u>o</u>t	/nat/	n<u>o</u>t
7.	c<u>u</u>t	/kət/	c<u>u</u>t
8.	n<u>u</u>t	/nət/	n<u>u</u>t
9.	b<u>oa</u>t	/bowt/	b<u>oa</u>t
10.	b<u>o</u>ne	/bown/	b<u>o</u>ne

3. CHECK YOUR LISTENING

You will hear words with the sounds /ow/, /ɔ/, /a/, and /ə/. First, cover the words in the following list. Then listen to each word. Concentrate on the sound, not the spelling. Which vowel sound do you hear? Write a check mark in the correct column.

	/ow/ as in "n<u>o</u>"	/ɔ/ as in "<u>a</u>ll"	/a/ as in "n<u>o</u>t"	/ə/ as in "<u>u</u>p"
1. b<u>ow</u>l	_____	_____	_____	_____
2. b<u>a</u>ll	_____	_____	_____	_____
3. c<u>oa</u>t	_____	_____	_____	_____
4. c<u>u</u>t	_____	_____	_____	_____
5. l<u>aw</u>n	_____	_____	_____	_____
6. p<u>o</u>t	_____	_____	_____	_____
7. b<u>u</u>t	_____	_____	_____	_____
8. c<u>o</u>me	_____	_____	_____	_____
9. c<u>a</u>lm	_____	_____	_____	_____
10. b<u>oa</u>t	_____	_____	_____	_____

💡 4. PRACTICE THE CONTRAST: /ow/ AS IN "N<u>O</u>" WITH /ɔ/ AS IN "<u>A</u>LL"

A. Practice these contrasting sounds. Listen and repeat each word pair.

	/ow/	/ɔ/			/ow/	/ɔ/
1.	b<u>ow</u>l	b<u>a</u>ll		6.	b<u>oa</u>t	b<u>ou</u>ght
2.	p<u>o</u>le	P<u>au</u>l		7.	w<u>o</u>ke	w<u>a</u>lk
3.	c<u>oa</u>l	c<u>a</u>ll		8.	ch<u>o</u>ke	ch<u>a</u>lk
4.	c<u>oa</u>st	c<u>o</u>st		9.	s<u>ew</u>	s<u>aw</u>
5.	c<u>oa</u>t	c<u>au</u>ght		10.	cl<u>o</u>se	cl<u>au</u>se

B. Now practice the contrasting sounds in sentence pairs. The first sentence of each pair has the sound /ow/ and the second has the sound /ɔ/. Listen and repeat. Notice the change in meaning. Visual clues can help. Make a simple drawing in each blank box. *Capital letters indicate syllable stress.*

☐	1a. b<u>ow</u>l	A b<u>ow</u>l is on the TAble.
☐	b. b<u>a</u>ll	A b<u>a</u>ll is on the TAble.

2a. h<u>o</u>le	Put it in the h<u>o</u>le.
b. h<u>a</u>ll	Put it in the h<u>a</u>ll.
3a. l<u>oa</u>n	Let's look at the l<u>oa</u>n.
b. l<u>aw</u>n	Let's look at the l<u>aw</u>n.
4a. c<u>oa</u>l	I got the c<u>oa</u>l.
b. c<u>a</u>ll	I got the c<u>a</u>ll.
5a. l<u>ow</u>	His voice is l<u>ow</u>.
b. l<u>aw</u>	His voice is l<u>aw</u>.

6a. p<u>o</u>se   Can you p<u>o</u>se by the desk?

  b. p<u>au</u>se   Can you p<u>au</u>se by the desk?

5. PRACTICE THE CONTRAST: /ow/ AS IN "N<u>O</u>," /a/ AS IN "N<u>OT</u>," AND /ə/ AS IN "<u>U</u>P"

A. Practice these contrasting sounds. Listen and repeat each group of three words.

	/ow/	/a/	/ə/
1.	n<u>o</u>te	n<u>o</u>t	n<u>u</u>t
2.	c<u>o</u>mb	c<u>a</u>lm	c<u>o</u>me
3.	s<u>oa</u>k	s<u>o</u>ck	s<u>u</u>ck
4.	c<u>oa</u>t	c<u>o</u>t	c<u>u</u>t
5.	r<u>o</u>be	r<u>o</u>b	r<u>u</u>b
6.	ph<u>o</u>ned	f<u>o</u>nd	f<u>u</u>nd

B. Now practice the contrasting sounds in sentences. The first sentence of each group has the sound /ow/, the second has the sound /a/, and the third has the sound /ə/. Listen and repeat. Notice the change in meaning. Visual clues can help. Make a simple drawing in each blank box.

  1a. n<u>o</u>te   Did you see the n<u>o</u>te?

   b. kn<u>o</u>t   Did you see the kn<u>o</u>t?

   c. n<u>u</u>t   Did you see the n<u>u</u>t?

2a. c<u>o</u>mb   Try to c<u>o</u>mb down.

  b. c<u>a</u>lm   Try to c<u>a</u>lm down.

  c. c<u>o</u>me   Try to c<u>o</u>me down.

3a. c<u>oa</u>t   He has a c<u>oa</u>t.

  b. c<u>o</u>t   He has a c<u>o</u>t.

  c. c<u>u</u>t   He has a c<u>u</u>t.

4a. r<u>o</u>be   I said "r<u>o</u>be."

  b. r<u>o</u>b   I said "r<u>o</u>b."

  c. r<u>u</u>b   I said "r<u>u</u>b."

5a. s<u>oa</u>k   We'll s<u>oa</u>k it.

  b. s<u>o</u>ck   We'll s<u>o</u>ck it.

  c. s<u>u</u>ck   We'll s<u>u</u>ck it.

6a. ph<u>o</u>ned   Was it ph<u>o</u>ned?

  b. f<u>o</u>nd   Was it "f<u>o</u>nd?"

  c. f<u>u</u>nd   Was it "f<u>u</u>nd?"

⟳ **6.** CHECK YOUR LISTENING

Work with a partner. Read a sentence from 4B or 5B to your partner. Can your partner define the sentence? He or she must be truthful.

Your partner will: • Say: I know what _____ means.
                    It means _____. (definition or paraphrase)
                    or
       • Act out what the word means.
                    or
       • Make a simple drawing.

Or your partner will ask: What does _____ mean? Then you must define the sentence, act it out, or make a drawing.

☻ **7.** STRESS AND INTONATION

Each of these sentences contains the vowel sound /ow/. You will hear each sentence four times:

1. Listen for the vowel sound /ow/ as in "n<u>o</u>." (The letters for this sound are underlined.)
2. Listen for syllable stress and word stress. *Capital letters indicate syllable stress.* Mark the word stress that you hear. Put a stress mark (´) over the stressed word or words.
3. Listen for rising or falling intonation at the end of the sentence. Mark intonation with the symbol "↗" or "↘."
4. Listen to the sentence again and repeat it. Pay attention to pauses and linking of words.

The first sentence is marked for you.

1. The TÓASTer is BRÓKen.↘
2. He t<u>o</u>ld a j<u>o</u>ke.
3. They kn<u>ow</u> I'm aL<u>O</u>NE.
4. He's a h<u>o</u>me <u>OW</u>Ner.
5. Let's g<u>o</u> SL<u>OW</u>ly.
6. He had <u>O</u>Nly his cl<u>o</u>thes.
7. Is that the <u>O</u>Nly aPPR<u>OA</u>CH?
8. P<u>o</u>TAt<u>oes</u> were on the b<u>oa</u>t.
9. Do you kn<u>ow</u> your zip c<u>o</u>de?
10. The ph<u>o</u>ne has a DIal t<u>o</u>ne.

8. DIALOG

You will hear a dialog with words that contain the sounds /ow/ as in "n<u>o</u>," /ɔ/ as in "<u>a</u>ll," /a/ as in "n<u>o</u>t," and /ə/ as in "<u>u</u>p." Listen to the dialog five times:

1. Concentrate on the meaning. Discuss any new vocabulary with your teacher and classmates.
2. Listen for the vowel sounds /ow/, /ɔ/, /a/, and /ə/. (The letters for these sounds are underlined.)
3. Listen for syllable stress and word stress. *Capital letters indicate syllable stress.* Mark the word stress that you hear. Put a stress mark (′) over the stressed word or words.
4. Listen for rising or falling intonation at the end of each sentence. Mark intonation with the symbol "⌇" or "⌇."
5. Listen to each sentence of the dialog again and repeat it. Pay attention to pauses and linking of words.

The first sentence is marked for you. Notice that unstressed /ə/ is marked for function words, like "t<u>o</u>." "To" is pronounced /tə/ in conversational speech. (See Unit 6.)

Joe: "Óh, hó, hó, and a BÓTTle of rúm!"

ANNa: Whąt in thę world ąre yǫu READing?

Joe: That's Lǫng Jǫhn SILver in *TREAsure ISląnd,* by ROBert LOUis
        STEvensǫn. Lǫng Jǫhn is ąn Evil PIrate. He has ONly ǫne eye and
        a WOODen peg leg. And he has a PARRǫt fǫr a pet. Well, I'm
        nǫt sure he EVer TREATed it like a pet. He's whąt we cąll a "bad
        guy."

ANNa: Ǫh, well, how bad is he? Let me try it, Jǫe.

        "Ǫh, hǫ, hǫ, and a BOTTle ǫf rǫm!"

        How's that? He's nǫt exACTly like SANta Claus² with his "Hǫ,
        hǫ, hǫ," is he?

Joe: AbsǫLUTEly nǫt! Whąt a CONtrast!

ANNa: Well, now I'm INterested.³ Let me read it when you've FINished,
        will you?

Joe: Sure thing!

⟳ 9. ROLE PLAY

Practice the dialog with a partner. Help each other with correct sounds,
stress, and intonation.

🏠 10. HOME ASSIGNMENT

1. Read the following Arabic proverb aloud. You can use a dictionary to help
   you with the pronunciation of new words.
2. Draw a single line under all words that have the sound /ow/ as in
   "nǫ."
3. Mark stressed words with a stress mark (´).
4. Read the proverb aloud one more time.

The first sentence is marked for you.

²Santa Claus: mythical character who brings gifts for children at Christmas (Christian holiday
celebrating the birth of Jesus Christ).
³See page 116 for alternate pronunciation.

He who <u>knows</u>, and <u>knows</u> he <u>knows</u>,

He is wise—FOLLow him.

He who knows, and knows not he knows,

He is aSLEEP—wake him.

He who knows not, and knows not he knows not,

He is a fool—shun[4] him.

He who knows not, and knows he knows not,

He is a child—teach him.

[4]shun: turn away from.

UNIT 19

/uw/ as in <u>do</u>
/ʊ/ as in <u>book</u>

1. PRODUCING /uw/[1]

Examples: thr<u>ough</u>, wh<u>ose</u>, j<u>ui</u>ce, t<u>oo</u>, sh<u>oe</u>, tr<u>ue</u>, bl<u>ew</u>

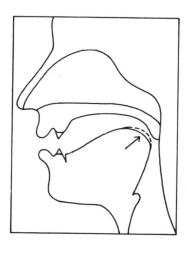

- Hold the front part of your tongue low in your mouth, with the tip lightly touching the lower front teeth.
- Raise the back of your tongue toward the roof (soft palate) of your mouth.
- Round your lips and push them out. The opening is smaller than for the sound /ow/ as in "n<u>o</u>."
- Place your thumb underneath your chin to feel the tense muscles.

[1]The combination /yuw/ is very common and occurs in words such as "union," "cute," "beauty," and "few." See Unit 30 for other examples and practice.

2. PRODUCING /ʊ/

Examples: p<u>u</u>t, B<u>U</u>TCHer, c<u>oo</u>k, S<u>U</u>Gar, w<u>o</u>lf, w<u>ou</u>ld

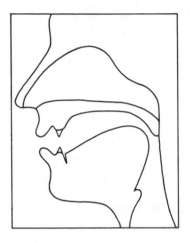

- Hold the front part of your tongue low in your mouth, with the tip lightly touching the lower front teeth.
- Raise the back of your tongue toward the roof (soft palate) of the mouth, but lower than for the sound /uw/ as in "d<u>o</u>."
- Your lips should be close together, but not rounded or pushed out.
- Place your thumb underneath your chin. You should feel no tense muscles; the muscles are *relaxed*.

3. CONTRAST: /uw/, /ʊ/, AND /ə/

A. Students may confuse the sounds /uw/ as in "d<u>o</u>," /ʊ/ as in "b<u>oo</u>k," and /ə/ as in "<u>u</u>p." Practice these sounds, first normally, then with exaggeration, then normally. Listen and repeat.

1.	/uw/	/uw. . . ./	/uw/
2.	/ʊ/	/ʊ. . . . ./	/ʊ/
3.	/ə/	/ə . . . . ./	/ə/

B. Now practice these sounds in words. Notice the phonetic spelling. Listen and repeat each word twice.

1.	tw<u>o</u>	/tuw/	tw<u>o</u>
2.	wh<u>o</u>	/huw/	wh<u>o</u>
3.	b<u>oo</u>k	/bʊk/	b<u>oo</u>k
4.	t<u>oo</u>k	/tʊk/	t<u>oo</u>k
5.	s<u>u</u>n	/sən/	s<u>u</u>n
6.	m<u>u</u>st	/məst/	m<u>u</u>st
7.	f<u>oo</u>d	/fuwd/	f<u>oo</u>d
8.	w<u>ou</u>ld	/wʊd/	w<u>ou</u>ld

🎧 **4.** CHECK YOUR LISTENING

You will hear words with the sounds /uw/, /ʊ/, and /ə/. First, cover the words in the following list. Then listen to each word. Concentrate on the sound, not the spelling. Which vowel sound do you hear? Write a check mark in the correct column.

	/uw/ as in "d<u>o</u>"	/ʊ/ as in "b<u>oo</u>k"	/ə/ as in "<u>u</u>p"
1. d<u>o</u>	———	———	———
2. b<u>oo</u>k	———	———	———
3. <u>u</u>p	———	———	———
4. f<u>u</u>n	———	———	———
5. c<u>u</u>t	———	———	———
6. t<u>oo</u>k	———	———	———
7. sch<u>oo</u>l	———	———	———
8. st<u>oo</u>d	———	———	———
9. tr<u>ue</u>	———	———	———
10. c<u>ou</u>ld	———	———	———

🎧 **5.** PRACTICE THE CONTRAST: /uw/ AS IN "D<u>O</u>" WITH /ʊ/ AS IN "B<u>OO</u>K"

A. Practice these contrasting sounds. Listen and repeat each word pair.

	/uw/	/ʊ/			/uw/	/ʊ/
1.	p<u>oo</u>l	p<u>u</u>ll	4.		c<u>oo</u>ed	c<u>ou</u>ld
2.	f<u>oo</u>l	f<u>u</u>ll	5.		wh<u>o</u>'d	h<u>oo</u>d
3.	L<u>u</u>ke	l<u>oo</u>k	6.		st<u>ew</u>ed	st<u>oo</u>d

B. Now practice the contrasting sounds in sentence pairs. The first sentence of each pair has the sound /uw/ and the second has the sound /ʊ/. Listen and repeat. Notice the change in meaning. Visual clues can help. Make a simple drawing in each blank box.

1a. p<u>oo</u>l   Don't p<u>oo</u>l it.

   b. p<u>u</u>ll   Don't p<u>u</u>ll it.

2a. f<u>oo</u>l   I said "f<u>oo</u>l."

   b. f<u>u</u>ll   I said "f<u>u</u>ll."

3a. L<u>u</u>ke   We said "L<u>u</u>ke."

   b. l<u>oo</u>k   We said "l<u>oo</u>k."

4a. c<u>oo</u>ed   He said they c<u>oo</u>ed.

   b. c<u>ou</u>ld   He said they c<u>ou</u>ld.

5a. wh<u>o</u>'d   Did you say "wh<u>o</u>'d?"

   b. h<u>oo</u>d   Did you say "h<u>oo</u>d?"

6a. st<u>ew</u>ed   It st<u>ew</u>ed all day.

b. st<u>oo</u>d   It st<u>oo</u>d all day.

🎧 **6. PRACTICE THE CONTRAST: /ʊ/ AS IN "B<u>OO</u>K" WITH /ə/ AS IN "<u>U</u>P"**

A. Practice these contrasting sounds. Listen and repeat each word pair.

	/ʊ/	/ə/		/ʊ/	/ə/
1.	l<u>oo</u>k	l<u>u</u>ck	4.	p<u>u</u>t	p<u>u</u>tt
2.	t<u>oo</u>k	t<u>u</u>ck	5.	st<u>oo</u>d	st<u>u</u>d
3.	b<u>oo</u>k	b<u>u</u>ck	6.	h<u>oo</u>ks	H<u>u</u>ck's

B. Now practice the contrasting sounds in sentence pairs. The first sentence of each pair has the sound /ʊ/ and the second has the sound /ə/. Listen and repeat. Notice the change in meaning. Visual clues can help. Make a simple drawing in each blank box. _Capital letters indicate syllable stress._

1a. l<u>oo</u>k   Her l<u>oo</u>k is new.

b. l<u>u</u>ck   Her l<u>u</u>ck is new.

2a. t<u>oo</u>k   They t<u>oo</u>k it in.

b. t<u>u</u>ck   They t<u>u</u>ck it in.

3a. b<u>oo</u>k   Give me a b<u>oo</u>k.

b. b<u>u</u>ck   Give me a b<u>u</u>ck.

4a. p<u>u</u>t   Will he p<u>u</u>t the ball there?

  b. p<u>u</u>tt   Will he p<u>u</u>tt the ball there?

5a. st<u>oo</u>d   Did he say "st<u>oo</u>d?"

  b. st<u>u</u>d   Did he say "st<u>u</u>d?"

6a. h<u>oo</u>ks   H<u>oo</u>ks are BETTer.

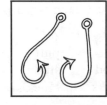

  b. H<u>u</u>ck's   H<u>u</u>ck's are BETTer.

↻ 7. CHECK YOUR LISTENING

Work with a partner. Read a sentence from 5B or 6B to your partner. Can your partner define the sentence? He or she must be truthful.

Your partner will: • Say: I know what _____ means.
                   It means _____. (definition or paraphrase)
                   or
               • Act out what the word means.
                   or
               • Make a simple drawing.

Or your partner will ask: What does _____ mean? Then you must define the sentence, act it out, or make a drawing.

🎙 8. STRESS AND INTONATION

The following sentences contain the vowel sounds /uw/ as in "d<u>o</u>," /ʊ/ as in "b<u>oo</u>k," and /ə/ as in "<u>u</u>p." You will hear each sentence four times.

1. Listen for the vowel sounds /uw/, /ʊ/, and /ə/. The letters for these sounds are underlined.
2. Listen for syllable stress and word stress. *Capital letters indicate syllable stress.* Put a stress mark (ˊ) over the stressed word or words.
3. Listen for rising or falling intonation at the end of the sentence. Mark intonation with the symbol "⤴" or "⤵."
4. Listen to the sentence again and repeat it. Pay attention to pauses and linking of words.

The first sentence is marked for you. Notice that unstressed /ə/ is marked for function words, like "to." "To" is pronounced /tə/ in conversational speech. (See Unit 6.)

1. The f<u>oo</u>l was pushed.
2. I ch<u>oo</u>se the w<u>oo</u>l.
3. It w<u>a</u>s <u>a</u> n<u>ew</u> b<u>oo</u>k.
4. The s<u>ou</u>p is f<u>u</u>ll <u>o</u>f salt.
5. Wh<u>o</u> is that W<u>O</u>Man?

6. He sh<u>ou</u>ld make <u>a</u> lot <u>o</u>f M<u>O</u>Ney.
7. L<u>oo</u>k on the <u>O</u>THer page.
8. C<u>ou</u>ld he go f<u>o</u>r lunch?
9. W<u>ou</u>ld y<u>ou</u> go with my <u>U</u>Ncle?
10. That W<u>O</u>Man has M<u>U</u>SCles.

🎙 9. DIALOG

You will hear a dialog with words that contain the sounds /uw/ as in "d<u>o</u>" and /ʊ/ as in "b<u>oo</u>k." Listen to the dialog five times:

1. Concentrate on the meaning. Discuss any new vocabulary with your teacher and classmates.
2. Listen for the vowel sounds /uw/ and /ʊ/. (The letters for these sounds are underlined.)
3. Listen for syllable stress and word stress. *Capital letters indicate syllable stress.* Mark the word stress that you hear. Put a stress mark (ˊ) over the stressed word or words.
4. Listen for rising or falling intonation at the end of each sentence. Mark intonation with the symbol "⤴" or "⤵."
5. Listen to each sentence of the dialog again and repeat it. Pay attention to pauses and linking of words.

The first sentence is marked for you.

MIchiko: Do yóu know ANYthing about Lúke—the FELĹow whǫ was in
the REStaurant toNÍGHT?

ToMÁS: Luke? He's the cǫok!

MIchiko: Lúke's the cǫok? I COULDn't be more surPRISED. He's PRETTy
young, and he's ALso PRETTy gǫod! I think the fǫod was suPERB
—REALLy VERy, VERy gǫod.

ToMÁS: That's trúe. Why dǫ yǫu think I tǫok you there? I WANTed to
please yǫu.

MIchiko: Well, yǫu did please me VERy much. I had a WONderful time.
Thank yǫu!

ToMÁS: Thank yǫu! It was my PLEASure. Dǫ yǫu think we cǫuld go out
aGAIN sǫon?

MIchiko: I'd like tǫ. I cǫuld call you next week. I'm GOing home to VISit
my PARents and YOUNGer BROTHer for a few days. He's
GOing back to schǫol on TUESday.

ToMÁS: Cǫuld I call you at your PARents' home beFORE TUESday? We
cǫuld make a date then.

MIchiko: All right. Gǫod. Here's the phone NUMber. Thank yǫu aGAIN,
and gǫod night.

ToMÁS: Gǫod night.

⟳ 10. ROLE PLAY

Practice the dialog with a partner. Help each other with correct sounds,
stress, and intonation.

🏠 11. HOME ASSIGNMENT

Some common English expressions are listed below. The underlined letters
represent either /uw/ as in "dǫ" or /ʊ/ as in "bǫok." A definition for each
expression appears in parentheses.

1. Read each expression and the sentence aloud. Use a dictionary to help you with the pronunciation of any new words.
2. In the spaces that follow the expressions, list all words that contain the sounds /uw/ or /ʊ/. *(Hint: There is a total of nine words.)*
3. Mark stressed words with a stress mark (ˊ).
4. Read the expressions and sentences aloud one more time.

Example: p<u>u</u>ll thr<u>ou</u>gh   (get better after an illness)

The ACcident was so SÉRious that the DÓCtor

DOESn't think he'll p<u>u</u>ll thr<u>ou</u>gh.

1. Once in a bl<u>ue</u> m<u>oo</u>n   (very seldom)
He sees his UNcle once in a bl<u>ue</u> m<u>oo</u>n.

2. C<u>oo</u>k up.   (to think up something)
Don't WORRy, we'll c<u>oo</u>k up a STORy, ANy STORy.

3. F<u>OO</u>Ling aROUND   (doing useless things)
Stop F<u>OO</u>Ling aROUND and get back to work.

4. C<u>OU</u>LDn't care less   (not to mind at all)
I C<u>OU</u>LDn't care less if I NEVer see him aGAIN.

5. To d<u>o</u> a g<u>oo</u>d turn   (to do something that benefits someone else)
He did me a g<u>oo</u>d turn when he recoMMENDed me for the job.

6. On D<u>U</u>ty; off D<u>U</u>ty   (working at one's job; not working)
The nurse went on D<u>U</u>ty at ten and off D<u>U</u>ty at four.

7. L<u>oo</u>k down on   (to regard as inferior)
He l<u>oo</u>ks down on ANYone making less MONey than he does.

	/uw/ as in "d<u>o</u>"	/ʊ/ as in "b<u>oo</u>k"
Example:	through	pull
	_____	_____
	_____	_____
	_____	_____
	_____	_____
	_____	

PART 4

Consonants

Check the consonant sounds of American English on pages 170-1. You will practice all these sounds. There are three major things to consider when producing consonant sounds:

1. <u>Place of Articulation.</u> Which articulators (lips, teeth, tongue, etc.) help us shape the sound? Say /m/ as in "<u>m</u>e." Your lips are closed. Say /f/ as in "<u>f</u>ood." Your upper teeth touch the inner part of your lower lip. Say /d/ as in "<u>d</u>ay." Your tongue touches your upper gum ridge.
2. <u>Manner of Production.</u> How does the air flow out of the mouth or nose?
   a. For some sounds the flow of air is stopped and then continued. Say /d/ as in "<u>d</u>ay." Your tongue stops the flow of air for a moment. As you complete the sound, a puff of air escapes. This type of sound is called <u>stop-plosive.</u>[1]
   b. For some sounds a little noise (friction) is created when the air flows out. Say /f/ as in "<u>f</u>ood." Do you hear the noise? This type of sound is called <u>fricative.</u>[1]
   c. For some sounds the air flows out of the nose. Say /m/ as in "<u>m</u>e." Place your finger underneath your nose and feel the air flowing out. This type of sound is called <u>nasal.</u>[1] All sounds that are not stop-plosives (with one exception) are called <u>continuants</u>[1] because they can be held as long as your breath allows.

[1]This term is for your reference. See chart on pages 170-1.

   d. For some sounds the air flows out of the mouth, in the same
      way it does for vowel sounds, as the lips and tongue move
      smoothly (or glide) from one position to another. Say /w/
      as in "<u>w</u>alk." Do you feel the air flowing out evenly? This
      type of sound is called <u>glide</u>[2] or <u>semi-vowel.</u>[2]
3. <u>Voiced or Voiceless Sounds.</u> In Unit 2 you practiced placing 2
   fingers on your throat while saying /z/ as in "<u>z</u>oo" and /s/ as
   in "<u>s</u>ee." When you say /z/ your vocal cords vibrate. Sounds
   made with vocal cords vibrating are <u>voiced.</u> When you say /s/
   your vocal cords do not vibrate. Sounds made with no vibration
   of the vocal cords are <u>voiceless.</u>

[2]This term is for your reference. See chart on pages 170-1.

Consonant Chart

Manner of Production

Place of Articulation	Stop-plosives VL	Stop-plosives VD	Fricatives VL	Fricatives VD	Nasals VD	Glides/Semi-Vowels VD	Affricates VL	Affricates VD
					CONTINUANTS			
Two lips	/p/ (pen)	/b/ (boy) Lips closed; air builds up and is released when lips part.			/m/ (me) Lips are closed; air passes out through nose.	/w/ (walk) Back of tongue is high in mouth; lips are rounded.		
Teeth and lip			/f/ (fat)	/v/ (voice) Upper teeth contact inside of lower lip; air is forced through.				
Tongue tip and teeth			/θ/ (thin)	/ð/ (the) Tip of tongue between teeth; air is forced through.				

Manner of Production

Place of Articulation	Stop-plosives		Fricatives		Nasals	Glides/Semi-Vowels	Affricates	
	VL	VD	VL	VD	VD	VD	VL	VD
Tongue tip and upper gum ridge	/t/ (ten) Tongue tip on upper gum ridge; air builds up and is released when tongue tip is removed.	/d/ (day)	/s/ (see) Tongue tip is close to upper gum ridge; air is forced through narrow opening formed by tongue.	/z/ (zoo)	/n/ (no) Tip of tongue on upper gum ridge; air passes out through nose.	/l/ (like) Tongue tip on upper gum ridge; air passes over sides of tongue. /r/ (red) Tongue tip points to upper gum ridge; air passes over tongue.		
Front of tongue and roof of mouth (hard palate)			/ʃ/ (she) Front part of tongue is raised toward roof of mouth; air passes over tongue; lips are rounded.	/ʒ/ (pleasure)		/y/ (yes) Center part of tongue is raised toward roof of mouth; air passes over tongue.	/tʃ/ (child) Combination of /t/ and /ʃ/; combination of /d/ and /ʒ/. Both are said quickly.	/dʒ/ (job)
Back of tongue and back of roof of mouth (soft palate)	/k/ (cat) Back of tongue touches soft palate; air builds up and is released when back of tongue is lowered.	/g/ (go)			/ŋ/ (king) Back of tongue touches soft palate; air passes out through nose.			
Glottis			h - (he) Formed at the vocal folds as air passes through small opening between them.					

UNIT 20 /l/ as in like

1. PRODUCING /l/

Examples: love, land, luck, beLOW, COLor, YELLow,
aLONE, FInal, fall, LITTle[1]

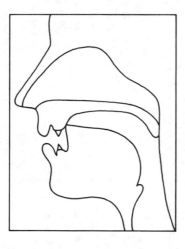

- Place the tip of your tongue against your upper gum ridge.
- As you make the sound, air flows out over the sides of your tongue.
- Your vocal cords vibrate.

2. PRACTICE THE SOUND

A. Practice the sound /l/ as in "like," first normally, then with exaggeration, then normally. Listen and repeat.

/l/   /l. . . ./   /l/

[1]The last sound of "little" is an example of a "syllabic /l/." See pages 201-2.

B. Now practice the sound in words. Notice the phonetic spelling. Listen and repeat each word twice.

1. <u>l</u>aw	/lɔ/	<u>l</u>aw
2. <u>l</u>eg	/lɛg/	<u>l</u>eg
3. BA<u>L</u>ance	/bæləns/	BA<u>L</u>ance
4. TE<u>L</u>ephone	/tɛləfown/	TE<u>L</u>ephone
5. schoo<u>l</u>	/skuwl/	schoo<u>l</u>
6. ki<u>ll</u>	/kɪl/	ki<u>ll</u>

3. CHECK YOUR LISTENING

In the following pairs of words, one word ends with the sound /l/. Circle the word in which you hear the sound /l/.

1.	me	mea<u>l</u>	5.	so	sou<u>l</u>
2.	my	mi<u>l</u>e	6.	say	sa<u>l</u>e
3.	boy	boi<u>l</u>	7.	pay	pai<u>l</u>
4.	too	too<u>l</u>	8.	why	whi<u>l</u>e

4. DIFFERENT POSITIONS OF /l/

Practice the sound /l/ as in "<u>l</u>ike" in several different positions. Listen and repeat these words. *Capital letters indicate syllable stress.*

/l/ IN INITIAL POSITION

1. <u>l</u>ook	5. <u>L</u>Abor	9. <u>L</u>Icense
2. <u>l</u>unch	6. <u>L</u>Egal	10. <u>L</u>AWyer
3. <u>l</u>augh	7. <u>L</u>ECture	11. <u>L</u>EADer
4. <u>l</u>oud	8. <u>L</u>OVer	12. <u>L</u>ITerature

/l/ IN MEDIAL POSITION

1. a<u>L</u>IVE	5. CO<u>LL</u>ege	9. REa<u>l</u>ize
2. a<u>L</u>ARM	6. FAMi<u>l</u>y	10. IS<u>l</u>and[2]
3. be<u>L</u>IEVE	7. po<u>L</u>ITE	11. POPu<u>l</u>ar
4. DO<u>LL</u>ar	8. TOI<u>l</u>et	12. inTE<u>LL</u>igent

[2]The "s" in "island" is not pronounced.

/l/ IN FINAL POSITION

1. a<u>ll</u>	5. hee<u>l</u>	9. ANNua<u>l</u>
2. poo<u>l</u>	6. DIa<u>l</u>	10. inSTA<u>LL</u>
3. ki<u>ll</u>	7. FEma<u>l</u>e	11. conTRO<u>L</u>
4. we<u>ll</u>	8. Apri<u>l</u>	12. SCHEDu<u>l</u>e

5. NO SOUND FOR "L"

In some words, the letter "l" is not pronounced. Listen and repeat the following words and sentences.

1. pa̸lm	There's a pa̸lm tree GROWing in front of my house.
2. ca̸lm	The WAter was ca̸lm AFter the storm.
3. ta̸lk	Don't ta̸lk to your ENemies.
4. wa̸lk	Don't wa̸lk on that path.
5. cha̸lk	Use the cha̸lk when you write on the CHA̸LKboard.
6. cou̸ld	I said you cou̸ld go.
7. wou̸ld	He said he wou̸ld go.
8. shou̸ld	We said they shou̸ld go.
9. ha̸lf	May I have ha̸lf of that?
10. beHA̸LF	I'll do it on your beHA̸LF.
11. SA̸LMon	I like to eat SA̸LMon for lunch.
12. LINco̸ln	Abraham LINco̸ln was our SIXteenth PRESident.

6. STRESS AND INTONATION

Each of these sentences contains the sound /l/ as in "<u>l</u>ike." You will hear each sentence four times:

1. Listen for the sound /l/. (The letter or letters for this sound are underlined.)
2. Listen for syllable stress and word stress. *Capital letters indicate syllable stress.* Mark the word stress that you hear. Put a stress mark (´) over the stressed word or words.
3. Listen for rising or falling intonation at the end of the sentence. Mark intonation with the symbol "⤴" or "⤵."
4. Listen to the sentence again and repeat it. Pay attention to pauses and linking of words.

The first sentence is marked for you.

1. Bíll, Phíl, LILĹian and LÚcy met for lunch at eLÉVen o'CLÓCK.

2. Phil told LILLian she looked BEAUtiful.

3. LILLian told Phil he was WONderful.

4. LUcy told Bill he looked old.

5. Bill told LUcy she was a spoiled child.

6. LILLian had a SALMon SALad and lemonADE for lunch.

7. Phil and Bill had FILLet of sole and MELon for lunch.

8. LUcy had leg of lamb and YELLow JELL-o for lunch.

9. LUcy spilled her YELLow JELL-o on Bill's lap.

10. Bill and LUcy no LONGer lunch toGETHer.

7. HOME ASSIGNMENT

A. A proverb is a short saying that gives advice or a warning. The following proverbs contain words with the sound /l/ as in "like." Read each proverb aloud. Then try to explain the proverb in different words. (You may ask a native speaker for help.) Write down your explanations.

1. Live and learn.
2. Live and let live.
3. Look beFORE you leap.
4. Like FAther, like son.
5. The love of MONey is the root of all Evil.

B. Bring your work to class. Work with a partner or small group. Share and compare your explanations of the proverbs.

UNIT 21 /r/ as in red

1. PRODUCING /r/

Examples: <u>r</u>an, <u>r</u>ead, <u>wr</u>ite,[1] a<u>R</u>OUND, toMO<u>RR</u>ow, a<u>r</u>e

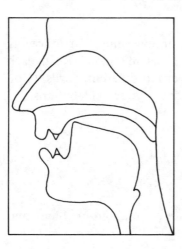

- Raise the tip of your tongue towards the upper gum ridge but do not touch it. The tip of your tongue should not touch anything.
- Press the sides of your tongue against your upper back teeth.
- Lips are slightly open.
- As you make the sound, air flows out over the tip of your tongue.
- Your vocal cords vibrate.

🎧 2. PRACTICE THE SOUND

A. Practice the sound /r/ as in "<u>r</u>ed," first normally, then with exaggeration, then normally. Listen and repeat.

/r/   /r. . . ./   /r/

---

[1]The "w" in "write" is not pronounced. See pages 292-3 for other words like "write."

176

B. Now practice the sound in words. Notice the phonetic spelling. Listen and repeat each word twice.

1. <u>r</u>ed	/rɛd/	<u>r</u>ed
2. <u>wr</u>ite	/rayt/	<u>wr</u>ite
3. a<u>RR</u>IVE	/ərayv/	a<u>RR</u>IVE
4. BO<u>RR</u>ow	/barow/	BO<u>RR</u>ow
5. ca<u>r</u>	/kar/	ca<u>r</u>
6. fa<u>r</u>	/far/	fa<u>r</u>

🍭 3. CHECK YOUR LISTENING

A. The following words contain the sounds /r/ as in "<u>r</u>ed," /w/ as in "<u>w</u>alk," and /l/ as in "<u>l</u>ike." You will hear one word from each group. Circle the word that you hear.

1. <u>r</u>aid	<u>w</u>eighed	<u>l</u>aid
2. <u>r</u>ate	<u>w</u>ait	<u>l</u>ate
3. <u>r</u>ay	<u>w</u>ay	<u>l</u>ay
4. <u>r</u>ed	<u>w</u>ed	<u>l</u>ed
5. <u>r</u>ot	<u>w</u>hat²	<u>l</u>ot
6. <u>r</u>ye	<u>w</u>hy²	<u>l</u>ie
7. <u>r</u>ide	<u>w</u>ide	<u>l</u>ied
8. <u>r</u>ight	<u>w</u>hite²	<u>l</u>ight

B. The following words contain the sounds /r/ as in "<u>r</u>ed," and /l/ as in "<u>l</u>ike." You will hear one word from each pair. Circle the word you hear.

1. BU<u>R</u>y	BE<u>LL</u>y	5. c<u>r</u>ime	c<u>l</u>imb
2. a<u>RR</u>IVE	a<u>L</u>IVE	6. f<u>r</u>ee	f<u>l</u>ee
3. e<u>R</u>ECT	e<u>L</u>ECT	7. c<u>r</u>own	c<u>l</u>own
4. g<u>r</u>ass	g<u>l</u>ass	8. c<u>r</u>owd	c<u>l</u>oud

²Some American speakers pronounce "<u>wh</u>at," "<u>wh</u>y" and "<u>wh</u>ite" with an initial /h/ sound: /hwət/, /hway/, /hwayt/. See Unit 32.

🔦 4. PRACTICE THE CONTRAST: /r/ AS IN "RED" WITH /l/ AS IN "LIKE"

A. Some students may confuse /r/ with /l/. Remember that /l/ is made by placing your tongue tip on the upper gum ridge. You make /r/ with the tongue tip pointing toward the gum ridge but not touching it.
Practice these contrasting sounds. Listen and repeat each word pair. *Capital letters indicate syllable stress.*

	/r/	/l/		/r/	/l/
1.	rock	lock	6.	wrong	long
2.	race	lace	7.	coRRECT	coLLECT
3.	red	lead	8.	PIrate	PIlot
4.	road	load	9.	fry	fly
5.	right	light	10.	crown	clown

B. Now practice the contrasting sounds in sentence pairs. The first sentence of each pair has the sound /r/ and the second has the sound /l/. Listen and repeat. Notice the change in meaning. Visual clues can help. Make a simple drawing in each blank box. *Capital letters indicate syllable stress.*

	1a. rock	He has a rock.

	b. lock	He has a lock.

2a. <u>r</u>ace   It's a good <u>r</u>ace.

  b. <u>l</u>ace   It's a good <u>l</u>ace.

3a. <u>r</u>ed   Can it be <u>r</u>ed?

  b. <u>l</u>ead   Can it be <u>l</u>ead?

4a. <u>r</u>oad   Where's the <u>r</u>oad?

  b. <u>l</u>oad   Where's the <u>l</u>oad?

5a. <u>r</u>ight   Give me a <u>r</u>ight one.

  b. <u>l</u>ight   Give me a <u>l</u>ight one.

6a. <u>wr</u>ong   It's the <u>wr</u>ong one.

  b. <u>l</u>ong   It's the <u>l</u>ong one.

7a. co<u>RR</u>ECT   Can you co<u>RR</u>ECT it?

  b. co<u>LL</u>ECT   Can you co<u>LL</u>ECT it?

8a. PIrate   It's aBOUT a PIrate.

b. PIlot   It's aBOUT a PIlot.

9a. fry   Let's fry it.

b. fly   Let's fly it.

10a. crown   Where's the crown?

b. clown   Where's the clown?

5. PRACTICE THE CONTRAST: /r/ AS IN "RED" WITH /w/ AS IN "WALK"

A. Some students may confuse /r/ with /w/. Remember that /r/ is made with the tongue tip pointing toward the gum ridge but not touching it. Make /w/ with your tongue tip resting against your bottom teeth and rounding your lips.

Practice these contrasting sounds. Listen and repeat each word pair.

	/r/	/w/			/r/	/w/
1.	ray	way		6.	red	wed
2.	rage	wage		7.	rent	went
3.	raced	waste		8.	rest	west
4.	rate	weight		9.	ripe	wipe
5.	rip	whip		10.	right	white

B. Now practice the contrasting sounds in sentence pairs. The first sentence of each pair has the sound /r/ and the second has the sound /w/. Listen and repeat. Notice the change in meaning. Visual clues can help. Make a simple drawing in each blank box.

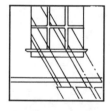

1a. ray   Is it a long ray?

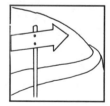

b. way   Is it a long way?

2a. rage   He had a rage.

b. wage   He had a wage.

3a. raced   They raced a lot.

b. waste   They waste a lot.

4a. <u>r</u>ate   Is it the <u>r</u>ate?

  b. <u>w</u>eight   Is it the <u>w</u>eight?

5a. <u>r</u>ip   It's a long <u>r</u>ip.

  b. <u>wh</u>ip   It's a long <u>wh</u>ip.

6a. <u>r</u>ed   Are they <u>r</u>ed?

  b. <u>w</u>ed   Are they <u>w</u>ed?

7a. <u>r</u>ent   Did I hear "<u>r</u>ent?"

  b. <u>w</u>ent   Did I hear "<u>w</u>ent?"

8a. <u>r</u>est   Let's go <u>r</u>est.

  b. <u>w</u>est   Let's go <u>w</u>est.

9a. <u>r</u>ipe   It's not "<u>r</u>ipe."

  b. <u>w</u>ipe   It's not "<u>w</u>ipe."

10a. <u>r</u>ight   Is it <u>r</u>ight?

   b. <u>wh</u>ite   Is it <u>wh</u>ite?

↻ 6. CHECK YOUR LISTENING

Work with a partner. Read a sentence from 4B or 5B to your partner. Can your partner define the sentence? He or she must be truthful.

Your partner will: • Say: I know what _____ means.
                     It means _____. (definition or paraphrase)
                     or
                   • Act out what the word means.
                     or
                   • Make a simple drawing.

Or your partner will ask: What does _____ mean? Then you must define the sentence, act it out, or make a drawing.

🎧 7. DIFFERENT POSITIONS OF /r/

Note: In some areas of the eastern and southern United States, and in other English-speaking countries, /r/ may not be pronounced in medial and in final positions. For example, the word "farm" might be pronounced /fam/, and the word "more" might be pronounced /mɔ/. In both cases the vowel sounds are lengthened. However, the majority of Americans pronounce /r/ in all positions. Practice the sound /r/ in several different positions. Listen and repeat. *Capital letters indicate syllable stress.*

/r/ IN INITIAL POSITION

1. <u>r</u>ug	4. <u>r</u>ight	7. <u>R</u>EADy	10. <u>r</u>eCEIVE
2. <u>r</u>oad	5. <u>r</u>ound	8. <u>R</u>EAson	11. <u>R</u>Ecent
3. <u>r</u>ich	6. <u>R</u>IVer	9. <u>R</u>Ealize	12. <u>R</u>ECognize

/r/ IN MEDIAL POSITION

1. CA<u>RR</u>y	4. O<u>R</u>ange	7. di<u>R</u>ECtion	10. PE<u>R</u>iod
2. CHO<u>R</u>us	5. pa<u>R</u>ADE	8. SAL<u>r</u>y	11. VA<u>R</u>ious
3. FO<u>R</u>eign	6. STO<u>R</u>y	9. TE<u>RR</u>ible	12. INvento<u>r</u>y

/r/ IN FINAL POSITION

1. ca<u>r</u>e	4. sta<u>r</u>	7. hou<u>r</u>	10. guiTA<u>R</u>
2. doo<u>r</u>	5. you<u>r</u>	8. beFO<u>R</u>E	11. igNO<u>R</u>E
3. fou<u>r</u>	6. sha<u>r</u>e	9. EMpi<u>r</u>e	12. inSU<u>R</u>E

♥ 8. STRESS AND INTONATION

Each of these sentences contains the sound /r/ as in "red." You will hear each sentence four times:

1. Listen for the sound /r/. (The letters for this sound are underlined.)
2. Listen for syllable stress and word stress. *Capital letters indicate syllable stress.* Mark the word stress that you hear. Put a stress mark (ʹ) over the stressed word or words.
3. Listen for rising or falling intonation at the end of the sentence. Mark intonation with the symbol "⤴" or "⤵."
4. Listen to the sentence again and repeat it. Pay attention to pauses and linking of words.

The first sentence is marked for you.

1. SORRy, I gave you the wrong diRECtions.
2. RONald ran aROUND the CORner.
3. Would you RATHer have rice with the roast?
4. When in Rome, do as the ROmans do.
5. Was Ruth in a HURRy to MARRy?
6. DIDn't you REalize it was RAINing when you ran out?
7. Don't WORRy, my CAMera is VERy good.
8. They had a TERRible QUARRel about the red ROSes.
9. Please show me the coRRECT way to OPerate the MIcrophone.
10. They CARRied all the chairs INto the room beFORE it STARTed to rain.

9. HOME ASSIGNMENT

1. Read the following riddle aloud. You can use a dictionary to help you with the meaning and pronunciation of new words.
2. Mark the passage for stress and intonation.
3. Be prepared to read the passage aloud in class.
4. Can you answer the riddle?

<u>R</u>ound and <u>r</u>ound the <u>R</u>UGGed <u>r</u>ock

The <u>R</u>AGGed <u>R</u>AScal <u>r</u>an.

How MANy <u>r</u>'s a<u>r</u>e the<u>r</u>e in that?

Now tell me if you can.

<table>
<tr><td>

UNIT
22

</td><td>

/p/ as in <u>p</u>en
/b/ as in <u>b</u>oy

</td></tr>
</table>

1. PRODUCING /p/

Examples: <u>p</u>ay, <u>p</u>ut, <u>p</u>lay, <u>p</u>rice, s<u>p</u>eak, s<u>p</u>ring, sle<u>p</u>t, ma<u>p</u>s, jum<u>p</u>, hel<u>p</u>

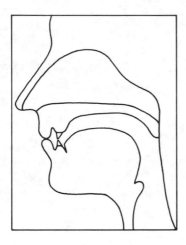

- First press your lips together, to stop the flow of air.
- Then open your lips and produce the sound with a strong puff of air.
- Your vocal cords do not vibrate.
- Hold a piece of paper in front of your lips. It should move when you produce the sound. Or hold your hand in front of your lips to feel the puff of air.

2. PRODUCING /b/

Examples: be, best, brain, black, aBOUT, oBEY, Able, job, tribe

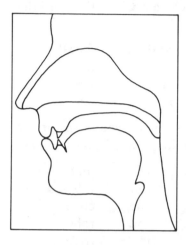

- This sound is produced the same way as /p/, except that /b/ is voiced and the puff of air is not as strong.
- First press your lips together, to stop the flow of air.
- Then open your lips and produce the sound with a puff of air.
- Your vocal cords should vibrate.
- Use a piece of paper or your hand to make sure a puff of air is released.

3. CONTRAST: /p/ AND /b/

A. Some students may confuse the sound /p/ as in "pen" with the sound /b/ as in "boy." Practice these two sounds, first normally, then with exaggeration, then normally. Listen and repeat.

Place your hand in front of your lips to feel a puff of air.

1.	/p/	/p. . . . ./	/p/
2.	/b/	/b. . . . ./	/b/

B. Now practice the sounds in words. Notice the phonetic spelling. Listen and repeat each word twice.

1.	pan	/pæn/	pan
2.	piece	/piys/	piece
3.	rePAIR	/rɪpɛr/	rePAIR
4.	type	/tayp/	type
5.	bake	/beyk/	bake
6.	bad	/bæd/	bad
7.	MAYbe	/meybiy/	MAYbe
8.	robe	/rowb/	robe

🔦 4. CHECK YOUR LISTENING

A. The following pairs of words contain the sounds /p/ as in "pen" and /b/ as in "boy." You will hear one word from each pair. Circle the word that you hear.

1.	pie	buy	5.	SIMple	SYMbol
2.	pack	back	6.	STAple	STAble
3.	peach	beach	7.	lap	lab
4.	pest	best	8.	rip	rib

B. In the following pairs of words, one word ends with the sound /p/ or /b/. You will hear one word from each pair. Circle the word that you hear.

1.	so	soap	6.	Ma	mob
2.	key	keep	7.	too	tube
3.	row	rope	8.	cue	cube
4.	why	wipe	9.	row	robe
5.	bum	bump	10.	try	tribe

🔦 5. PRACTICE THE CONTRAST: /p/ AS IN "PEN" WITH /b/ AS IN "BOY"

A. Practice these contrasting sounds. Listen and repeat each word pair. *Capital letters indicate syllable stress. Note:* When /p/ or /b/ appears at the end of a word, the sound is produced with a weak puff of air.

	/p/	/b/		/p/	/b/
1.	pig	big	6.	cap	cab
2.	pill	bill	7.	tap	tab
3.	pat	bat	8.	mop	mob
4.	pet	bet	9.	rope	robe
5.	PALate	BALLot	10.	lap	lab

B. Now practice the contrasting sounds in sentence pairs. The first sentence of each pair has the sound /p/ and the second has the sound /b/. Listen and repeat. Notice the change in meaning. Visual clues can help. Make a simple drawing in each blank box. *Capital letters indicate syllable stress.*

1a. pat   Give him a pat.

  b. bat   Give him a bat.

2a. pet   This is my pet.

  b. bet   This is my bet.

3a. <u>p</u>ill   Did you take the <u>p</u>ill?

b. <u>b</u>ill   Did you take the <u>b</u>ill?

4a. <u>P</u>ALate   I see the <u>P</u>ALate.

b. <u>B</u>ALLot   I see the <u>B</u>ALLot.

5a. <u>p</u>ig   Is it a LITTle <u>p</u>ig?

b. <u>b</u>ig   Is it a LITTle <u>b</u>ig?

6a. <u>c</u>ap   She took the ca<u>p</u>.

b. <u>c</u>ab   She took the ca<u>b</u>.

7a.	rope	John has a rope.
b.	robe	John has a robe.
8a.	tap	Did you find the tap?

b.	tab	Did you find the tab?

9a.	mop	Did you see the mop?
b.	mob	Did you see the mob?
10a.	lap	Put it in his lap.
b.	lab	Put it in his lab.

◐ 6. CHECK YOUR LISTENING

Work with a partner. Read a sentence from 5B to your partner. Can your partner define the sentence? He or she must be truthful.

Your partner will:
- Say: I know what _____ means.
  It means _____. (definition or paraphrase)
  or
- Act out what the word means.
  or
- Make a simple drawing.

Or your partner will ask: What does _____ mean? Then you must define the sentence, act it out, or make a drawing. Do two or three sentences each.

7. CONSONANT CLUSTERS WITH /p/ AS IN "PEN" AND /b/ AS IN "BOY"

When one consonant sound is combined with one or more other consonants, it is called a *cluster*.

A. When /p/ occurs in a cluster, the puff of air is weak. However, make sure your lips close to stop the flow of air. Listen and repeat. *Capital letters indicate syllable stress.*

Initial /pl/	Medial /pl/	Final /pl/
1. plan	1. aPPLY	1. APPle
2. plane	2. suPPLY	2. COUPle
3. plus	3. rePLY	3. PEOple
4. plate	4. emPLOY	4. PARticiple

Initial /pr/	Medial /pr/	Medial /rp/
1. pray	1. Apron	1. AIRplane
2. PRIson	2. aPPROACH	2. CARpet
3. PROMise	3. aPPROVE	3. PURple
4. preFER	4. imPROVE	4. SURplus

B. When /b/ occurs in a cluster, there is no puff of air. However, make sure your lips close and your vocal cords vibrate. *Capital letters indicate syllable stress.*

Initial /bl/	Medial /bl/	Final /bl/
1. black	1. PROBlem	1. TAble
2. blank	2. PROBably	2. POSSible
3. blame	3. PUBlic	3. TROUBle
4. blood	4. PUBlish	4. TERRible

Initial /br/	Medial /br/	Medial & Final /rb/
1. brain	1. aBROAD	1. URban
2. break	2. aBBREviate	2. ORbit
3. brown	3. ALgebra	3. GARbage
4. bridge	4. LIbrary	4. CARbon
		5. HARbor
		6. curb
		7. verb
		8. disTURB

🎧 8. NO SOUND FOR "b" AND "p"

A. The letter "b" is usually not pronounced when it follows the letter "m." It is also not pronounced before the letter "t" in the same syllable. Listen and repeat. *Capital letters indicate syllable stress.*

1.	climb̷	Don't climb̷ up the tree.
2.	comb̷	May I use your comb̷?
3.	dumb̷	That's a dumb̷ thing I did.
4.	lamb̷	A lamb̷ is a young sheep.
5.	limb̷	A limb̷ is an arm or a leg.
6.	numb̷	To be numb̷ is to feel no pain.
7.	thumb̷	Your thumb̷ is a short, thick FINger.
8.	tomb̷	A tomb̷ is a place where SOMEone is BURied.
9.	bomb̷	A bomb̷ went off in the MARket.
10.	PLUMB̷er	A PLUMB̷er rePAIRS WAter pipes.
11.	doub̷t	When in doub̷t, don't use it.
12.	deb̷t	A deb̷t is SOMEthing owed to SOMEone else.

B. When the letters "ps" begin a word, the "p" is not pronounced. "P" is also not pronounced in a few other words. Listen and repeat.

1.	p̷sal̷m	A p̷sal̷m is a reLIGious song or POem. ("l" is also not pronounced.)
2.	p̷syCHIatrist	A p̷syCHIatrist is a MEDical DOCtor who treats MENtal ILLness.
3.	p̷syCHOLogist	A p̷syCHOLogist ALso treats MENtal ILLness but has no MEDical deGREE.
4.	corp̷s̷	The MaRINE Corp̷s̷ is part of the Armed FORCes. ("s" in "Corps" is also not pronounced.)
5.	reCEIP̷T	You should get a reCEIP̷T when you pay the rent.

🎧 9. STRESS AND INTONATION

Each of these sentences contains the sound /p/ as in "<u>p</u>en," the sound /b/ as in "<u>b</u>oy," or both. You will hear each sentence four times:

1. Listen for the sounds /p/ and /b/. (Letters that stand for these sounds are underlined. Clusters with /p/ and /b/ are also underlined.)
2. Listen for syllable stress and word stress. *Capital letters indicate syllable stress.* Mark the word stress that you hear. Put a stress mark (ʹ) over the stressed word or words.

3. Listen for rising or falling intonation at the end of the sentence. Mark intonation with the symbol "⤴" or "⤵."

4. Listen to the sentence again and repeat it. Pay attention to pauses and linking of words.

The first sentence is marked for you.

1. Take the SU<u>B</u>way to the <u>P</u>U<u>B</u>lic LI<u>b</u>rary.

2. Did you <u>b</u>uy the A<u>PP</u>le?

3. <u>P</u>ark the car at the cur<u>b</u>.

4. Take the ex<u>PRESS</u> <u>b</u>us to the AI<u>R</u>port.

5. Is this <u>b</u>louse WASHa<u>b</u>le?

6. Are these ma<u>p</u>s VALua<u>b</u>le?

7. Did he come to in<u>SP</u>ECT the CA<u>R</u>pet?

8. Is the <u>b</u>iOLogy la<u>b</u> on CAMpus?

9. My <u>b</u>oss <u>b</u>ought a new <u>B</u>USiness.

10. <u>BROOK</u>lyn and the <u>B</u>ronx are <u>p</u>art of New York CITy.

11. The CA<u>R</u>bon <u>P</u>Aper is in the GA<u>R</u>bage.

12. <u>P</u>lease <u>p</u>ass the s<u>p</u>oon with the sou<u>p</u>.

13. Did your em<u>PLO</u>Yer <u>b</u>uy the <u>PROP</u>erty?

14. Did he eSCA<u>P</u>E from <u>PR</u>Ison?

10. HOME ASSIGNMENT

A. Review the clusters in Exercise 7. Choose one word from each cluster and use it in an original sentence. When you finish you should have twelve sentences. Mark the sentences for stress and rising or falling intonation.

B. Bring your list to class. Work with a partner. Your partner may read your sentences aloud, using your stress and intonation marking. Is the meaning clear?

<table>
<tr><td>UNIT
23</td><td># /t/ as in <u>t</u>en
/d/ as in <u>d</u>ay</td></tr>
</table>

1. PRODUCING /t/

Examples: <u>t</u>o, <u>t</u>ime, s<u>t</u>op, LI<u>TT</u>le, AU<u>t</u>o, a<u>t</u>e, walk<u>ed</u>

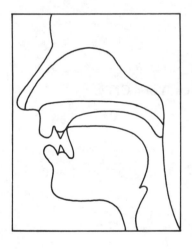

- First press the tip of your tongue on your upper gum ridge, to stop the flow of air.
- Then quickly drop the tongue tip to produce the sound with a strong puff of air.
- Your vocal cords do not vibrate.
- Hold a piece of paper in front of your lips. It should move when you produce the sound. Or hold your hand in front of your lips to feel the puff of air.

2. PRODUCING /d/

Examples: <u>d</u>o, <u>d</u>ark, CAN<u>d</u>y, LOU<u>D</u>er, POW<u>d</u>er, nee<u>d</u>, si<u>d</u>e, call<u>ed</u>

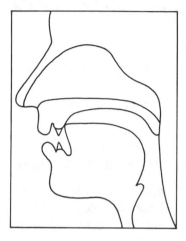

- This sound is produced the same way as /t/ except that /d/ is voiced and the puff of air is not as strong.
- First press your tongue tip on your upper gum ridge, to stop the flow of air.
- Then drop your tongue tip and produce the sound with a puff of air.
- Your vocal cords should vibrate.

3. CONTRAST: /t/ AND /d/

A. Some students may confuse the sound /t/ as in "<u>t</u>en" with the sound /d/ as in "<u>d</u>ay." Practice these two sounds, first normally, then with exaggeration, then normally. Listen and repeat. Place your hand in front of your lips to feel a puff of air.

        1. /t/   /t . . . . ./   /t/
        2. /d/   /d. . . . ./   /d/

B. Now practice the sounds in words. Notice the phonetic spelling. Listen and repeat each word twice.

1. <u>t</u>ea	/tiy/	<u>t</u>ea
2. <u>t</u>ell	/tɛl/	<u>t</u>ell
3. a<u>TT</u>ACK	/ətæk/	a<u>TT</u>ACK
4. coa<u>t</u>	/kowt/	coa<u>t</u>
5. <u>d</u>eep	/diyp/	<u>d</u>eep
6. <u>d</u>ig	/dɪg/	<u>d</u>ig
7. a<u>D</u>ULT	/ədəlt/	a<u>D</u>ULT
8. nee<u>d</u>	/niyd/	nee<u>d</u>

🔘 **4.** CHECK YOUR LISTENING

A. The following pairs of words contain the sounds /t/ as in "<u>t</u>en" and /d/ as in "<u>d</u>ay." You will hear one word from each pair. Circle the word that you hear.

1.	<u>t</u>ear	<u>d</u>ear	6.	ba<u>t</u>	ba<u>d</u>
2.	<u>t</u>ie	<u>d</u>ie	7.	nea<u>t</u>	nee<u>d</u>
3.	<u>t</u>ime	<u>d</u>ime	8.	ha<u>t</u>	ha<u>d</u>
4.	<u>t</u>o	<u>d</u>o	9.	coa<u>t</u>	co<u>d</u>e
5.	<u>t</u>own	<u>d</u>own	10.	hi<u>t</u>	hi<u>d</u>

B. In the following pairs of words, one word ends with the sound /t/ or /d/. You will hear one word from each pair. Circle the word that you hear.

1.	spy	spi<u>t</u>e	6.	may	ma<u>d</u>e
2.	he	hea<u>t</u>	7.	knee	nee<u>d</u>
3.	plan	plan<u>t</u>	8.	car	car<u>d</u>
4.	see	sea<u>t</u>	9.	rye	ri<u>d</u>e
5.	go	goa<u>t</u>	10.	plan	plann<u>ed</u>

🔘 **5.** PRACTICE THE CONTRAST: /t/ AS IN "<u>T</u>EN" WITH /d/ AS IN "<u>D</u>AY"

A. Practice these contrasting sounds. Listen and repeat each word pair.

	/t/	/d/		/t/	/d/
1.	<u>t</u>ear	<u>d</u>ear	6.	a<u>t</u>	a<u>dd</u>
2.	<u>t</u>ie	<u>d</u>ye	7.	nea<u>t</u>	nee<u>d</u>
3.	<u>t</u>ime	<u>d</u>ime	8.	coa<u>t</u>	co<u>d</u>e
4.	<u>t</u>ile	<u>D</u>Ial	9.	deb<u>t</u>	dea<u>d</u>
5.	<u>t</u>own	<u>d</u>own	10.	brigh<u>t</u>	bri<u>d</u>e

B. Now practice the contrasting sounds in sentence pairs. The first sentence of each pair has the sound /t/ and the second has the sound /d/. Listen and repeat. Notice the change in meaning. Visual clues can help. Make a simple drawing in each blank box.

1a. <u>t</u>ime   Do you have the <u>t</u>ime?

b. <u>d</u>ime   Do you have the <u>d</u>ime?

2a. <u>t</u>ile   Can you <u>t</u>ile it?

b. <u>DI</u>al   Can you <u>DI</u>al it?

3a. <u>t</u>ore   Did you say "<u>t</u>ore?"

b. <u>d</u>oor   Did you say "<u>d</u>oor?"

4a. <u>t</u>ie   I like the <u>t</u>ie.

b. <u>d</u>ye   I like the <u>d</u>ye.

5a. wri<u>t</u>e   Will you wri<u>t</u>e?

b. ri<u>d</u>e   Will you ri<u>d</u>e?

6a. sea<u>t</u>   Do you want the sea<u>t</u>?

b. see<u>d</u>   Do you want the see<u>d</u>?

7a. ca<u>r</u>t   I gave him my ca<u>r</u>t.

b. ca<u>r</u>d   I gave him my ca<u>r</u>d.

8a. be<u>t</u>   It's a good be<u>t</u>.

b. be<u>d</u>   It's a good be<u>d</u>.

9a. deb<u>t</u>   I saw the deb<u>t</u>.

b. dea<u>d</u>   I saw the dea<u>d</u>.

10a. pa<u>t</u>   Give her a pa<u>t</u>.

b. pa<u>d</u>   Give her a pa<u>d</u>.

↻ 6. CHECK YOUR LISTENING

Work with a partner. Read a sentence from 5B to your partner. Can your partner define the sentence? He or she must be truthful.

Your partner will: • Say: I know what _____ means.
It means _____. (definition or paraphrase)
or
• Act out what the word means.
or
• Make a simple drawing.

Or your partner will ask: What does _____ mean? Then you must define the sentence, act it out, or make a drawing.

🎧 7. WHEN /t/ SOUNDS LIKE /d/

When the sound /t/ occurs between two vowel sounds, in an unstressed syllable, or at the end of a stressed syllable, it is pronounced quickly, without a puff of air. Many educated Americans pronounce this sound like /d/. You will hear two pronunciations for each word. The first will have the /t/ sound and the second the /d/ sound. Listen and repeat.

1. CI<u>T</u>y	4. DAUGH<u>t</u>er	7. FOR<u>t</u>y	10. BU<u>TT</u>er
2. SI<u>TT</u>ing	5. WRI<u>T</u>er	8. DIR<u>t</u>y	11. MA<u>TT</u>er
3. WA<u>t</u>er	6. WRI<u>T</u>ing	9. BE<u>TT</u>er	12. LI<u>TT</u>le

🎧 8. CONSONANT CLUSTERS /lt/ AND /ld/

A. Practice these clusters. Listen to the contrast between the single sound and the cluster; then repeat each word pair.

	/l/	/lt/		/l/	/ld/
1.	fe<u>ll</u>	fe<u>lt</u>	6.	coa<u>l</u>	co<u>ld</u>
2.	hau<u>l</u>	ha<u>lt</u>	7.	goa<u>l</u>	go<u>ld</u>
3.	fa<u>ll</u>	fau<u>lt</u>	8.	bi<u>ll</u>	bui<u>ld</u>
4.	be<u>ll</u>	be<u>lt</u>	9.	ho<u>le</u>	ho<u>ld</u>
5.	ma<u>ll</u>	ma<u>lt</u>	10.	so<u>le</u>	so<u>ld</u>

B. Now practice the sounds in sentence pairs. The first sentence of each pair has a word that ends in /l/. The second has a word that ends in /lt/ or /ld/. Listen and repeat. Notice the change in meaning. Visual clues can help. Make a simple drawing in each blank box.

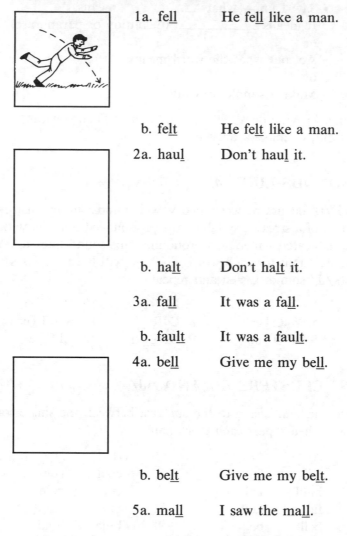

1a. fe<u>ll</u>   He fe<u>ll</u> like a man.

  b. fe<u>lt</u>   He fe<u>lt</u> like a man.

2a. hau<u>l</u>   Don't hau<u>l</u> it.

  b. ha<u>lt</u>   Don't ha<u>lt</u> it.

3a. fa<u>ll</u>   It was a fa<u>ll</u>.

  b. fau<u>lt</u>   It was a fau<u>lt</u>.

4a. be<u>ll</u>   Give me my be<u>ll</u>.

  b. be<u>lt</u>   Give me my be<u>lt</u>.

5a. ma<u>ll</u>   I saw the ma<u>ll</u>.

  b. ma<u>lt</u>   I saw the ma<u>lt</u>.

6a. co<u>al</u>   It's not coa<u>l</u>.

b. co<u>ld</u>   It's not co<u>ld</u>.

7a. go<u>al</u>   Was it your goa<u>l</u>?

b. go<u>ld</u>   Was it your go<u>ld</u>?

8a. bi<u>ll</u>   Will you bi<u>ll</u> it?

b. bui<u>ld</u>   Will you bui<u>ld</u> it?

9a. ho<u>le</u>   Put it in the ho<u>le</u>.

b. ho<u>ld</u>   Put it in the ho<u>ld</u>.

10a. so<u>le</u>   The fish is so<u>le</u>.

b. so<u>ld</u>   The fish is so<u>ld</u>.

9. SYLLABIC /l/ AFTER /t/ AND /d/

A. When /l/ is in an unstressed syllable following /t/ or /d/ no vowel sound is produced. This occurs even when a vowel letter appears between /t/ and /l/ and /d/ and /l/. For example,

1. LITTle	/lɪtl̩/	3. TOtal	/towtl̩/
2. MIDDle	/mɪdl̩/	4. MEDal	/mɛdl̩/

This /l/ sound is called *syllabic* because it forms a syllable without a vowel sound (indicated by the symbol /l̩/).

B. Remember that /t/, /d/, and /l/ are all made with the tongue tip pressed against the upper gum ridge.

• To produce /t/ or /d/, press your tongue tip against the upper gum ridge. This action stops the flow of air.
• Instead of releasing the tongue tip, keep it in place. Let the air escape over the sides of your tongue as you make the sound /l/.

C. Listen and repeat these words and sentences. Note that some educated speakers may use a "soft /t/" in words spelled with "t" or "tt." (See page 199.) *Capital letters indicate syllable stress.*

1. BOTTle	/batl̩/	Did you give the BAby the BOTTle?
2. BATTle	/bætl̩/	The SOLdiers fought in a big BATTle.
3. KETTle	/kɛtl̩/	Boil the WAter in the KETTle.
4. SETTle	/sɛtl̩/	Don't SETTle for less than what it's worth.
5. HOSpital	/haspɪtl̩/	We took him to the HOSpital.
6. CANdle	/kændl̩/	Light a CANdle when it gets dark.
7. RIDDle	/rɪdl̩/	What's the ANswer to the RIDDle?
8. SADDle	/sædl̩/	Put a SADDle on the horse.
9. NEEdle	/niydl̩/	Do you have a NEEdle and thread?
10. SANdals	/sændl̩z/	I like to wear SANdals, not closed shoes.

10. STRESS AND INTONATION

Each of these sentences contains the sound /t/ as in "<u>t</u>en," the sound /d/ as in "<u>d</u>ay," or both. You will hear each sentence four times:

1. Listen for the sounds /t/ and /d/. (Letters for these sounds are underlined.)
2. Listen for syllable stress and word stress. *Capital letters indicate syllable stress.* Mark the word stress that you hear. Put a stress mark (ʹ) over the stressed word or words.
3. Listen for rising or falling intonation at the end of the sentence. Mark intonation with the symbol "⤴" or "⤵."
4. Listen to the sentence again and repeat it. Pay attention to pauses and linking of words.

The first sentence is marked for you.

1. DURing the WINter the days are short.
2. Does your TEACHer get paid on FRIdays?
3. I ate all the toMAtoes YESterday.
4. She told us a roMANtic STORy.
5. Tom bought a lot of DOUGHnuts.

6. The <u>D</u>OORman <u>told</u> us <u>to</u> go <u>d</u>own.

7. The PILgrims came here in SIX<u>t</u>een TWENty.

8. SA<u>T</u>ur<u>d</u>ay nigh<u>t</u> is the LONElies<u>t</u> nigh<u>t</u> of the week.

9. I Usually VISi<u>t</u> my aun<u>t</u> on MON<u>d</u>ays.

10. <u>Did</u> you make an aPPOIN<u>T</u>men<u>t</u> with your DOC<u>t</u>or?

11. PRONUNCIATION OF THE "-ed" ENDING

Form the past tense of regular verbs by adding the ending "-ed" to the base form. The ending has three different pronunciations. The pronunciation of "-ed" depends on which sound comes before it.

A. Verbs Ending in Voiceless Consonants

When a verb ends in a voiceless consonant (except for /t/), pronounce "-ed" as /t/. Voiceless consonants include /p/, /k/, /f/, /s/, /θ/, /ʃ/, and /tʃ/. Listen and repeat.

1a.	ki<u>ss</u>	/kɪs/	Did you ki<u>ss</u> me?
b.	ki<u>ssed</u>	/kɪst/	I ki<u>ssed</u> you beFORE.
2a.	wal<u>k</u>	/wɔk/	I'll wal<u>k</u> aLONE.
b.	wal<u>ked</u>	/wɔkt/	I wal<u>ked</u> aLONE.

B. Verbs Ending in Voiced Consonants

When a verb ends in a voiced consonant (except for /d/), pronounce "-ed" as /d/. Voiced consonants are those not listed above. Listen and repeat.

1a.	ca<u>ll</u>	/kɔl/	Did you ca<u>ll</u> me?
b.	ca<u>lled</u>	/kɔld/	Yes, I ca<u>lled</u> you.
2a.	beLIE<u>VE</u>	/bəliyv/	I beLIE<u>VE</u> it's OK.
b.	beLIE<u>VED</u>	/bəliyvd/	I beLIE<u>VED</u> it was OK.

Remember that all vowels are voiced. Thus, when a verb ends in a vowel sound, "-ed" is pronounced /d/. Listen and repeat.

1a.	pl<u>ay</u>	/pley/	Did you pl<u>ay</u> drums?
b.	pl<u>ayed</u>	/pleyd/	No, I pl<u>ayed</u> piANo.
2a.	sh<u>ow</u>	/ʃow/	I'll sh<u>ow</u> it to you.
b.	sh<u>owed</u>	/ʃowd/	I sh<u>owed</u> it to you.

C. Verbs Ending in /t/ or /d/

When a verb ends in /t/ or /d/, pronounce "-ed" as /ɪd/. In this case, "-ed" is a separate syllable. Listen and repeat.

1a.	pain<u>t</u>	/peynt/	Pain<u>t</u> one wall.
b.	PAIN<u>Ted</u>	/peyntɪd/	I PAIN<u>Ted</u> one wall.
2a.	wan<u>t</u>	/want/	I wan<u>t</u> a piece.
b.	WAN<u>Ted</u>	/wantɪd/	I WAN<u>Ted</u> a piece.
3a.	nee<u>d</u>	/niyd/	I nee<u>d</u> it now.
b.	NEE<u>Ded</u>	/niydɪd/	I NEE<u>Ded</u> it YESterday.
4a.	deCI<u>DE</u>	/dɪsayd/	Don't deCI<u>DE</u> toDAY.
b.	deCI<u>Ded</u>	/dɪsaydɪd/	I deCI<u>Ded</u> toDAY.

🎧 12. PRACTICE /t/, /d/, AND /ɪd/ ENDINGS

A. /t/ ending

1. I bak<u>ed</u> a cake.
2. I wrapp<u>ed</u> the PACKage.
3. We reach<u>ed</u> the top.
4. I help<u>ed</u> him with his work.
5. He miss<u>ed</u> BREAKfast toDAY.

B. /d/ ending

1. The BAby scream<u>ed</u> all night.
2. He liv<u>ed</u> a long time.
3. I reCEIV<u>ED</u> a bill for it.
4. He conTINu<u>ed</u> to win at cards.
5. They ADvertis<u>ed</u> in the PAper.

C. /ɪd/ ending

1. He recoMMEND<u>ed</u> me for the job.
2. We BOARD<u>ed</u> the plane on time.
3. She was adMITT<u>ed</u> to the HOSpital.
4. I reQUEST<u>ed</u> a room with a view.
5. They deCID<u>ed</u> to go by train.

🐎 13. HOME ASSIGNMENT

Form the past tense of the following verbs.

1. Pronounce the base form of the verb. You can use a dictionary to help you with the pronunciation.
2. Write the past tense form in the space provided. Then write the phonetic symbol for the "-ed" ending (/t/, /d/, or /ɪd/).
3. Pronounce the past tense form.

Examples:		
add	added	/ɪd/
elect	elected	/ɪd/
laugh	laughed	/t/
delay	delayed	/d/

1. travel _____ _____
2. dream _____ _____
3. wash _____ _____
4. receive _____ _____
5. study _____ _____
6. report _____ _____
7. type _____ _____
8. stop _____ _____
9. vote _____ _____
10. expect _____ _____

<table>
<tr><td>UNIT
24</td><td></td></tr>
</table>

/k/ as in <u>c</u>at
/g/ as in <u>g</u>o

1. PRODUCING /k/

Examples: <u>k</u>iss, <u>c</u>ame, <u>k</u>ey, <u>CH</u>ARacter, QUIet, LIQuid,
PI<u>C</u>ture, CHI<u>CK</u>en, A<u>C</u>cident, si<u>ck</u>, boo<u>k</u>, bra<u>k</u>e

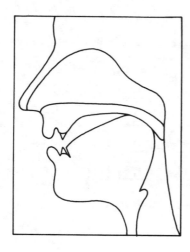

- First press the back part of your tongue to the back of the roof of your mouth (soft palate). This stops the flow of air.
- Then quickly lower the back of your tongue. Produce the sound with a strong puff of air.
- Your vocal cords do not vibrate.
- Hold a piece of paper in front of your lips. It should move when you produce the sound. Or hold your hand in front of your lips to feel the puff of air.

2. PRODUCING /g/

Examples: get, ghost, guest, forGET, beGAN, bag, egg, league

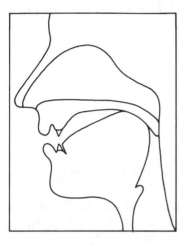

- This sound is produced the same way as /k/, except that /g/ is voiced and the puff of air is not as strong.
- First press the back part of your tongue to the back of the roof of your mouth (soft palate). This stops the flow of air.
- Then quickly lower the back of your tongue. Produce the sound with a puff of air.
- Your vocal cords should vibrate.

3. CONTRAST: /k/ AND /g/

A. Some students may confuse the sound /k/ as in "cat" with the sound /g/ as in "go." Practice these two sounds, first normally, then with exaggeration, then normally. Listen and repeat.

Place your hand in front of your lips to feel a puff of air.

1. /k/	/k. . . . ./	/k/
2. /g/	/g. . . . ./	/g/

B. Now practice the sounds in words. Notice the phonetic spelling. Listen and repeat each word twice.

1. can	/kæn/	can
2. key	/kiy/	key
3. beCAME	/bɪkeym/	beCAME
4. make	/mayk/	make
5. go	/gow/	go
6. give	/gɪv/	give
7. aGAIN	/əgɛn/	aGAIN
8. bag	/bæg/	bag

🎧 4. CHECK YOUR LISTENING

A. The following pairs of words contain the sounds /k/ as in "cat" and /g/ as in "go." You will hear one word from each pair. Circle the word that you hear.

1.	came	game		6.	snack	snag
2.	come	gum		7.	lack	lag
3.	cane	gain		8.	duck	dug
4.	coal	goal		9.	pick	pig
5.	class	glass		10.	frock	frog

B. In the following pairs of words, one word ends with the sound /k/ or /g/. You will hear one word from each pair. Circle the word that you hear.

1.	see	seek		6.	Lee	league
2.	stay	steak		7.	play	plague
3.	way	wake		8.	more	morgue
4.	we	week		9.	row	rogue
5.	lay	lake		10.	few	fugue

🎧 5. PRACTICE THE CONTRAST: /k/ AS IN "CAT" WITH /g/ AS IN "GO"

A. Practice these contrasting sounds. Listen and repeat each word pair. *Capital letters indicate syllable stress.*

	/k/	/g/			/k/	/g/
1.	curl	girl		6.	ANkle	ANgle
2.	card	guard		7.	lock	log[1]
3.	could	good		8.	rack	rag
4.	coast	ghost		9.	leak	league
5.	cold	gold		10.	back	bag

[1]Some Americans say /lɔg/ rather than /lag/.

B. Now practice the contrasting sounds in sentence pairs. The first sentence of each pair has the sound /k/ and the second has the sound /g/. Listen and repeat. Notice the change in meaning. Visual clues can help. Make a simple drawing in each blank box. *Capital letters indicate syllable stress.*

1a. curl   That's a nice curl.

  b. girl   That's a nice girl.

2a. card   Watch the card.

  b. guard   Watch the guard.

3a. could   I said "could."

  b. good   I said "good."

4a. coast   I see the coast.

  b. ghost   I see the ghost.

5a. <u>c</u>old   It was <u>c</u>old.

b. gold   It was gold.

6a. AN<u>k</u>le   Is the AN<u>k</u>le BETTer?

b. ANgle   Is the ANgle BETTer?

7a. lo<u>ck</u>   Is that a lo<u>ck</u>?

b. lo<u>g</u>   Is that a lo<u>g</u>?

8a. ra<u>ck</u>   A ra<u>ck</u> is on the wall.

b. ra<u>g</u>   A ra<u>g</u> is on the wall.

9a. lea<u>k</u>   It's a big lea<u>k</u>.

b. lea<u>gu</u>e   It's a big lea<u>gu</u>e.

10a. ba<u>ck</u>   It's in the ba<u>ck</u>.

b. ba<u>g</u>   It's in the ba<u>g</u>.

↻ 6. CHECK YOUR LISTENING

Work with a partner. Read a sentence from 5B to your partner. Can your partner define the sentence? He or she must be truthful.

Your partner will: • Say: I know what _____ means.
                 It means _____. (definition or paraphrase)
                 or
             • Act out what the word means.
                 or
             • Make a simple drawing.

Or your partner will ask: What does _____ mean? Then you must define the sentence, act it out, or make a drawing. You may do two or three sentences each.

♥ 7. SOUNDS FOR THE LETTERS "cc"

A. The letters "cc" sometimes represent the sound /k/ as in "<u>c</u>at." Listen and repeat. *Capital letters indicate syllable stress.*

1. a<u>CC</u>OUNT   Open an a<u>CC</u>OUNT.
2. a<u>CC</u>USE   Don't a<u>CC</u>USE me.
3. o<u>CC</u>UR   When did it o<u>CC</u>UR?
4. SO<u>CC</u>er   Do you play SO<u>CC</u>er?

     5. aCCOMplish   I'll aCCOMplish it.
     6. aCCORdion   He plays the aCCORdion.
     7. oCCAsion   What's the oCCAsion?
     8. aCCOUNtant   He's an aCCOUNtant.

B. Sometimes the letters "cc" represent the sounds /ks/. Notice the syllable break in this form of "cc." Listen and repeat.

     1. acCELerate   To acCELerate means to move FASTer.
     2. VACcine   A VACcine proTECTS us aGAINST diSEASE.
     3. ACcent   He speaks with an ACcent.
     4. acCEDE   To acCEDE means to aGREE.
     5. acCEPT   We all acCEPT it.
     6. ACcident   It was an ACcident.
     7. sucCEED   She'll sucCEED in her work.
     8. sucCESS   The PARty was a sucCESS.

8. SOUNDS FOR THE LETTER "x"

A. In the middle of a word, the letter "x" usually represents the sounds /ks/. Listen and repeat.

     1. EXercise   I ALways EXercise.
     2. exPLAIN   Don't exPLAIN it.
     3. EXtra   He has an EXtra one.
     4. exPECT   We exPECT him.
     5. exPENSE   Spare no exPENSE.

B. At the end of a word, the letter "x" always represents /ks/. Listen and repeat.

     1. ax   Chop the wood with an ax.
     2. fix   Did he fix the pipe?
     3. tax   We all pay INcome tax.
     4. mix   Did you mix the paint?
     5. reLAX   Don't WORRy, reLAX!

C. Sometimes "x" represents /gz/. Listen and repeat.

     1. exAMple   Please read the exAMple.
     2. exIST   How do we know that we exIST?
     3. exHIBit   Did you see the art exHIBit?
     4. exACT   I have the exACT change.
     5. exAGGerate   Don't exAGGerate the sound.

♟ 9. SOUNDS FOR THE LETTERS "qu"

A. In the initial (beginning) position, "qu" usually represents the sounds /kw/. Listen and repeat.

1.	quiz	My TEACHer gave us a quiz.
2.	quick	Take a quick SHOWer.
3.	queen	She's queen for a day.
4.	QUIet	The house is QUIet.
5.	quite	It's REALLy quite good.

B. In the medial (middle) position, "qu" also usually represents /kw/. Listen and repeat.

1.	Equal	We're all Equal.
2.	eQUAtion	It's a math eQUAtion.
3.	LIQuid	Pour the LIQuid.
4.	squeeze	Did you squeeze it?
5.	square	It's square, not round.

♟ 10. NO SOUND FOR "k" AND "g"

A. When the letters "kn" begin a word, the "k" is not pronounced.

1.	Knee	The Knee is a joint in the leg.
2.	Kneel	To Kneel means to get down on your Knees.
3.	Know	Did you know that?
4.	Knew	I knew that.
5.	Knife	Use a Knife to cut the bread.

B. When the letter "g" comes before the letters "n" or "m" in the same syllable, it is not pronounced.

1.	sign	Did you see the sign in the WINdow?
2.	reSIGN	I'll reSIGN from my job at the end of the year.
3.	reign	The reign of the queen is a long one.
4.	FOReign	The ship docked at FOReign ports.
5.	deSIGNer	She ALways buys deSIGNer clothes.
6.	DIaphragm	The DIaphragm is a MUSCle that SEParates the lungs from the STOMach.

🎧 11. STRESS AND INTONATION

The first five sentences contain the sound /k/. The last five contain the sound /g/. You will hear each sentence four times:

1. Listen for the sounds /k/ and /g/. (The letters for these sounds are underlined.)
2. Listen for syllable stress and word stress. *Capital letters indicate syllable stress.* Mark the word stress that you hear. Put a stress mark (´) over the stressed word or words.
3. Listen for rising or falling intonation at the end of the sentence. Mark intonation with the symbol "⤴" or "⤵."
4. Listen to the sentence again and repeat it. Pay attention to pauses and linking of words.

The first sentence is marked for you.

1. The meCHANic said the car was READy.

2. Come and carve the TURkey.

3. We can't pay for the PACKage.

4. The bank is near the school.

5. DIFFerent kinds of ARchitecture can be found in New York.

6. I need a GALLon of gas.

7. Did he GRADuate in AUgust?

8. She goes JOGGing EVery day.

9. Is JOGGing good for your health?

10. I'm GIVing you a good REAson for not GOing.

🐎 12. HOME ASSIGNMENT

1. Read the following poems aloud (authors unknown). Use a dictionary to help you with the pronunciation and meaning of new words.
2. Draw a single line under all letters representing the sound /k/ as in "<u>c</u>at." Draw a double line under all letter representing the sound /g/ as in "<u>g</u>o."
3. Mark the poems for stress and intonation.

Example: Hár<u>k</u>! Hár<u>k</u>! the dó<u>g</u>s do bár<u>k</u>,

Hark! Hark!

Hark! Hark! the dogs do bark,

The BEGGars have come to town;

Some in rags, some in tags,

And some in VELvet gowns.

KITTens

A KITTen with a black nose
  Will sleep all the day;
A KITTen with a white nose
  Is ALways glad to play;
A KITTen with a YELLow nose
  Will come when you call;
But a KITTen with a gray nose
  I like best of all.

<table>
<tr><td>

UNIT

25

</td><td>

/f/ as in <u>food</u>
/v/ as in <u>voice</u>

</td></tr>
</table>

1. PRODUCING /f/

Examples: <u>f</u>un, <u>ph</u>one, re<u>F</u>ER, COF<u>F</u>ee, LAU<u>GH</u>ing, gra<u>ph</u>, stu<u>ff</u>, rou<u>gh</u>

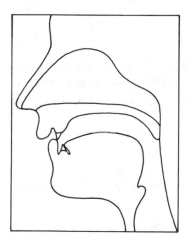

- Lightly touch the upper teeth with the *inner* part of the lower lip.
- Produce the sound by forcing air out through the opening. Do not stop the flow of air.
- Your vocal cords do not vibrate.
- Hold your hand in front of your lips to feel the flow of air.

2. PRODUCING /v/

Examples: <u>v</u>erb, <u>VILL</u>age, O<u>v</u>er, CLE<u>V</u>er, bra<u>v</u>e, gi<u>v</u>e

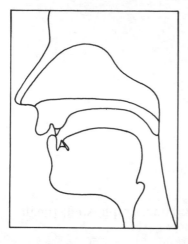

- This sound is produced the same way as /f/, except that /v/ is voiced.
- Lightly touch the upper teeth with the *inner* part of the lower lip.
- Produce the sound by forcing air out through the opening. Do not stop the flow of air.
- Your vocal cords should vibrate.
- Hold your hand in front of your lips to feel the flow of air.

3. CONTRAST: /f/ AND /v/

A. Some students may confuse the sound /f/ as in "<u>f</u>ood" with the sound /v/ as in "<u>v</u>oice." Practice these two sounds, first normally, then with exaggeration, then normally. Listen and repeat. Place your hand in front of your lips to feel the flow of air.

1. /f/	/f...../	/f/
2. /v/	/v...../	/v/

B. Now practice the sounds in words. Notice the phonetic spelling. Listen and repeat each word twice.

1. <u>f</u>ood	/fuwd/	<u>f</u>ood
2. a<u>FF</u>ORD	/əfɔrd/	a<u>FF</u>ORD
3. bee<u>f</u>	/biyf/	bee<u>f</u>
4. tou<u>gh</u>	/təf/	tou<u>gh</u>
5. <u>v</u>oice	/vɔys/	<u>v</u>oice
6. DRI<u>V</u>er	/drayvər/	DRI<u>V</u>er
7. a<u>BOV</u>E	/əbəv/	a<u>BOV</u>E
8. ca<u>v</u>e	/keyv/	ca<u>v</u>e

🔊 4. CHECK YOUR LISTENING

A. The following pairs of words contain the sounds /f/ as in "food" and /v/ as in "voice." You will hear one word from each pair. Circle the word that you hear.

1.	fast	vast		5.	SURface	SERvice
2.	fan	van		6.	reFUSE	reVIEWS
3.	FERRy	VERy		7.	safe	save
4.	few	view		8.	half	have

B. In the following pairs of words, one word ends with the sound /f/ or /v/. You will hear one word from each pair. Circle the word that you hear.

1.	say	safe		6.	say	save
2.	bee	beef		7.	dry	drive
3.	lie	life		8.	lie	live
4.	why	wife		9.	we	we've
5.	low	loaf		10.	way	wave

🔊 5. PRACTICE THE CONTRAST: /f/ AS IN "FOOD" WITH /v/ AS IN "VOICE"

A. Practice these contrasting sounds. Listen and repeat each word pair. *Capital letters indicate syllable stress.*

	/f/	**/v/**			**/f/**	**/v/**
1.	fan	van		6.	SAFer	SAVer
2.	FERRy	VERy		7.	half	have
3.	fault	vault		8.	safe	save
4.	few	view		9.	leaf	leave
5.	RIfle	RIval		10.	life	live

B. Now practice the contrasting sounds in sentence pairs. The first sentence of each pair has the sound /f/ and the second has the sound /v/. Listen and repeat. Notice the change in meaning. Visual clues can help. Make a simple drawing in each blank box. *Capital letters indicate syllable stress.*

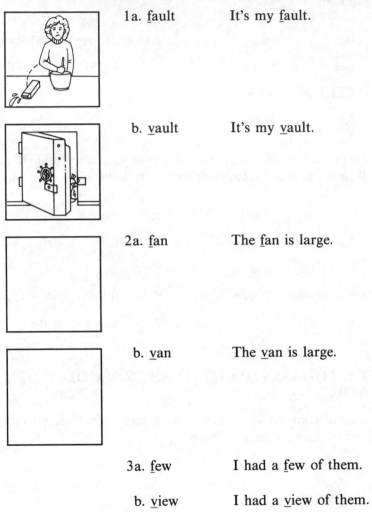

1a. <u>f</u>ault   It's my <u>f</u>ault.

  b. <u>v</u>ault   It's my <u>v</u>ault.

2a. <u>f</u>an   The <u>f</u>an is large.

  b. <u>v</u>an   The <u>v</u>an is large.

3a. <u>f</u>ew   I had a <u>f</u>ew of them.

  b. <u>v</u>iew   I had a <u>v</u>iew of them.

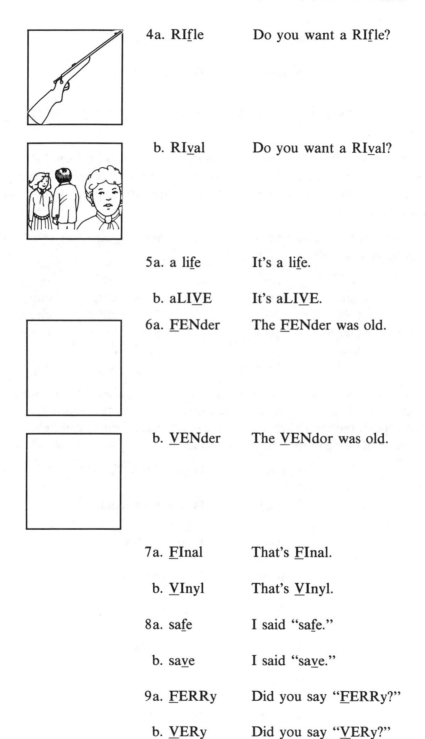

4a. RIfle   Do you want a RIfle?

b. RIval   Do you want a RIval?

5a. a life   It's a life.

b. aLIVE   It's aLIVE.

6a. FENder   The FENder was old.

b. VENder   The VENdor was old.

7a. FInal   That's FInal.

b. VInyl   That's VInyl.

8a. safe   I said "safe."

b. save   I said "save."

9a. FERRy   Did you say "FERRy?"

b. VERy   Did you say "VERy?"

10a. half   Who said "half?"

  b. have   Who said "have?"

6. PRACTICE THE CONTRAST: /f/ AS IN "FOOD" WITH /p/ AS IN "PEN"

Some speakers may confuse /f/ as in "food," with /p/ as in "pen." Remember that when you pronounce /f/, the air flows out without stopping. When you say /p/, you stop the air flow and then let it escape with a puff. Both of these sounds are voiceless.

A. Practice these contrasting sounds. Listen and repeat each word pair. *Capital letters indicate syllable stress.*

	/f/	/p/		/f/	/p/
1.	fade	paid	6.	cliff	clip
2.	fool	pool	7.	chief	cheap
3.	fork	pork	8.	laugh	lap
4.	fast	past	9.	cuff	cup
5.	SUFFer	SUPPer	10.	wife	wipe

B. Now practice the contrasting sounds in sentence pairs. The first sentence of each pair has the sound /f/ and the second has the sound /p/. Listen and repeat. Notice the change in meaning. Visual clues can help. Make a simple drawing in each blank box. *Capital letters indicate syllable stress.*

1a. fade   Is the word "fade?"

  b. paid   Is the word "paid?"

2a. fool   I saw the fool.

  b. pool   I saw the pool.

3a. fork   Do you want the fork?

  b. pork   Do you want the pork?

4a. fast   It's not fast.

  b. past   It's not past.

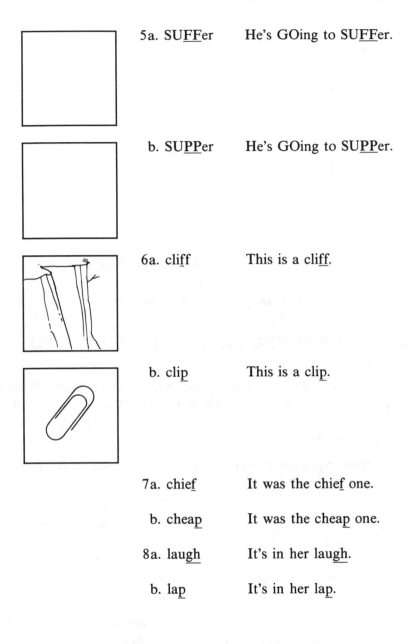

5a. SUFFer   He's GOing to SUFFer.

b. SUPPer   He's GOing to SUPPer.

6a. cli<u>ff</u>   This is a cli<u>ff</u>.

b. cli<u>p</u>   This is a cli<u>p</u>.

7a. chie<u>f</u>   It was the chie<u>f</u> one.

b. chea<u>p</u>   It was the chea<u>p</u> one.

8a. lau<u>gh</u>   It's in her lau<u>gh</u>.

b. la<u>p</u>   It's in her la<u>p</u>.

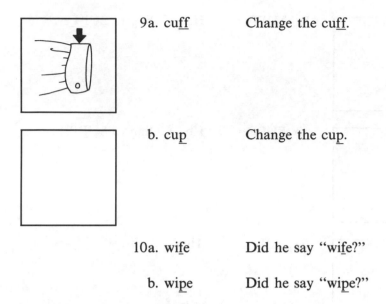

9a. cuff   Change the cu**ff**.

b. cup   Change the cu**p**.

10a. wife   Did he say "wi**fe**?"

b. wipe   Did he say "wi**pe**?"

🔊 7. PRACTICE THE CONTRAST: /v/ AS IN "<u>V</u>OICE" WITH /b/ AS IN "<u>B</u>OY"

Some speakers may confuse /v/ as in "<u>v</u>oice" with /b/ as in "<u>b</u>oy." Remember that when you pronounce /v/, the air flows out without stopping. When you say /b/, you stop the air flow and then let it escape with a puff. Both of these sounds are voiced.

A. Practice these contrasting sounds. Listen and repeat each word pair. *Capital letters indicate syllable stress.*

	/v/	/b/			/v/	/b/
1.	"V"	be		6.	vent	bent
2.	veil	bail		7.	van	ban
3.	VERy	BURy		8.	vote	boat
4.	vet	bet		9.	vow	bow
5.	vest	best		10.	curve	curb

B. Now practice the contrasting sounds in sentence pairs. The first sentence of each pair has the sound /v/ and the second has the sound /b/. Listen and repeat. Notice the change in meaning. Visual clues can help. Make a simple drawing in each blank box. *Capital letters indicate syllable stress.*

1a. vest   It's the vest.

b. best   It's the best.

2a. v̲eil   I have the v̲eil.

b. b̲ail   I have the b̲ail.

3a. V̲ERy   Is the word "V̲ERy?"

b. B̲URy   Is the word "B̲URy?"

4a. v̲et   I like that v̲et.

b. b̲et   I like that b̲et.

5a. "v"   The letter is "v."

b. "b"   The letter is "b."

6a. v̲ent   I said "v̲ent."

b. b̲ent   I said "b̲ent."

7a. v̲an   Did you hear aBOUT the v̲an?

b. b̲an   Did you hear aBOUT the b̲an?

8a. <u>v</u>ote   Do you want the <u>v</u>ote?

b. <u>b</u>oat   Do you want the <u>b</u>oat?

9a. <u>v</u>ow   Take a <u>v</u>ow.

b. <u>b</u>ow   Take a <u>b</u>ow.

10a. cur<u>ve</u>   The car is on the cur<u>ve</u>.

b. cur<u>b</u>   The car is on the cur<u>b</u>.

↻ 8. CHECK YOUR LISTENING

Work with a partner. Read a sentence from 5B, 6B, or 7B to your partner. Can your partner define the sentence? He or she must be truthful.

Your partner will:
- Say: I know what _____ means.
  It means _____. (definition or paraphrase)
  or
- Act out what the word means.
  or
- Make a simple drawing.

Or your partner will ask: What does _____ mean? Then you must define the sentence, act it out, or make a drawing. You may do two or three sentences each.

🎧 9. STRESS AND INTONATION

These sentences contain the sounds /f/ as in "food" and /v/ as in "voice." You will hear each sentence four times:

1. Listen for the sounds /f/ and /v/. (The letters for these sounds are underlined.)
2. Listen for syllable stress and word stress. *(Capital letters indicate syllable stress.)* Mark the word stress that you hear. Put a stress mark (′) over the stressed word or words.
3. Listen for rising or falling intonation at the end of the sentence. Mark intonation with the symbol "⤴" or "⤵."
4. Listen to the sentence again and repeat it. Pay attention to pauses and linking of words.

The first sentence is marked for you.

1. "V" is a CONsonant, not a VOWel.

2. Was the COFFee served at five o'CLOCK?

3. The vote was NEGative, not POSitive.

4. He found VARious PHOtos in the file.

5. What's the DIFFerence beTWEEN the graphs?

6. Does he have his own knife and fork?

7. I beLIEVE the roof is unEven.

8. Can you prove it?

9. Did the CHAUffeur have a converSAtion with your wife?

10. The SHERiff caught the thieves STEALing the loaves of bread.

🎧 10. DIALOG

You will hear a dialog with words that contain the sounds /f/ as in "food," /v/ as in "voice," /p/ as in "pen" and /b/ as in "boy." Listen to the dialog five times:

1. Concentrate on the meaning. Discuss any new vocabulary with your teacher and classmates.
2. Listen for the consonant sounds /f/, /v/, /p/, and /b/. (The letters for these sounds are underlined.)

3. Listen for syllable stress and word stress. *Capital letters indicate syllable stress.* Mark the word stress you hear. Put a stress mark (´) over the stressed word or words.
4. Listen for rising or falling intonation at the end of each sentence. Mark intonation with the symbol "⤴" or "⤵."
5. Listen to each sentence of the dialog again and repeat it. Pay attention to pauses and linking of words.

The first sentence is marked for you.

Phil: What are you DÓing, V̇ic?⤴

Vic: I'm MAKing a list o̲f̲ f̲ood and suPPLIES.

Phil: What f̲or?

Vic: What f̲or? F̲or the PARty, o̲f̲ course!

Phil: PARty? What PARty?

Vic: Did you f̲orGET that we're HAVing a VALentine's day PARty?

Phil: Oh, I did f̲orGET. Who's inVITed?

Vic: We'v̲e inVITed all our f̲riends f̲rom the SOPHomore class.

Phil: Can I help you with the prepaRAtions?

Vic: Well, here's a list of some of the food you could buy.

Phil: Mmm. Five pounds of roast beef and four pounds of french fries. Will that be eNOUGH?

Vic: It'll have to be eNOUGH.

Phil: Should I ALso buy PLAStic forks, knives, plates, cups and PAper NAPkins?

Vic: Fine! That'll be a big help.

Phil: OK, leave it to me. I'll take care of it.

Vic: OK. I'll see you at the aPARTment at five. Don't forGET!

Phil: Don't WORRy, I won't forGET.

11. ROLE PLAY

Practice the dialog with a partner. Help each other with correct sounds, stress, and intonation.

12. HOME ASSIGNMENT

A. Make up a sentence for each of the following phrases. Underline the phrase in each sentence. Mark them for stress and intonation. Read them aloud.

1. french fries
2. flew to FREEdom
3. scarf on the floor
4. aFRAID of inFLAtion
5. deFROST the reFRIGerator
6. COVer the TELevision
7. save the VEGetables
8. knives on the stove
9. vote for SEVen
10. twelve vans

B. Bring your list to class. Work with a partner. Your partner may read your sentences using your stress and intonation marks. Is the meaning clear?

<table>
<tr><td>

UNIT

26

</td><td>

/θ/ as in <u>th</u>in
/ð/ as in <u>the</u>

</td></tr>
</table>

1. PRODUCING /θ/

Examples: <u>th</u>ank, <u>TH</u>IRty, NO<u>TH</u>ing, HEAL<u>TH</u>y, SYMpa<u>th</u>y, fif<u>th</u>, tru<u>th</u>

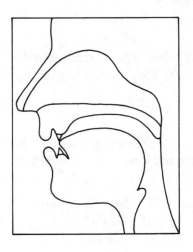

- Lightly place your tongue tip between your upper and lower front teeth (not between your lips).
- Produce the sound by forcing air out through the opening between your teeth and tongue.
- Your vocal cords do not vibrate.
- Hold your hand in front of your lips to feel the flow of air.

2. PRODUCING /ð/

Examples: this, they, BOTHer, FAther, SOUTHern, clothe

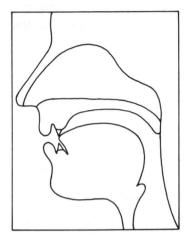

- This sound is produced the same way as /θ/, except that /ð/ is voiced.
- Lightly place your tongue tip between your upper and lower front teeth (not between your lips).
- Produce the sound by forcing air out through the opening between your teeth and tongue.
- Say /ð/ with less force than you use for /θ/.
- Your vocal cords should vibrate.
- Hold your hand in front of your lips to feel the flow of air.

3. CONTRAST: /θ/ AND /ð/

A. Some speakers may confuse the sound /θ/ as in "thin" with the sound /ð/ as in "the." Practice these two sounds, first normally, then with exaggeration, then normally. Listen and repeat. Place your hand in front of your lips to feel the stream of air.

1. /θ/   /θ. . . . ./   /θ/
2. /ð/   /ð. . . . ./   /ð/

B. Now practice the sounds in words. Notice the phonetic spelling. Listen and repeat each word twice.

1. thumb	/θəm/	thumb
2. AUthor	/ɔθər/	AUthor
3. path	/pæθ/	path
4. they	/ðey/	they
5. FAther	/faðər/	FAther
6. smooth	/smuwð/	smooth
7. thick	/θɪk/	thick
8. those	/ðowz/	those

4. CHECK YOUR LISTENING

You will hear words with the sounds /θ/ and /ð/. First, cover the words in the following list. Then listen to each word. Concentrate on the sound, not the spelling. Which consonant sound do you hear? Write a check mark in the correct column.

	/θ/ as in "thin"	/ð/ as in "the"
1. this	___	___
2. then	___	___
3. three	___	___
4. bath	___	___
5. both	___	___
6. bathe	___	___
7. south	___	___
8. fifth	___	___
9. these	___	___
10. breathe	___	___

5. PRACTICE THE CONTRAST: /θ/ AS IN "THIN" WITH /t/ AS IN "TEN"

Some students may confuse /θ/ as in "thin" with /t/ as in "ten." When you pronounce /θ/, air flows out without stopping. When you pronounce /t/, the air stops, then escapes with a puff.

A. Practice these contrasting sounds. Listen and repeat each word pair.

	/t/	/θ/		/t/	/θ/
1.	taught	thought	5.	tent	tenth
2.	team	theme	6.	debt	death
3.	tree	three	7.	boot	booth
4.	true	through	8.	mat	math

B. Now practice the contrasting sounds in sentence pairs. The first sentence of each pair has the sound /t/ and the second has the sound /θ/. Listen and repeat. Notice the change in meaning. Visual clues can help. Make a simple drawing in each blank box.

1a. taught   He taught a lot.

b. thought   He thought a lot.

2a. team   I need a team.

b. theme   I need a theme.

3a. tree   Which tree is it?

b. three   Which three is it?

4a. true   Is she true?

b. through   Is she through?

5a. tent   It's my tent.

b. tenth   It's my tenth.

6a. debt   It's not his debt.

b. death   It's not his death.

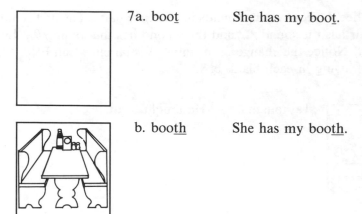

7a. boo<u>t</u>   She has my boo<u>t</u>.

b. boo<u>th</u>   She has my boo<u>th</u>.

8a. ma<u>t</u>   It's my ma<u>t</u>.

b. ma<u>th</u>   It's my ma<u>th</u>.

6. PRACTICE THE CONTRAST: /ð/ AS IN "<u>TH</u>E" WITH /d/ AS IN "<u>D</u>AY"

Some students may confuse /ð/ as in "<u>th</u>e" with /d/ as in "<u>d</u>ay." When you pronounce /ð/, the air flows out without stopping. When you pronounce /d/, the air stops, then escapes with a puff.

A. Practice these contrasting sounds. Listen and repeat each word pair. *Capital letters indicate syllable stress.*

	/d/	/ð/			/d/	/ð/
1.	<u>d</u>ay	<u>th</u>ey		5.	LA<u>DD</u>er	LA<u>TH</u>er
2.	<u>d</u>oze	<u>th</u>ose		6.	LOA<u>D</u>ing	LOA<u>TH</u>ing
3.	<u>d</u>ough	<u>th</u>ough		7.	WOR<u>D</u>y	WOR<u>TH</u>y
4.	<u>d</u>are	<u>th</u>ere		8.	sue<u>d</u>	soo<u>th</u>e

B. Now practice the contrasting sounds in sentence pairs. The first sentence of each pair has the sound /d/ and the second has the sound /ð/. Listen and repeat. Notice the change in meaning. *Capital letters indicate syllable stress.*

1a. <u>d</u>ay   Will <u>d</u>ay come?

b. <u>th</u>ey   Will <u>th</u>ey come?

2a. <u>d</u>oze   It's not fair to <u>d</u>oze in class.

 b. <u>th</u>ose   It's not fair to <u>th</u>ose in class.

3a. <u>d</u>ough   Can you spell "<u>d</u>ough"?

 b. <u>th</u>ough   Can you spell "<u>th</u>ough"?

4a. LA<u>DD</u>er   Look at the LA<u>DD</u>er.

 b. LA<u>TH</u>er   Look at the LA<u>TH</u>er.

5a. LOA<u>D</u>ing   He was LOA<u>D</u>ing it.

 b. LOA<u>TH</u>ing   He was LOA<u>TH</u>ing it.

6a. WOR<u>D</u>y   It's not WOR<u>D</u>y.

 b. WOR<u>TH</u>y   It's not WOR<u>TH</u>y.

7a. sue<u>d</u>   We sue<u>d</u> him.

 b. soo<u>th</u>e   We soo<u>th</u>e him.

♀ 7. PRACTICE THE CONTRAST: /θ/ AS IN "THIN" WITH /f/ AS IN "FOOD"

Some students may confuse /θ/ as in "thin" with /f/ as in "food." When you pronounce /θ/, place your tongue tip between your teeth. When you say /f/, touch your upper teeth with the inner part of your lower lip.

A. Practice these contrasting sounds. Listen and repeat each word pair.

	/f/	/θ/			/f/	/θ/
1.	first	thirst		6.	deaf	death
2.	fought	thought		7.	oaf	oath
3.	Fred	thread		8.	roof	Ruth
4.	frill	thrill		9.	miff	myth
5.	free	three		10.	reef	wreath

B. Now practice the contrasting sounds in sentence pairs. The first sentence of each pair has the sound /f/ and the second has the sound /θ/. Listen and repeat. Notice the change in meaning. Visual clues can help. Make a simple drawing in each blank box.

1a. first   It's my first.

  b. thirst   It's my thirst.

2a. fought   He fought a lot.

  b. thought   He thought a lot.

3a. Fred   Was it Fred?

b. thread   Was it thread?

4a. frill   It's not a frill.

b. thrill   It's not a thrill.

5a. free   Is it free?

b. three   Is it three?

6a. deaf   It's deaf.

b. death   It's death.

7a. oaf   I hear an oaf.

b. oath   I hear an oath.

8a. roof   My roof is good.

b. Ruth   My Ruth is good.

9a. miff   He said, "miff."

b. myth   He said, "myth."

10a. reef   It's a nice reef.

b. wreath   It's a nice wreath.

💡 8. PRACTICE THE CONTRAST: /ð/ AS IN "T<u>HE</u>" WITH /v/ AS IN "<u>V</u>OICE"

Some students may confuse /ð/ as in "<u>the</u>" with /v/ as in "<u>v</u>oice." When you pronounce /ð/, place your tongue tip between your teeth. When you say /v/, touch your upper teeth with the *inner* part of your lower lip.

A. Listen and repeat these contrasting sounds. *Capital letters indicate syllable stress.*

	/v/	/ð/
1.	"<u>V</u>"	<u>th</u>ee
2.	<u>v</u>an	<u>th</u>an
3.	<u>v</u>at	<u>th</u>at
4.	<u>v</u>eil	<u>th</u>ey'll
5.	<u>v</u>ine	<u>th</u>ine
6.	LE<u>V</u>er	LEA<u>TH</u>er

B. Now practice the contrasting sounds in sentence pairs. The first sentence of each pair has the sound /v/ and the second has the sound /ð/. Listen and repeat. Notice the change in meaning. Visual clues can help. Make a simple drawing in each blank box. *Capital letters indicate syllable stress.*

1a. <u>v</u>at   It's one <u>v</u>at I want.

b. <u>th</u>at   It's one <u>th</u>at I want.

2a. <u>v</u>eil   It's not "<u>v</u>eil."

b. <u>th</u>ey'll   It's not "<u>th</u>ey'll."

3a. <u>v</u>ine   Can you spell "<u>v</u>ine?"

b. <u>th</u>ine   Can you spell "<u>th</u>ine?"

4a. LEVer   He held the LEVer.

b. LEATHer   He held the LEATHer.

⟳ 9. CHECK YOUR LISTENING

Work with a partner. Read a sentence from 5B, 6B, 7B, or 8B to your partner. Can your partner define the sentence? He or she must be truthful.

Your partner will: • Say: I know what _____ means.
                    It means _____. (definition or paraphrase)
                  • Act out what the word means.
                    or
                  • Make a simple drawing.

Or your partner will ask: What does _____ mean? Then you must define the sentence, act it out, or make a drawing. You may do two or three sentences each.

👤 10. STRESS AND INTONATION

The first five sentences contain the sound /ð/ as in "<u>the</u>." The last five contain the sound /θ/ as in "<u>thin</u>." You will hear each sentence four times:

1. Listen for the sounds /ð/ and /θ/. (The letters for these sounds are underlined.)
2. Listen for syllable stress and word stress. *Capital letters indicate syllable stress.* Mark the word stress that you hear. Put a stress mark (´) over the stressed word or words.
3. Listen for rising or falling intonation at the end of the sentence. Mark intonation with the symbol "⟋" or "⟍."
4. Listen to the sentence again and repeat it. Pay attention to pauses and linking of words.

The first sentence is marked for you.

1. My MOTHer gave me a LEATHer belt.

2. Breathe in and then breathe out.

3. This is the house that Jack built.

4. We went there toGETHer.

5. AlTHOUGH the WEATHer is bad, they'll still go.

6. Thanks for THINKing of me.

7. She wants three things for her BIRTHday.

8. He wants EVerything or NOTHing.

9. Both are HEALTHy, WEALTHy, and wise.

10. I thought I saw him go through a door.

11. HOME ASSIGNMENT

1. Read the following poems (authors unknown) aloud. Use a dictionary to help you with the pronunciation and meaning of new words.
2. Draw a single line under all letters representing the sound /θ/ as in "thin." Draw a double line under all letters representing the sound /ð/ as in "the."
3. Mark the poems for stress and intonation. Then read the poems aloud again.

> **Example:**   In THIRty-three days
>
> Will come the HOLidays.

THIRty THOUsand THOUGHTless Boys

THIRty THOUsand THOUGHTless boys

Thought they'd make a THUNdering noise;

So with THIRty THOUsand thumbs,

They thumped on THIRty THOUsand drums.

The Old WOMan

There was an old WOMan
    And NOTHing she had;
And so this old WOMan
    Was said to be mad.
She'd NOTHing to eat,
    She'd NOTHing to wear,
She'd NOTHing to lose,
    She'd NOTHing to fear,
She'd NOTHing to ask,
    And NOTHing to leave,
And when she did die
    NObody grieved.

UNIT 27

/s/ as in see
/z/ as in zoo

1. PRODUCING /s/

Examples: so, cent, scene, MISSing, deCIDE, race, kiss, cease

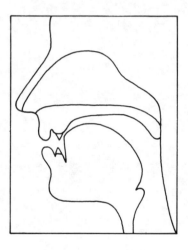

- Raise the front part of your tongue and point the tip toward the upper gum ridge, but do not touch it.
- Press the sides of your tongue against the upper teeth.
- Produce the sound by forcing air over the tongue and through the opening between your tongue and teeth.
- Your vocal cords do not vibrate.

2. PRODUCING /z/

Examples: <u>Z</u>Ero, CRA<u>z</u>y, DI<u>ZZ</u>y, NOI<u>S</u>y, bu<u>zz</u>, the<u>s</u>e, crie<u>s</u>

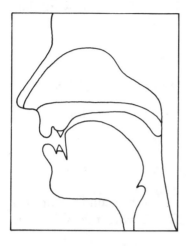

- This sound is produced the same way as /s/ except that /z/ is voiced.
- Raise the front part of your tongue and point the tip toward the upper gum ridge, but do not touch it.
- Press the sides of your tongue against the upper teeth.
- Produce the sound by forcing air over the tongue and through the opening between your tongue and teeth.
- Your vocal cords should vibrate.

🎧 3. CONTRAST: /s/ AND /z/

A. Some students may confuse the sound /s/ as in "<u>s</u>ee" with the sound /z/ as in "<u>z</u>oo." Practice these two sounds, first normally, then with exaggeration, then normally. Listen and repeat. Place your hand in front of your lips to feel the stream of air.

1. /s/	/s. . . . ./	/s/
2. /z/	/z. . . . ./	/z/

B. Now practice the sound in words. Notice the phonetic spelling. Listen and repeat each word twice.

1. <u>s</u>ad	/sæd/	<u>s</u>ad
2. <u>s</u>afe	/seyf/	<u>s</u>afe
3. E<u>SS</u>ay	/ɛsey/	E<u>SS</u>ay
4. i<u>c</u>e	/ays/	i<u>c</u>e
5. "z"	/ziy/	"z"
6. FREE<u>Z</u>er	/friyzər/	FREE<u>Z</u>er
7. pau<u>s</u>e	/pɔz/	pau<u>s</u>e
8. <u>z</u>ip	/zɪp/	<u>z</u>ip

🔆 4. CHECK YOUR LISTENING

A. The following pairs of words contain the sounds /s/ as in "see" and /z/ as in "zoo." You will hear one word from each pair. Circle the word that you hear.

1.	sue	zoo	6.	rice	rise
2.	sip	zip	7.	adVICE	adVISE
3.	sink	zinc	8.	dice	dies
4.	sewn	zone	9.	race	rays
5.	sing	zing	10.	loss	laws

B. In the following pairs of words, one word ends with the sound /s/ or /z/. You will hear one word from each pair. Circle the word that you hear.

1.	den	dense	6.	who	whose
2.	sin	since	7.	go	goes
3.	for	force	8.	though	those
4.	saw	sauce	9.	no	nose
5.	see	cease	10.	pray	praise

🔆 5. PRACTICE THE CONTRAST: /s/ AS IN "SEE" WITH /z/ AS IN "ZOO"

A. Practice these contrasting sounds. Listen and repeat each word pair. *Capital letters indicate syllable stress.*

	/s/	/z/			/s/	/z/
1.	seal	zeal		6.	niece	knees
2.	sink	zinc		7.	ice	eyes
3.	sip	zip		8.	place	plays
4.	deCEASED	diSEASED		9.	price	prize
5.	RACing	RAISing		10.	spice	spies

B. Now practice the contrasting sounds in sentence pairs. The first sentence of each pair has the sound /s/ and the second has the sound /z/. Listen and repeat. Notice the change in meaning. Visual clues can help. Make a simple drawing in each blank box. *Capital letters indicate syllable stress.*

1a. <u>s</u>eal   Say "<u>s</u>eal."

 b. <u>z</u>eal   Say "<u>z</u>eal."

2a. <u>s</u>ink   Take the <u>s</u>ink.

 b. <u>z</u>inc   Take the <u>z</u>inc.

3a. <u>s</u>ip   He'll <u>s</u>ip it.

 b. <u>z</u>ip   He'll <u>z</u>ip it.

4a. de<u>CEAS</u>ED   She's de<u>CEAS</u>ED.

 b. di<u>SEAS</u>ED   She's di<u>SEAS</u>ED.

5a. RA<u>C</u>ing   He's RA<u>C</u>ing the dog.

 b. RAI<u>S</u>ing   He's RAI<u>S</u>ing the dog.

6a. nie<u>c</u>e   Did you see her nie<u>c</u>e?

 b. knee<u>s</u>   Did you see her knee<u>s</u>?

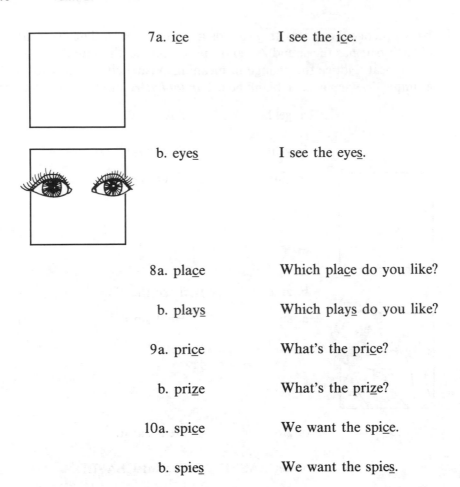

7a. i<u>c</u>e   I see the i<u>c</u>e.

b. eye<u>s</u>   I see the eye<u>s</u>.

8a. pla<u>c</u>e   Which pla<u>c</u>e do you like?

b. play<u>s</u>   Which play<u>s</u> do you like?

9a. pri<u>c</u>e   What's the pri<u>c</u>e?

b. pri<u>z</u>e   What's the pri<u>z</u>e?

10a. spi<u>c</u>e   We want the spi<u>c</u>e.

b. spie<u>s</u>   We want the spie<u>s</u>.

🎧 6. PRACTICE THE CONTRAST: /θ/ AS IN "<u>TH</u>IN" WITH /s/ AS IN "<u>S</u>EE"

Some speakers may confuse /θ/ as in "<u>th</u>in" with /s/ as in "<u>s</u>ee." When you pronounce /θ/, place your tongue tip between your teeth. When you pronounce /s/, raise your tongue tip toward your upper gum ridge.

A. Practice these contrasting sounds. Listen and repeat each word pair.

	/s/	/θ/		/s/	/θ/
1.	<u>s</u>ick	<u>th</u>ick	5.	fa<u>c</u>e	fai<u>th</u>
2.	<u>s</u>igh	<u>th</u>igh	6.	ten<u>s</u>e	ten<u>th</u>
3.	<u>s</u>eam	<u>th</u>eme	7.	mou<u>s</u>e	mou<u>th</u>
4.	<u>s</u>ank	<u>th</u>ank	8.	u<u>s</u>e	you<u>th</u>

B. Now practice the contrasting sounds in sentence pairs. The first sentence of each pair has the sound /s/ and the second has the sound /θ/. Listen and repeat. Notice the change in meaning. Visual clues can help. Make a simple drawing in each blank box.

1a. <u>s</u>ick   It's <u>s</u>ick.

  b. <u>th</u>ick   It's <u>th</u>ick.

2a. <u>s</u>igh   It's a <u>s</u>igh.

  b. <u>th</u>igh   It's a <u>th</u>igh.

3a. <u>s</u>eam   I need a <u>s</u>eam.

  b. <u>th</u>eme   I need a <u>th</u>eme.

4a. <u>s</u>ank   I said "<u>s</u>ank."

  b. <u>th</u>ank   I said "<u>th</u>ank."

5a. fa<u>c</u>e   He lost fa<u>c</u>e.

  b. fai<u>th</u>   He lost fai<u>th</u>.

6a. ten<u>s</u>e   Are you ten<u>s</u>e?

  b. ten<u>th</u>   Are you ten<u>th</u>?

7a. mouse   It's my mouse.

  b. mouth   It's my mouth.

8a. use   It's for your use.

  b. youth   It's for your youth.

7. PRACTICE THE CONTRAST: /ð/ AS IN "THE" WITH /z/ AS IN "ZOO"

Some speakers may confuse /ð/ as in "the" with /z/ as in "zoo." When you pronounce /ð/, place your tongue tip between your teeth. When you pronounce /z/, raise your tongue tip toward your upper gum ridge.

A. Practice these contrasting sounds. Listen and repeat each word pair. *Capital letters indicate syllable stress.*

	/z/	/ð/
1.	"Z"	thee
2.	Zen	then
3.	TEASing	TEETHing
4.	CLOSing	CLOTHing
5.	tease	teethe
6.	close	clothe

B. Now practice the contrasting sounds in sentence pairs. The first sentence of each pair has the sound /z/ and the second has the sound /ð/. Listen and repeat. Notice the change in meaning. Visual clues can help. Make a simple drawing in the blank box. *Capital letters indicate syllable stress.*

1a. "Z"   Is it "Z?"

  b. thee   Is it thee?

2a. Zen   It was Zen.

  b. then   It was then.

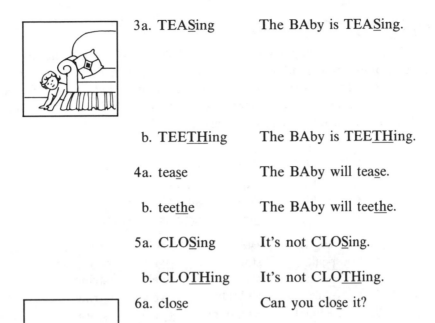

3a. TEA<u>S</u>ing The BAby is TEA<u>S</u>ing.

b. TEE<u>TH</u>ing The BAby is TEE<u>TH</u>ing.

4a. tea<u>s</u>e The BAby will tea<u>s</u>e.

b. tee<u>th</u>e The BAby will tee<u>th</u>e.

5a. CLO<u>S</u>ing It's not CLO<u>S</u>ing.

b. CLO<u>TH</u>ing It's not CLO<u>TH</u>ing.

6a. clo<u>s</u>e Can you clo<u>s</u>e it?

b. clo<u>th</u>e Can you clo<u>th</u>e it?

☞ 8. CHECK YOUR LISTENING

Work with a partner. Read a sentence from 5B, 6B, or 7B to your partner. Can your partner define the sentence? He or she must be truthful.

Your partner will: • Say: I know what _____ means.
It means _____. (definition or paraphrase)
or
• Act out what the word means.
or
• Make a simple drawing.

Or your partner will ask: What does _____ mean? Then you must define the sentence, act it out, or make a drawing. You may do two or three sentences each.

🔊 **9.** CONSONANT CLUSTERS WITH /s/

Many English words begin with the sound /s/ followed by one or more consonants (for example, <u>sch</u>ool, <u>st</u>op). Some students have difficulty pronouncing these clusters. They may say the sound /ɛ/ as in "m<u>e</u>t" before /s/. "School" then sounds like /ɛskuwl/. To correct this problem, try to hold the /s/ sound longer than usual. Listen and repeat these words.

	/sk/	/sl/	/sm/	/sn/
1.	<u>sk</u>i	<u>sl</u>ow	<u>sm</u>ack	<u>sn</u>ow
2.	<u>sk</u>y	<u>sl</u>ap	<u>sm</u>all	<u>sn</u>ap
3.	<u>sk</u>irt	<u>sl</u>eep	<u>sm</u>art	<u>sn</u>ob
4.	<u>sk</u>in	<u>sl</u>ip	<u>sm</u>oke	<u>sn</u>eeze

	/sp/	/st/	/sw/	/str/
5.	<u>sp</u>eak	<u>st</u>op	<u>sw</u>im	<u>str</u>eet
6.	<u>sp</u>oon	<u>st</u>ay	<u>sw</u>ell	<u>str</u>ing
7.	<u>sp</u>ell	<u>STU</u>Dy	<u>sw</u>eet	<u>str</u>ike
8.	<u>SPE</u>cial	<u>STU</u>dent	<u>sw</u>ear	<u>str</u>ess

🔊 **10.** CONSONANT CLUSTERS /sks/, /sps/, AND /sts/

A. Students may have difficulty with the consonant cluster /sks/. Practice the following words and sentences with this combination.

1. a<u>sks</u>   She ALways a<u>sks</u> STUdents to VISit her home.
2. ma<u>sks</u>   The CHILdren wear ma<u>sks</u> for the COStume PARty.
3. ba<u>sks</u>   The cat ba<u>sks</u> in the sun for hours.
4. ta<u>sks</u>   A MOTHer has MANy ta<u>sks</u> to do at home.
5. de<u>sks</u>   How MANy de<u>sks</u> are there?

B. Practice the following words and sentences with /sps/ and /sts/.

1. gra<u>sps</u>   A FRIGHTened child gra<u>sps</u> a MOTHer's skirt.
2. ga<u>sps</u>   A man with a heart aTTACK ga<u>sps</u> for air.
3. te<u>sts</u>   The inSTRUCtor gives MANy te<u>sts</u>.
4. pe<u>sts</u>   Flies and ants are pe<u>sts</u>.
5. li<u>sts</u>   All the li<u>sts</u> are on the wall.

💡 11. STRESS AND INTONATION

The first five sentences contain the sound /s/ as in "<u>s</u>ee." The last five contain the sound /z/ as in "<u>z</u>oo." You will hear each sentence four times:

1. Listen for the sounds /s/ and /z/. (Letters for these sounds are underlined.)
2. Listen for syllable stress and word stress. *Capital letters indicate syllable stress.* Mark the word stress that you hear. Put a stress mark (´) over the stressed word or words.
3. Listen for rising or falling intonation at the end of the sentence. Mark intonation with the symbol "⤴" or "⤵."
4. Listen to the sentence again and repeat it. Pay attention to pauses and linking of words.

The first sentence is marked for you.

1. LÍ<u>s</u>a'<u>s</u> OLDe<u>s</u>t SÍSter has a SPEcial <u>s</u>kill that aCCÓUNT<u>S</u> for her sucCE<u>SS</u>⤵.

2. LÍ<u>s</u>a's YOUNGe<u>s</u>t SISter, <u>S</u>ADly, is MISSing thi<u>s</u> SPEcial <u>s</u>kill.

3. <u>S</u>ome STUdent<u>s</u> ju<u>s</u>t NEVer <u>s</u>eem to <u>s</u>tay in cla<u>ss</u> all <u>s</u>eMESter.

4. <u>S</u>till, STUdent<u>s</u> ARen't all the <u>s</u>ame.

5. LÍ<u>s</u>ten to your STUdent<u>s</u>; <u>s</u>ome are SMARTer than their proFE<u>SS</u>ors.

6. Just a<u>s</u> I wa<u>s</u> LEAVing, tho<u>s</u>e boy<u>s</u> walked past our HOU<u>S</u>es.

7. Tho<u>s</u>e boy<u>s</u> made a lot of noi<u>s</u>e; their crie<u>s</u> could be heard for mile<u>s</u>.

8. I wa<u>s</u> plea<u>s</u>ed to leave; that kind of noi<u>s</u>e drive<u>s</u> me CRA<u>z</u>y.

9. I went to see tho<u>s</u>e one-act play<u>s</u> on TUE<u>S</u>day; one wa<u>s</u> aBOUT spie<u>s</u>.

10. It WA<u>S</u>n't ANy pri<u>z</u>e, I'd say; but some PEOple will prai<u>s</u>e ANything.

🔊 12. PRONUNCIATION OF THE "-s" ENDING

Form many plurals, possessives, and contractions by adding "-s" to a noun. Form the "s-form" of a verb by adding "-s" to the base form. This ending has three different pronunciations. The pronunciation of "-s" depends on which sound comes before it.

A. Nouns Ending in Voiceless Consonants

When a noun ends in the voiceless consonants /p/, /t/, /f/, /k/, and /θ/, pronounce "-s" as /s/, as in "see." Listen and repeat.

	Singular	Plural	Possessive	Contraction
1.	one sho<u>p</u>	two shop<u>s</u>	the sho<u>p's</u> WINdow	The sho<u>p's</u> closed.
2.	one boa<u>t</u>	two boat<u>s</u>	the boa<u>t's</u> CAPtain	The boa<u>t's</u> in the WAter.
3.	one chie<u>f</u>	two chief<u>s</u>	the chie<u>f's</u> son	The chie<u>f's</u> in his OFFice.
4.	one bi<u>ke</u>	two bi<u>kes</u>	the bi<u>ke's</u> tire	The bi<u>ke's</u> in the house.
5.	one mon<u>th</u>	two mon<u>ths</u>	in a mon<u>th's</u> time	The mon<u>th's</u> here.

B. Nouns Ending in Voiced Sounds

When a noun ends in the voiced consonants /b/, /d/, /g/, /v/, /m/, /n/, /ŋ/, /l/, or /r/, pronounce "-s" as /z/, as in "zoo." Listen and repeat.

	Singular	Plural	Possessive	Contraction
1.	one ca<u>b</u>	two cab<u>s</u>	the ca<u>b's</u> lights	The ca<u>b's</u> late.
2.	one be<u>d</u>	two bed<u>s</u>	the be<u>d's</u> frame	The be<u>d's</u> BROken.
3.	one ba<u>g</u>	two bag<u>s</u>	the ba<u>g's</u> COLor	The ba<u>g's</u> torn.
4.	one glo<u>ve</u>	two glo<u>ves</u>	the glo<u>ve's</u> COLor	The glo<u>ve's</u> torn.
5.	one far<u>m</u>	two far<u>ms</u>	the far<u>m's</u> crop	The far<u>m's</u> in New York.

Remember that all vowels are voiced. Thus, when a noun ends in a vowel sound, "-s" is pronounced /z/. Listen and repeat.

	Singular	Plural	Possessive	Contraction
1.	one da<u>y</u>	two da<u>ys</u>	a da<u>y's</u> JOURney	The da<u>y's</u> Over.
2.	one be<u>e</u>	two be<u>es</u>	the be<u>e's</u> hive	The be<u>e's</u> on the FLOWer.
3.	one bo<u>y</u>	two bo<u>ys</u>	the bo<u>y's</u> toy	The bo<u>y's</u> COMing.
4.	one CI<u>Ty</u>	two CI<u>Ties</u>	the CI<u>Ty's</u> stores	The CI<u>Ty's</u> near.
5.	one fl<u>y</u>	two fl<u>ies</u>	the fl<u>y's</u> wings	The fl<u>y's</u> all Over.

C. "-s" or "-es" Pronounced as /ɪz/

When a noun ends in /s/, /z/, /ʃ/ as in "bru<u>sh</u>," /ʒ/ as in "gaRA<u>GE</u>,"[1] /tʃ/ as in "bea<u>ch</u>," or /dʒ/ as in "bri<u>dge</u>," pronounce "-s" or "-es" as /ɪz/. Pronounce /ɪz/ as a separate syllable. Listen and repeat.

	Singular	Plural	Singular Possessive	Plural Possessive
1.	one bo<u>ss</u>	two BO<u>SS</u>es	the BO<u>SS</u>'s store	the BO<u>SS</u>es' MEETing
2.	one chee<u>se</u>	many CHEE<u>S</u>es	the CHEE<u>SE</u>'s Odor	the CHEE<u>S</u>es' Odor
3.	one bru<u>sh</u>	two BRU<u>SH</u>es	the bru<u>sh</u>'s HANdle	the BRU<u>SH</u>es' HANdles
4.	one gaRA<u>GE</u>	two gaRA<u>G</u>es	the gaRA<u>GE</u>'s door	the gaRA<u>G</u>es' doors
5.	one ben<u>ch</u>	two BEN<u>CH</u>es	the BEN<u>CH</u>'s paint	the BEN<u>CH</u>es' paint
6.	one bri<u>dge</u>	two BRI<u>DG</u>es	the BRI<u>DGE</u>'s ropes	the BRI<u>DG</u>es' ropes

D. Verbs Ending in Voiceless Consonants

When a verb ends in the voiceless consonants /p/, /t/, /f/, or /k/, pronounce "-s" as /s/, as in "<u>s</u>ee." Listen and repeat.

1. I jum<u>p</u>.   He jum<u>ps</u>.
2. I si<u>t</u>.   She si<u>ts</u>.
3. I lau<u>gh</u>.   He lau<u>ghs</u>.
4. I spea<u>k</u>.   She spea<u>ks</u>.

E. Verbs Ending in Voiced Sounds

When a verb ends in the voiced consonants /b/, /d/, /g/, /v/, /ð/, /m/, /n/, /ŋ/, /l/, or /r/, pronounce "-s" as /z/, as in "<u>z</u>oo." Listen and repeat.

1. I ru<u>b</u>.   He ru<u>bs</u>.
2. I nee<u>d</u>.   She nee<u>ds</u>.
3. I be<u>g</u>.   He be<u>gs</u>.
4. I sa<u>ve</u>.   She sa<u>ves</u>.
5. I swi<u>m</u>.   He swi<u>ms</u>.
6. I wi<u>n</u>.   She wi<u>ns</u>.
7. I si<u>ng</u>.   He si<u>ngs</u>.

[1]American speakers may pronounce this word /ɡəraʒ/ or /ɡəradʒ/.

8. I fee<u>l</u>.   She fee<u>ls</u>.
9. I hea<u>r</u>.   He hea<u>rs</u>.
10. I brea<u>the</u>.   He brea<u>thes</u>.

Remember that all vowels are voiced. Thus, when a verb ends in a vowel sound, "-s" or "-es" is pronounced /z/. Listen and repeat.

1. I g<u>o</u>.   He g<u>oes</u>.
2. I s<u>ee</u>.   She s<u>ees</u>.
3. I w<u>eigh</u>.   He w<u>eighs</u>.
4. I fl<u>y</u>.   He fl<u>ies</u>.

F. "-s" or "-es" Pronounced /ɪz/

When a verb ends in /s/, /z/, /ʃ/ as in "wi<u>sh</u>," /ʒ/ as in "maSSA<u>GE</u>,"² /tʃ/ as in "tea<u>ch</u>," or /dʒ/ as in "ple<u>dge</u>," pronounce "-es" /ɪz/. Pronounce /ɪz/ as a separate syllable. Listen and repeat.

1. I mi<u>ss</u>.   He MI<u>SSes</u>.
2. I pau<u>se</u>.   She PAU<u>Ses</u>.
3. I wi<u>sh</u>.   He WI<u>SHes</u>.
4. I maSSA<u>GE</u>.   She maSSA<u>Ges</u>.
5. I tea<u>ch</u>.   He TEA<u>CHes</u>.
6. I ple<u>dge</u>.   He PLE<u>DGes</u>.

🔨 13. HOME ASSIGNMENT

Form the plural endings of the following nouns.

1. Pronounce the singular form of the noun.
   You may use a dictionary to help you with any new words.
2. Pronounce the plural form of the noun. Write it on the blank line in the second column.
3. Write the phonetic symbol(s) for the plural ending in the last column: /s/, /z/, or /ɪz/.

²American speakers may pronounce this word /məsaʒ/ or /məsadʒ/.

Examples:

lamp	lamps	/s/
FLOWer	flowers	/z/
cheese	cheeses	/ɪz/

1. bridge _____ ____
2. TRAVeler _____ ____
3. speed _____ ____
4. BIcycle _____ ____
5. horse _____ ____
6. hoTEL _____ ____
7. SUITcase _____ ____
8. shop _____ ____
9. MARket _____ ____
10. TOURist _____ ____
11. CABBage _____ ____
12. OLive _____ ____
13. meat _____ ____
14. spice _____ ____
15. baNANa _____ ____
16. COconut _____ ____
17. MANgo _____ ____
18. CEReal _____ ____
19. CARRot _____ ____
20. ORange _____ ____

UNIT 28 — /ʃ/ as in she /ʒ/ as in PLEASure

1. PRODUCING /ʃ/

Examples: shoe, sure, maCHINE, Ocean, NAtion, TENsion, PRECIous, rush

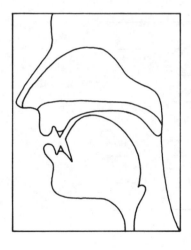

- First, raise the front part of your tongue toward the roof of the mouth, but do not touch it.
- Then press the sides of your tongue against the upper side teeth. Produce the sound by forcing air out over the tongue and through your teeth.
- Round your lips slightly.
- Your vocal cords do not vibrate.
- This is the sound you make when you want someone to be quiet (Sh!).

2. PRODUCING /ʒ/

Examples: TREASure, VISIon, exPLOsion, mirAGE

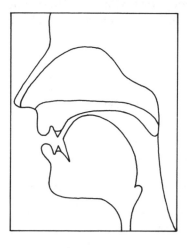

- This sound is produced the same way as /ʃ/, except that /ʒ/ is voiced.
- First, raise the front part of your tongue toward the roof of the mouth, but do not touch it.
- Then press the sides of your tongue against the upper side teeth. Produce the sound by forcing air out over the tongue and through your teeth.
- Round your lips slightly.
- Your vocal cords should vibrate.

3. CONTRAST: /ʃ/ AND /ʒ/

A. Some students may confuse the sound /ʃ/ as in "<u>she</u>" with the sound /ʒ/ as in "PLEA<u>S</u>ure." Practice these two sounds, first normally, then with exaggeration, then normally. Listen and repeat.

1. /ʃ/   /ʃ. . . . ./   /ʃ/
2. /ʒ/   /ʒ. . . . ./   /ʒ/

B. Now practice the sound in words. Notice the phonetic spelling. Listen and repeat each word twice.

1. <u>sh</u>ip	/ʃɪp/	<u>sh</u>ip
2. ma<u>CHINE</u>	/məʃiyn/	ma<u>CHINE</u>
3. wi<u>sh</u>	/wɪʃ/	wi<u>sh</u>
4. VI<u>S</u>ual	/vɪʒuwəl/	VI<u>S</u>ual
5. FU<u>s</u>ion	/fyuwʒən/	FU<u>s</u>ion
6. ESpiona<u>ge</u>	/ɛspiyənaʒ/	ESpiona<u>ge</u>
7. wa<u>sh</u>	/waʃ/	wa<u>sh</u>
8. TREA<u>S</u>ure	/trɛʒər/	TREA<u>S</u>ure

♀ 4. CHECK YOUR LISTENING

You will hear words with the sounds /ʃ/, /ʒ/, /s/, /z/, and /θ/. First, cover the words in the following list. Then listen to each word. Concentrate on the sound, not the spelling. Which consonant sound do you hear? Write a check mark in the correct column.

	/ʃ/ as in "she"	/s/ as in "see"	/θ/ as in "thin"	/ʒ/ as in "pleasure"	/z/ as in "zoo"
1. through	——	——	——	——	——
2. sue	——	——	——	——	——
3. CRAzy	——	——	——	——	——
4. shoe	——	——	——	——	——
5. truce	——	——	——	——	——
6. truth	——	——	——	——	——
7. days	——	——	——	——	——
8. miRAGE	——	——	——	——	——
9. brush	——	——	——	——	——
10. YOUTHful	——	——	——	——	——
11. occuPAtion	——	——	——	——	——
12. USEful	——	——	——	——	——
13. USer	——	——	——	——	——
14. USual	——	——	——	——	——

♀ 5. PRACTICE THE CONTRAST: /s/ AS IN "SEE" WITH /ʃ/ AS IN "SHE"

A. Practice these contrasting sounds. Listen and repeat each word pair. *Capital letters indicate syllable stress.*

	/s/	/ʃ/			/s/	/ʃ/
1.	sip	ship		4.	CLASSes	CLASHes
2.	sew	show		5.	class	clash
3.	leased	leashed		6.	bass	bash

B. Now practice the contrasting sounds in sentence pairs. The first sentence of each pair has the sound /s/, and the second has the sound /ʃ/. Listen and repeat. Notice the change in meaning. Visual clues can help. Make a simple drawing in each blank box. *Capital letters indicate syllable stress.*

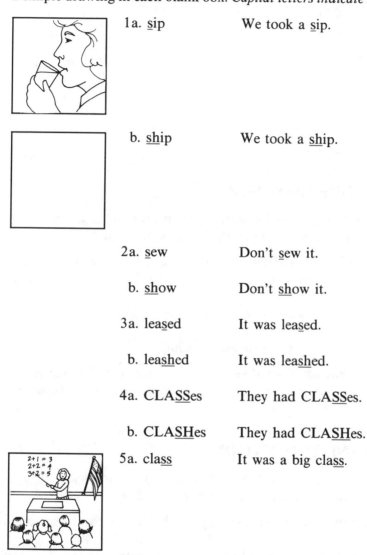

1a. <u>s</u>ip   We took a <u>s</u>ip.

b. <u>sh</u>ip   We took a <u>sh</u>ip.

2a. <u>s</u>ew   Don't <u>s</u>ew it.

b. <u>sh</u>ow   Don't <u>sh</u>ow it.

3a. lea<u>s</u>ed   It was lea<u>s</u>ed.

b. lea<u>sh</u>ed   It was lea<u>sh</u>ed.

4a. CLA<u>SS</u>es   They had CLA<u>SS</u>es.

b. CLA<u>SH</u>es   They had CLA<u>SH</u>es.

5a. cla<u>ss</u>   It was a big cla<u>ss</u>.

b. cla<u>sh</u>   It was a big cla<u>sh</u>.

6a. ba<u>ss</u>   They had a big ba<u>ss</u>.

b. ba<u>sh</u>   They had a big ba<u>sh</u>.

6. CHECK YOUR LISTENING

Work with a partner. Read a sentence from 5B to your partner. Can your partner define the sentence? He or she must be truthful.

Your partner will: • Say: I know what _____ means.
                        It means _____. (definition or paraphrase)
                        or
                      • Act out what the word means.
                        or
                      • Make a simple drawing.

Or your partner will ask: What does _____ mean? Then you must define the sentence, act it out, or make a drawing. You may do two or three sentences each.

7. STRESS AND INTONATION

Each of these sentences contains the sounds /ʃ/ as in "<u>sh</u>e" and /ʒ/ as in "PLEA<u>S</u>ure." You will hear each sentence four times:

1. Listen for the sounds /ʃ/ and /ʒ/. (The letters for these sounds are underlined.)
2. Listen for syllable stress and word stress. *Capital letters indicate syllable stress.* Mark the word stress that you hear. Put a stress mark (ʹ) over the stressed word or words.

3. Listen for rising or falling intonation at the end of the sentence. Mark intonation with the symbol "⤴" or "⤵."

4. Listen to the sentence again and repeat it. Pay attention to pauses and linking of words.

The first sentence is marked for you.

1. Don't wa<u>sh</u> the car in the gaRÁ<u>GE</u>.

2. Some of our NA<u>TI</u>onal TREA<u>S</u>ures are in the White House.

3. We ate the deLI<u>CI</u>ous food and we DIDn't need a great deal of per-SUA<u>si</u>on.

4. The <u>sh</u>ip has proVI<u>S</u>ions for a three-month cruise.

5. The inviTA<u>ti</u>on said to dress FORmally, not CA<u>S</u>ually.

6. The PA<u>ti</u>ent asked for a maSSA<u>GE</u>.

7. The day we met was a SPE<u>CI</u>al oCCA<u>s</u>ion.

8. He hurt his <u>SH</u>OULder in the coLLI<u>SI</u>on.

9. When you FINi<u>sh</u>, please give me your deCI<u>SI</u>on.

10. <u>SH</u>AKEspeare wrote the play, "MEA<u>S</u>ure for MEA<u>S</u>ure."

8. HOME ASSIGNMENT

1. Read the following poem (author unknown) aloud. Use a dictionary to help you with the pronunciation and meaning of new words.

2. Draw a single line under all letters representing the sound /ʃ/ as in "<u>sh</u>e." Draw a double line under all letters representing the sound /s/ as in "<u>s</u>ee."

3. Mark the poem for stress and intonation. Then read the poem aloud again.

Example: When I Go FISHing

When I go FISHing

I'm ALways WISHing

Some FISHes I will get;

But while I'm FISHing,

The fish are WISHing

I won't; just HARDer yet.

And all those WISHes,

Of the FISHes,

EVery one comes true;

So all my WISHes

To get FISHes

NEVer, NEVer do.

<table>
<tr><td>

UNIT
29

</td><td>

/tʃ/ as in <u>ch</u>ild
/dʒ/ as in jo<u>b</u>

</td></tr>
</table>

1. PRODUCING /tʃ/

Examples: <u>ch</u>eck, <u>ch</u>ur<u>ch</u>, TEA<u>CH</u>er, NA<u>T</u>ural, lun<u>ch</u>, mat<u>ch</u>

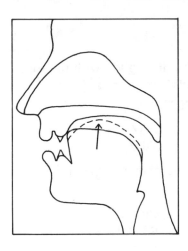

- This sound is a combination of /t/ as in "<u>t</u>en" and /ʃ/ as in "<u>sh</u>e."
- First, press the tip of your tongue against your gum ridge. This stops the flow of air.
- Then lower the tip of your tongue quickly, keeping the sides of your tongue pressed against the upper side teeth and forcing the air out over the tongue.
- Round your lips slightly.
- Your vocal cords do not vibrate.

2. PRODUCING /dʒ/

Examples: joy, germ, judge, enJOY, DANger, wage, cage

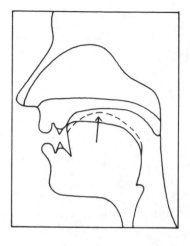

- This sound is a combination of /d/ as in day and /ʒ/ as in "pleasure." It is produced the same way as /tʃ/, except that /dʒ/ is voiced.
- First, press the tip of your tongue against your gum ridge. This stops the flow of air.
- Then lower the tip of your tongue quickly, keeping the sides of your tongue pressed against the upper side teeth and forcing the air out over the tongue.
- Round your lips slightly.
- Your vocal cords should vibrate.

3. CONTRAST: /tʃ/ AND /dʒ/

A. Some students may confuse the sound /tʃ/ as in "child" with the sound /dʒ/ as in "job." Practice these two sounds, first normally, then with exaggeration, then normally. Listen and repeat.

    1. /tʃ/   /tʃ . . . . ./   /tʃ/
    2. /dʒ/   /dʒ. . . . ./   /dʒ/

B. Now practice the sound in words. Notice the phonetic spelling. Listen and repeat each word twice.

1. cheese	/tʃiyz/	cheese
2. KITCHen	/kɪtʃən/	KITCHen
3. each	/iytʃ/	each
4. jam	/dʒæm/	jam
5. MAGic	/mædʒɪk/	MAGic
6. page	/peydʒ/	page
7. choose	/tʃuwz/	choose
8. joke	/dʒowk/	joke

🔦 4. CHECK YOUR LISTENING

A. The following pairs of words contain the sounds /tʃ/ as in "child" and /dʒ/ as in "job." You will hear one word from each pair. Circle the word that you hear.

1.	cheap	jeep	5.	RICHes	RIDGes
2.	choke	joke	6.	lunch	lunge
3.	chew	Jew	7.	match	Madge
4.	choice	Joyce	8.	etch	edge

B. In the following pairs of words, one word ends with the sound /tʃ/ or /dʒ/. You will hear one word from each pair. Circle the word that you hear.

1.	hat	hatch	5.	bad	badge
2.	hit	hitch	6.	aid	age
3.	it	itch	7.	paid	page
4.	beat	beach	8.	head	hedge

🔦 5. PRACTICE THE CONTRAST: /tʃ/ AS IN "CHILD" WITH /dʒ/ AS IN "JOB"

A. Practice these contrasting sounds. Listen and repeat each word pair. _Capital letters indicate syllable stress._

	/tʃ/	/dʒ/			/tʃ/	/dʒ/
1.	chin	gin	6.		ETCHing	EDGing
2.	chain	Jane	7.		batch	badge
3.	chest	jest	8.		March	Marge
4.	chills	Jill's	9.		"h"	age
5.	CHOKing	JOKing	10.		rich	ridge

B. Now practice the contrasting sounds in sentence pairs. The first sentence of each pair has the sound /tʃ/ and the second has the sound /dʒ/. Listen and repeat. Notice the change in meaning. Visual clues can help. Make a simple drawing in each blank box. *Capital letters indicate syllable stress.*

1a. <u>ch</u>in   I like his <u>ch</u>in.

  b. <u>g</u>in   I like his <u>g</u>in.

2a. <u>ch</u>ain   That's my <u>ch</u>ain.

  b. <u>J</u>ane   That's my <u>J</u>ane.

3a. <u>ch</u>est   It's a <u>ch</u>est.

  b. <u>j</u>est   It's a <u>j</u>est.

4a. <u>ch</u>ills   Is it <u>ch</u>ills?

  b. <u>J</u>ill's   Is it <u>J</u>ill's?

5a. <u>CHOK</u>ing   He's <u>CHOK</u>ing.

  b. <u>JOK</u>ing   He's <u>JOK</u>ing.

6a. <u>ETCH</u>ing   It's a nice <u>ETCH</u>ing.

  b. <u>EDG</u>ing   It's a nice <u>EDG</u>ing.

7a. bat<u>ch</u>   I saw his bat<u>ch</u>.

  b. ba<u>dge</u>   I saw his ba<u>dge</u>.

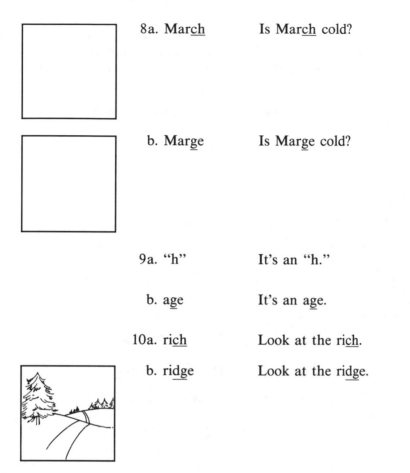

8a. Mar<u>ch</u>   Is Mar<u>ch</u> cold?

b. Mar<u>ge</u>   Is Mar<u>ge</u> cold?

9a. "h"   It's an "h."

b. a<u>ge</u>   It's an a<u>ge</u>.

10a. ri<u>ch</u>   Look at the ri<u>ch</u>.

b. ri<u>dge</u>   Look at the ri<u>dge</u>.

🎧 6. PRACTICE THE CONTRAST: FINAL /ts/ WITH FINAL /tʃ/

Some students may confuse /tʃ/ as in "cat<u>ch</u>" with /ts/ as in "ca<u>ts</u>."

A. Practice these contrasting sounds. Listen and repeat each word pair.

	/ts/	/tʃ/
1.	ma<u>ts</u>	mat<u>ch</u>
2.	ca<u>ts</u>	cat<u>ch</u>
3.	bee<u>ts</u>	bea<u>ch</u>
4.	ba<u>ts</u>	bat<u>ch</u>
5.	coa<u>ts</u>	coa<u>ch</u>

B. Now practice the contrasting sounds in sentence pairs. The first sentence of each pair has the sounds /ts/ and the second has the sound /tʃ/. Listen and repeat. Notice the change in meaning. Visual clues can help. Make a simple drawing in each blank box.

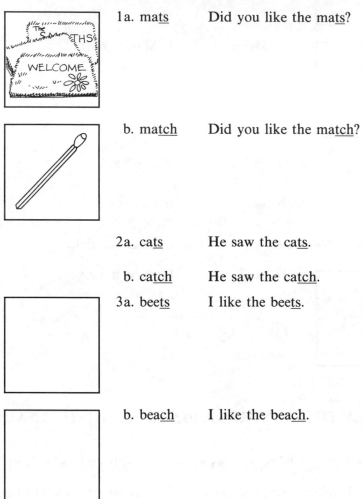

1a. ma<u>ts</u>   Did you like the ma<u>ts</u>?

b. ma<u>tch</u>   Did you like the ma<u>tch</u>?

2a. ca<u>ts</u>   He saw the ca<u>ts</u>.

b. ca<u>tch</u>   He saw the ca<u>tch</u>.

3a. bee<u>ts</u>   I like the bee<u>ts</u>.

b. bea<u>ch</u>   I like the bea<u>ch</u>.

4a. ba<u>ts</u>   Put the ba<u>ts</u> aWAY.

 b. ba<u>tch</u>   Put the ba<u>tch</u> aWAY.

5a. coa<u>ts</u>   We want the coa<u>ts</u>.

 b. coa<u>ch</u>   We want the coa<u>ch</u>.

☝ 7. PRACTICE THE CONTRAST: /tʃ/ AS IN "<u>CH</u>ILD" WITH /ʃ/ AS IN "<u>SH</u>E"

Some students may confuse /tʃ/ as in "<u>ch</u>ild" with /ʃ/ as in "<u>sh</u>e." When you pronounce /tʃ/, be sure to press your tongue tip to the upper gum ridge. Then drop the tip quickly and let the air rush out.

A. Practice these contrasting sounds. Listen and repeat each word pair. *Capital letters indicate syllable stress.*

	/ʃ/	/tʃ/
1.	<u>sh</u>are	<u>ch</u>air
2.	<u>sh</u>eet	<u>ch</u>eat
3.	<u>SH</u>OPPing	<u>CH</u>OPPing
4.	WA<u>SH</u>ing	WA<u>TCH</u>ing
5.	wa<u>sh</u>	wa<u>tch</u>

B. Now practice the contrasting sounds in sentence pairs. The first sentence of each pair has the sound /ʃ/ and the second has the sound /tʃ/. Listen and repeat. Notice the change in meaning. Visual clues can help. Make a simple drawing in each blank box. *Capital letters indicate syllable stress.*

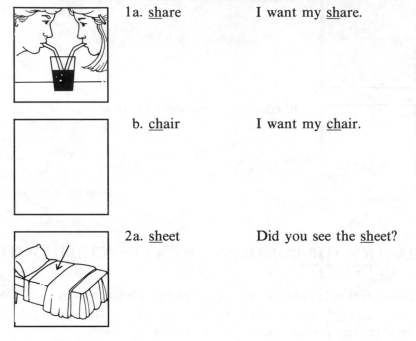

1a. <u>sh</u>are   I want my <u>sh</u>are.

b. <u>ch</u>air   I want my <u>ch</u>air.

2a. <u>sh</u>eet   Did you see the <u>sh</u>eet?

b. <u>ch</u>eat   Did you see the <u>ch</u>eat?

3a. <u>SH</u>OPPing   She did the <u>SH</u>OPPing.

b. <u>CH</u>OPPing   She did the <u>CH</u>OPPing.

4a. WA<u>SH</u>ing   He did the WA<u>SH</u>ing.

b. WA<u>TCH</u>ing   He did the WA<u>TCH</u>ing.

5a. wa<u>sh</u>   Did he take the wa<u>sh</u>?

b. wa<u>tch</u>   Did he take the wa<u>tch</u>?

↻ 8. CHECK YOUR LISTENING

Work with a partner. Read a sentence from 5B, 6B, or 7B to your partner. Can your partner define the sentence? He or she must be truthful.

Your partner will:
- Say: I know what _____ means.
  It means _____. (definition or paraphrase)
  or
- Act out what the word means.
  or
- Make a simple drawing.

Or your partner will ask: What does _____ mean? Then you must define the sentence, act it out, or make a drawing. You may do two or three sentences each.

🎧 9. STRESS AND INTONATION

Each of these sentences contains the sounds /tʃ/ as in "<u>ch</u>ild" and /dʒ/ as in "<u>j</u>ob." You will hear each sentence four times:

1. Listen for the sounds /tʃ/ and /dʒ/. (Letters for these sounds are under-lined.)
2. Listen for syllable stress and word stress. *Capital letters indicate syllable stress.* Mark the word stress that you hear. Put a stress mark (′) over the stressed word or words.
3. Listen for rising or falling intonation at the end of the sentence. Mark intonation with the symbol "⌣⌐" or "⌣⌐."
4. Listen to the sentence again and repeat it. Pay attention to pauses and linking of words.

The first sentence is marked for you.

1. Did you wat<u>ch</u> them go to <u>j</u>ail?
2. The high TEMpera<u>t</u>ure did a lot of DAMa<u>ge</u>.
3. Were you <u>CH</u>Osen to serve on the <u>J</u>URy?
4. Whi<u>ch</u> car can I rent with unLIMited MILEa<u>ge</u>?
5. The Fren<u>ch</u> LANguage is VERy MUsical.
6. The <u>ch</u>ild is <u>J</u>EALous of his SISter.
7. Is spee<u>ch</u> reQUIRED at your COLLe<u>ge</u>?
8. The FU<u>t</u>ure looks good for the SOL<u>d</u>ier.
9. Don't you have QUES<u>t</u>ions to ask aBOUT re<u>g</u>iSTRAtion?
10. <u>CH</u>OWder is a thick soup that is prePARED with fish, VE<u>G</u>etables, and milk.

📖 10. HOME ASSIGNMENT

In the following words, the underlined letters represent these sounds:

/tʃ/ as in "<u>ch</u>ild"   /ʃ/ as in "<u>sh</u>e"
/dʒ/ as in "<u>j</u>ob"   /z/ as in "<u>z</u>oo"
/s/ as in "<u>s</u>ee"

Say each word aloud, then write the correct phonetic symbol in the blank.

Examples:

a. <u>Ch</u>iCAgo	/ʃ/		d. eRA<u>S</u>er	/s/	
b. ed<u>g</u>e	/dʒ/		e. noi<u>s</u>e	/z/	
c. <u>CH</u>ILdren	/tʃ/				

1. Ju<u>L</u>Y	___		14. rai<u>s</u>e	___
2. sear<u>ch</u>	___		15. BI<u>c</u>ycle	___
3. lar<u>g</u>e	___		16. MA<u>j</u>or	___
4. <u>SC</u>Ience	___		17. cham<u>PAGN</u>E	___
5. REA<u>s</u>on	___		18. <u>j</u>ump	___
6. bru<u>sh</u>	___		19. beCAU<u>S</u>E	___
7. ri<u>ch</u>	___		20. BA<u>CH</u>elor	___
8. <u>ch</u>art	___		21. mi<u>ss</u>	___
9. <u>s</u>ee	___		22. inFEC<u>ti</u>on	___
10. plea<u>s</u>e	___		23. PACK<u>a</u><u>g</u>e	___
11. fiNAN<u>c</u>ial	___		24. MER<u>ch</u>andise	___
12. <u>ch</u>ase	___		25. the<u>s</u>e	___
13. RE<u>G</u>ister	___			

UNIT 30 /y/ as in "yes"

1. PRODUCING /y/

Examples: you, young, YESterday, ONion, MILLion

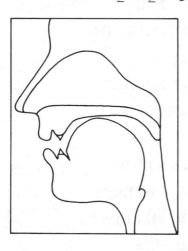

- This sound is always followed by a vowel sound. As you say /y/, your tongue and lips glide from their original position. Then they shape the vowel sound.
- Rest the tip of your tongue, lightly, against your bottom teeth.
- Raise the center part of your tongue toward the roof of your mouth, but do not touch it.
- Press the sides of your tongue against your top teeth. Produce the sound by letting air flow over your tongue. Then pronounce the vowel.
- Your vocal cords should vibrate.

2. PRACTICE THE SOUND

A. Remember to combine the sound /y/ with the vowel sound that follows it. Practice these sounds first normally, then with exaggeration, then normally. Listen and repeat.

/yɛs/   /y. . . .ɛs/   /yɛs/

274

B. Now practice the sound in words. Notice the phonetic spelling. Listen and repeat each word twice.

1.	yet	/yɛt/	yet
2.	you	/yuw/	you
3.	youth	/yuwθ/	youth
4.	MILLion	/mɪlyən/	MILLion
5.	ONion	/ənyən/	ONion
6.	JUNior	/dʒuwnyər/	JUNior

3. CHECK YOUR LISTENING

A. In the following pairs of words, one word begins with the sound /y/. You will hear one word from each pair. Circle the word that you hear.

1.	"S"	yes		5.	oak	yolk
2.	ear	year		6.	east	yeast
3.	ail	Yale		7.	am	yam
4.	or	your		8.	AWNing	YAWNing

4. PRACTICE THE CONTRAST: /y/ AS IN "YES" WITH /dʒ/ AS IN "JOB"

Some students may confuse /y/ as in "yes" with /dʒ/ as in "job." When you pronounce /y/, no part of your tongue touches the gum ridge. When you pronounce /dʒ/, the tongue tip touches the upper gum ridge, stopping the air flow for a moment.

A. Practice these contrasting sounds. Listen and repeat each word pair. *Capital letters indicate syllable stress.*

	/y/	/dʒ/			/y/	/dʒ/
1.	YELLow	JELL-o		5.	year	jeer
2.	Yale	jail		6.	yolk	joke
3.	yet	jet		7.	yam	jam
4.	yes	Jess				

B. Now practice the contrasting sounds in sentence pairs. The first sentence of each pair has the sound /y/ and the second has the sound /dʒ/. Listen and repeat. Notice the change in meaning. Visual clues can help. Make a simple drawing in each blank box. *Capital letters indicate syllable stress.*

1a. <u>Y</u>ELLow   Is it <u>Y</u>ELLow?

  b. <u>J</u>ELL-o   Is it <u>J</u>ELL-o?

- 2a. <u>Y</u>ale   He's GOing to <u>Y</u>ale.

  b. <u>j</u>ail   He's GOing to <u>j</u>ail.

3a. <u>y</u>et   Was it "<u>y</u>et?"

  b. <u>j</u>et   Was it "<u>j</u>et?"

4a. <u>y</u>es   I said "<u>Y</u>es."

  b. <u>J</u>ess   I said "<u>J</u>ess."

5a. <u>y</u>ear   It's an unPLEASant <u>y</u>ear.

  b. <u>j</u>eer   It's an unPLEASant <u>j</u>eer.

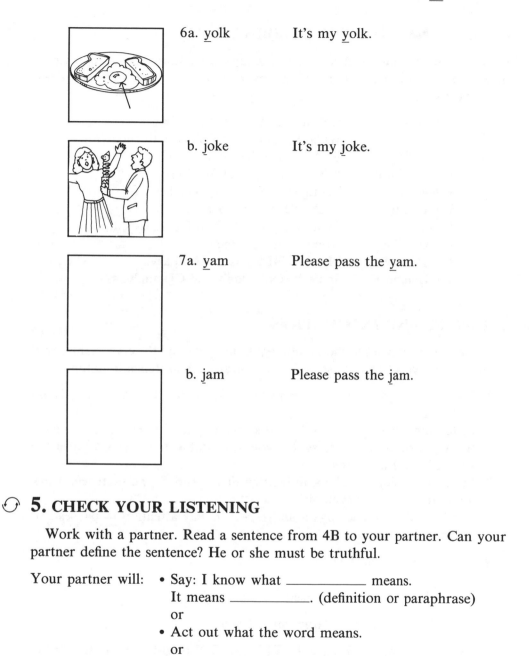

6a. yolk   It's my yolk.

b. joke   It's my joke.

7a. yam   Please pass the yam.

b. jam   Please pass the jam.

5. CHECK YOUR LISTENING

Work with a partner. Read a sentence from 4B to your partner. Can your partner define the sentence? He or she must be truthful.

Your partner will: • Say: I know what _____ means.
It means _____. (definition or paraphrase)
or
• Act out what the word means.
or
• Make a simple drawing.

Or your partner will ask: What does _____ mean? Then you must define the sentence, act it out, or make a drawing. You may do two or three sentences each.

☻ 6. CONSONANT-VOWEL COMBINATION /yuw/

The combined sound /yuw/ is very common. Sometimes it is not represented by a letter but is heard as the first part of the vowel sound. Listen and repeat these words and sentences.

1.	UNion	He's a MEMber of the UNion.
2.	Unit	We are ALmost FINished with this Unit.
3.	BEAUty	BEAUty is ONly skin deep.
4.	BEAUtiful	What a BEAUtiful SUNset!
5.	few	There are a few SANDwiches left.
6.	reFUSE	I reFUSE to be a part of this.
7.	cute	That BAby's OUTfit is REALLy cute.
8.	conFUSE	Don't conFUSE me.
9.	JANuary	My BIRTHday is in JANuary.
10.	CUcumber	Some PEOple don't like CUcumbers.

☻ 7. STRESS AND INTONATION

These sentences contain the sounds /y/ as in "yes" and the consonant-vowel combination /yuw/ as in "use." You will hear each sentence four times:

1. Listen for the sounds /y/ and /yuw/. (The letters for these sounds are underlined.)
2. Listen for syllable stress and word stress. *Capital letters indicate syllable stress.* Mark the word stress that you hear. Put a stress mark (´) over the stressed word or words.
3. Listen for rising or falling intonation at the end of the sentence. Mark intonation with the symbol "⤴" or "⤵."
4. Listen to the sentence again and repeat it. Pay attention to pauses and linking of words.

The first sentence is marked for you.

1. A yacht¹ is a small ship used for SAILing.

2. Yale is the name of a large uniVERsity.

3. The YELLow PAGes are the YELLow-COLored PAGes in the TELe-phone book that list you aCCORDing to your BUSiness.

¹In this word "ch" is not pronounced. The word is pronounced /yat/.

4. Yule is aNOTHer word you can use for CHRISTmas.

5. A mute PERson is one who does not use his voice to speak.

6. A BRILLiant PERson is Usually called a GENius.

7. CaliFORnia is LARGer than New York.

8. New York is LARGer than PennsylVANia.

9. PennsylVANia is LARGer than VirGINia.

10. VirGINia is LARGer than West VirGINia.

8. HOME ASSIGNMENT

A. 1. Make up a sentence for each of the words listed below. Use a dictionary to look up new words.
   2. Say each sentence aloud. Mark them for stress and intonation.

1. HUman	6. Uniform
2. MUsic	7. JANuary
3. SENior	8. POPular
4. VOLume	9. parTICular
5. FUneral	10. repuTAtion

B. Work with a partner. Read your sentences aloud, using your stress and intonation markings. Your partner will paraphrase the sentence or tell you what the sentence means. Did he or she understand your meaning?

UNIT 31	/h/ as in <u>house</u>

1. PRODUCING /h/

Examples: <u>h</u>e, <u>h</u>ow, <u>w</u>ho,[1] a<u>H</u>EAD, PER<u>h</u>aps

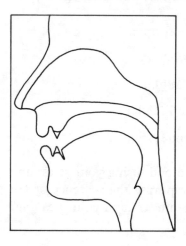

- This sound is always followed by a vowel sound. As you say /h/, your tongue and lips shape the vowel sound that follows.
- Lower your jaw slightly, and let your tongue rest in a relaxed position.
- Force air out of your throat, through open lips.
- Your vocal cords do not vibrate.

2. PRACTICE THE SOUND

A. Practice the sound /h/, first normally, then with exaggeration, then normally. Listen and repeat.

/h/   /h. . . ./   /h/

[1]The "w" is not pronounced in some words that begin with "wh." See page 293.

B. Now practice the sound in words. Notice the phonetic spelling. Listen and repeat each word twice.

1. <u>h</u>e	/hiy/	<u>h</u>e
2. <u>h</u>ome	/howm/	<u>h</u>ome
3. <u>h</u>ole	/howl/	<u>h</u>ole
4. <u>h</u>ave	/hæv/	<u>h</u>ave
5. re<u>H</u>EAT	/riyhiyt/	re<u>H</u>EAT
6. SOME<u>h</u>ow	/səmhaw/	SOME<u>h</u>ow

3. CHECK YOUR LISTENING

In the following pairs of words, one word begins with the sound /h/. You will hear one word from each pair. Circle the word that you hear.

1.	as	<u>h</u>as	5.	ear	<u>h</u>ear
2.	old	<u>h</u>old	6.	and	<u>h</u>and
3.	I'd	<u>h</u>ide	7.	am	<u>h</u>am
4.	all	<u>h</u>all	8.	at	<u>h</u>at

4. PRACTICE THE CONTRAST: WORDS WITH INITIAL /h/ AS IN "<u>H</u>OUSE" AND WORDS WITHOUT /h/

Some students may leave out the sound /h/ when it appears at the beginning of a word.

A. Listen and repeat each word pair.

	No /h/	/h/		No /h/	/h/
1.	art	<u>h</u>eart	6.	I	<u>h</u>igh
2.	eat	<u>h</u>eat	7.	arm	<u>h</u>arm
3.	air	<u>h</u>air	8.	it	<u>h</u>it
4.	ate	<u>h</u>ate	9.	owl	<u>h</u>owl
5.	add	<u>h</u>ad	10.	old	<u>h</u>old

B. The second sentence of each pair has the sound /h/. Listen and repeat. Notice the change in meaning. Visual clues can help. Make a simple drawing in each blank box.

1a. art   It's my art.

b. <u>h</u>eart   It's my <u>h</u>eart.

2a. eat   Did you eat it?

b. <u>h</u>eat   Did you <u>h</u>eat it?

3a. air   It's in the air.

b. <u>h</u>air   It's in the <u>h</u>air.

4a. I   It was I.

b. <u>h</u>igh   It was <u>h</u>igh.

5a. arm   Did you arm the man?

b. <u>h</u>arm   Did you <u>h</u>arm the man?

6a. it   She was it.

b. <u>h</u>it   She was <u>h</u>it.

5. PRACTICE THE CONTRAST: /h/ AS IN "<u>H</u>OUSE" WITH /f/ AS IN "<u>F</u>OOD"

Some students may confuse /h/ as in "<u>h</u>ouse" with /f/ as in "<u>f</u>ood." When you say /f/, touch your upper front teeth with the inner part of your lower lip. When you say /h/, let air flow out of your throat through open lips.

A. Practice these contrasting sounds. Listen and repeat each word pair.

	/h/	/f/
1.	<u>h</u>all	<u>F</u>all
2.	<u>h</u>at	<u>f</u>at
3.	<u>h</u>ate	<u>f</u>ate
4.	<u>h</u>ear	<u>f</u>ear
5.	<u>h</u>eal	<u>f</u>eel

B. Now practice the contrasting sounds in sentence pairs. The first sentence of each pair has the sound /h/ and the second has the sound /f/. Listen and repeat. Visual clues can help. Make a simple drawing in each blank box.

1a. <u>h</u>all   It was in the <u>h</u>all.

b. <u>F</u>all   It was in the <u>F</u>all.

2a. <u>h</u>at   Take off the <u>h</u>at.

b. <u>f</u>at   Take off the <u>f</u>at.

3a. <u>h</u>ate   It could be <u>h</u>ate.

b. <u>f</u>ate   It could be <u>f</u>ate.

4a. h̲ear   We h̲ear it.

b. f̲ear   We f̲ear it.

5a. h̲eal   I can't h̲eal it.

b. f̲eel   I can't f̲eel it.

↻ 6. CHECK YOUR LISTENING

Work with a partner. Read a sentence from 4B or 5B to your partner. Can your partner define the sentence? He or she must be truthful.

Your partner will:
- Say: I know what _____ means.
  It means _____. (definition or paraphrase)
  or
- Act out what the word means.
  or
- Make a simple drawing.

Or your partner will ask: What does _____ mean? Then you must define the sentence, act it out, or make a drawing. You may do two or three sentences each.

☝ 7. NO SOUND FOR "h" AND "gh"

A. The letter "h" is not pronounced in the following words. Listen and repeat these words and sentences. *Capital letters indicate syllable stress.*

1. h̷our	An h̷our is Equal to 60 MINutes.
2. H̷ONor	When you H̷ONor SOMEone you show your reSPECT.
3. H̷ONest	If you're H̷ONest, you tell the truth.
4. h̷eir	An h̷eir is SOMEone who reCEIVES MONey or PROPerty from one who has died.
5. h̷erb	An h̷erb is a plant that's used to give food FLAvor. (This word may also be pronounced with /h/.)
6. RH̷YTHm	MUsic beats out a RH̷YTHm you can dance to.
7. exh̷iBITIon	An exh̷iBITIon shows things in PUBlic.
8. gh̷ost	A gh̷ost is the SPIRit of a dead PERson who suPPOSedly aPPEARS aGAIN.
9. Joh̷n	Joh̷n is the name of my friend.
10. TH̷OMas	TH̷OMas is the name of John's friend.
11. VEh̷icle	A car is reFERRED to as a VEh̷icle.

B. The letters "gh" are not pronounced in the following words. Listen and repeat these words and sentences.

1. NEIG̷H̷bor	My NEIG̷H̷bor lives next door to me.
2. DOUG̷H̷nut	Did he eat a DOUG̷H̷nut with his COFFee?
3. thoug̷h̷t	I thoug̷h̷t I saw him.
4. throug̷h̷	Did you go throug̷h̷ my drawer?
5. THORoug̷h̷	I made a THORoug̷h̷ search.
6. alTHOUG̷H̷	I'll go, alTHOUG̷H̷ I'm aFRAID.
7. caug̷h̷t	I caug̷h̷t a cold.
8. foug̷h̷t	They foug̷h̷t like cats and dogs.
9. taug̷h̷t	Were you taug̷h̷t to do that?
10. fig̷h̷t	They fig̷h̷t EVery day.
11. heig̷h̷t	His heig̷h̷t is six feet.
12. nig̷h̷t	The house is QUIet at nig̷h̷t.

🎧 8. STRESS AND INTONATION

Each of these sentences contains the sound /h/ as in <u>h</u>ouse. You will hear each sentence four times:

1. Listen for the sound /h/. (The letters for this sound are underlined.)
2. Listen for syllable stress and word stress. *Capital letters indicate syllable stress.* Mark the word stress that you hear. Put a stress mark (ʹ) over the stressed word or words.
3. Listen for rising or falling intonation at the end of the sentence. Mark intonation with the symbol "⌐↗" or "⌐↘."
4. Listen to the sentence again and repeat it. Pay attention to pauses and linking of words.

The first sentence is marked for you.

1. <u>Wh</u>ose old <u>h</u>át is that on the <u>h</u>oók?↗
2. Don't <u>H</u>ESitate to go to the <u>H</u>OSpital.
3. <u>H</u>ARRy wants a <u>h</u>ot dog, and I want a <u>h</u>am on rye.
4. <u>H</u>URRy up, my <u>H</u>USband is <u>H</u>UNgry and he wants a <u>H</u>AMburger.
5. Did you <u>h</u>ear <u>H</u>al say <u>h</u>eLLO to <u>H</u>ELen?
6. <u>H</u>ow aBOUT TAKing <u>h</u>alf of it <u>h</u>ome?
7. I <u>h</u>urt my <u>h</u>ead when I fell in the <u>h</u>all.
8. The <u>H</u>EAVy smog in the air is bad for my <u>H</u>AIRdo.
9. It's in<u>H</u>Uman to <u>h</u>old a re<u>H</u>EARSal in such <u>h</u>ot WEATHer.
10. He <u>h</u>ad a <u>H</u>ORRible <u>H</u>EADache AFter in<u>H</u>ALing the ALco<u>h</u>ol.

9. HOME ASSIGNMENT

A. Make up five sentences with the the sound /h/ as in "<u>h</u>ouse" in initial position and five with /h/ in medial position. Choose words from the lists below. Underline the word in each sentence. (*Remember:* the sound /h/ never occurs in final position in English.)

/h/ IN INITIAL
POSITION

<u>h</u>im	<u>HOL</u>iday
<u>h</u>old	<u>HIS</u>tory
<u>h</u>ot	<u>HOS</u>pital
<u>HURR</u>y	ho<u>TEL</u>

/h/ IN MEDIAL POSITION

be<u>HAVE</u>	in<u>HER</u>it
be<u>HIND</u>	re<u>HEAT</u>
re<u>HEARSE</u>	SWEET<u>h</u>eart
SOME<u>h</u>ow	in<u>H</u>Uman

B. Work with a partner.

Your partner may read your sentences aloud and explain the meaning.

UNIT 32   /w/ as in <u>walk</u>

1. PRODUCING /w/

Examples: <u>w</u>ant, <u>w</u>ord, <u>w</u>hite¹, a<u>WHILE</u>,¹ a<u>WAKE</u>,
s<u>w</u>eet, HIGH<u>w</u>ay, q<u>u</u>art², <u>o</u>ne³, <u>o</u>nce³

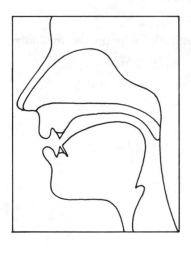

- This sound is always followed by a vowel sound. As you say /w/, your tongue and lips shape the vowel sound that follows.
- Raise the back of your tongue up toward the roof of your mouth (soft palate).
- Rest the tip of your tongue against your bottom teeth.
- First round your lips, then relax them, as you let air flow out through your lips.
- Your vocal cords should vibrate.

¹Some American speakers pronounce "wh" with an initial /h/ sound: "<u>wh</u>ite" /hwayt/, "a<u>wh</u>ile" /əhwayl/. In this text no distinction is made between voiceless /hw/ and voiced /w/ as in "<u>w</u>alk."
²See Unit 24, page 213, for words that begin with /kw/.
³/w/ is the first sound in "<u>o</u>ne" /wən/ and "<u>o</u>nce" /wəns/.

288

🔦 2. PRACTICE THE SOUND

A. Practice the sound /w/, first normally, then with exaggeration, then normally. Listen and repeat.

/w/   /w. . .iy/   /w/

B. Now practice the sound in words. Notice the phonetic spelling. Listen and repeat each word twice.

1. <u>w</u>ife   /wayf/   <u>w</u>ife
2. <u>w</u>ait   /weyt/   <u>w</u>ait
3. <u>w</u>eek   /wiyk/   <u>w</u>eek
4. <u>w</u>ell   /wɛl/   <u>w</u>ell
5. <u>wh</u>en   /wɛn/   <u>wh</u>en
6. a<u>W</u>AY   /əwey/   a<u>W</u>AY

🔦 3. CHECK YOUR LISTENING

Cover the list of words below. Listen and put a check mark under /w/ or /v/ for the sound that you hear.

	/w/	/v/
1. <u>v</u>erse	____	____
2. <u>wh</u>ile	____	____
3. <u>w</u>et	____	____
4. <u>v</u>est	____	____
5. <u>wh</u>eel	____	____
6. <u>w</u>ail	____	____
7. <u>v</u>eal	____	____
8. "V"	____	____

🎧 4. PRACTICE THE CONTRAST: /w/ AS IN "WALK" WITH /v/ AS IN "VOICE"

Some students may confuse /w/ as in "walk" with /v/ as in "voice." When you pronounce /v/, touch your upper teeth with the inner part of your lower lip. Do not touch your teeth with your lip when you say /w/.

A. Listen and repeat each word pair.

	/w/	/v/
1.	west	vest
2.	wine	vine
3.	worse	verse
4.	wail	veil
5.	we	"V"
6.	wet	vet
7.	wheel	veal
8.	while	vile

B. The first sentence of each pair has the sound /w/. The second sentence has the sound /v/. Listen and repeat. Notice the change in meaning. Visual clues can help. Make a simple drawing in each blank box.

1a. west   I like the west.

b. vest   I like the vest.

2a. <u>w</u>ine   It's a nice <u>w</u>ine.

 b. <u>v</u>ine   It's a nice <u>v</u>ine.

3a. <u>w</u>orse   Is it <u>w</u>orse?

 b. <u>v</u>erse   Is it <u>v</u>erse?

4a. <u>w</u>ail   It was a long <u>w</u>ail.

 b. <u>v</u>eil   It was a long <u>v</u>eil.

5a. <u>w</u>e   I said "<u>w</u>e."

 b. <u>V</u>   I said "V."

6a. <u>w</u>et   She said "<u>w</u>et."

 b. <u>v</u>et   She said "<u>v</u>et."

7a. <u>wh</u>eel   Take the <u>wh</u>eel.

b. <u>v</u>eal   Take the <u>v</u>eal.

8a. <u>wh</u>ile   Can it be "<u>wh</u>ile?"

b. <u>v</u>ile   Can it be "<u>v</u>ile?"

↻ 5. CHECK YOUR LISTENING

Work with a partner. Read a sentence from 4B to your partner. Can your partner define the sentence? He or she must be truthful.

Your partner will: • Say: I know what _____ means.
It means _____. (definition or paraphrase)
or
• Act out what the word means.
or
• Make a simple drawing.

Or your partner will ask: What does _____ mean? Then you must define the sentence, act it out, or make a drawing. You may do two or three sentences each.

💡 6. NO SOUND FOR "w"

A. The letter "w" is not pronounced in words that begin with "wr." Listen and repeat these words and sentences.

1. w̸rite   Will you w̸rite to me?
2. w̸rote   I w̸rote a long LETTer.
3. w̸rong   You're w̸rong, you DIDn't.
4. w̸rap   I'll w̸rap the PACKage.

5. ẉrist   I fell and hurt my ẉrist.
6. ẉreck   AFter the ACcident, the car was a ẉreck.
7. ẉreath   At CHRISTmas⁴ time we'll hang a ẉreath on the door.
8. WRINkle   Don't WRINkle the PAper.

B. The letter "w" is not pronounced in the following words that begin with "wh." (Not all words that begin with "wh" have a "w" that represents no sound.) Listen and repeat these words and sentences.

1. ẉho   The man ẉho saw us is here.
2. ẉhom   The man to ẉhom I spoke is here.
3. ẉhose   I don't know ẉhose it is.
4. ẉhole   Did you eat the ẉhole pie?
5. ẉhoEVer   I don't care, ẉhoEVer it is.

C. The letter "w" is also not pronounced in the following words. Listen and repeat.

1. tẉo   Did you buy tẉo of them?
2. toẉard   The car came toẉard us at a VERy high speed.
3. ANsẉer   Did you ANsẉer the QUEStion?
4. sẉord   FENCing is the art of FIGHTing with a sẉord.
5. KNOWLedge⁵   A LITTle KNOWLedge⁵ is a DANgerous thing.

🎧 7. STRESS AND INTONATION

Each of these sentences contains the sound /w/ as in "walk." You will hear each sentence four times:

1. Listen for the sound /w/. (The letters for this sound are underlined.)
2. Listen for syllable stress and word stress. *Capital letters indicate syllable stress.* Mark the word stress that you hear. Put a stress mark (ʹ) over the stressed word or words.
3. Listen for rising or falling intonation at the end of the sentence. Mark intonation with the symbol "⤴" or "⤵."
4. Listen to the sentence again and repeat it. Pay attention to pauses and linking of words.

The first sentence is marked for you.

---

⁴The "t" in "Christmas" is not pronounced.
⁵The "k" in "knowledge" is not pronounced.

1. I ALways eat SANDwiches for lunch.

2. There was a WARning SIGnal on the wet road.

3. Is that a wool SWEATer?

4. There were two world wars.

5. EVeryone who is ANyone was there.

6. "Where or When" is the name of a song.

7. The White House is in WASHington, D.C.

8. He takes the SUBway to work.

9. I don't know WHETHer I'll walk in this WEATHer.

10. The WAITer Opened the WINdow when it got warm.

8. HOME ASSIGNMENT

1. Read the following paragraph aloud. Use a dictionary to help you with any new words.
2. Underline all words that have the sound /w/ as in "walk."
3. Mark the paragraph for stress and intonation.
4. Read the paragraph aloud one more time.

My DAIly ROUtine

DURing the week I Usually wake up at a QUARter to SEVen. AFter I wash up I get dressed QUICKly. For BREAKfast, I have two SLICes of whole wheat toast and wash it down with COFFee. I leave for school at eight o'CLOCK. I Usually walk but when the WEATHer is bad, I take the SUBway. AFter school I go to work as a WAITress. When I come home from work I have just eNOUGH time to do my HOMEwork, write some LETTers, and watch TV. I go to sleep at twelve o'CLOCK. I also work on WEEKends.

<table>
<tr><td>UNIT
33</td><td># /m/ as in <u>me</u></td></tr>
</table>

1. PRODUCING /m/

Examples: <u>m</u>y, <u>m</u>ake, DA<u>M</u>age, FA<u>m</u>ous, SWI<u>MM</u>er, ai<u>m</u>, co<u>m</u>e, ha<u>m</u>

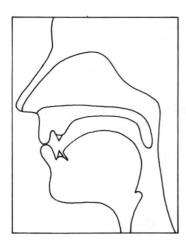

- Close your lips firmly. This stops the air from flowing out of your mouth.
- Produce the sound by letting air flow out through your nose. As you say the sound, you can feel your lips vibrate.
- Your vocal cords also vibrate.

🎧 2. PRACTICE THE SOUND

A. Practice the sound /m/, first normally, then with exaggeration, then normally. Listen and repeat.

/m/   /m. . . . ./   /m/

B. Now practice the sound in words. Notice the phonetic spelling. Listen and repeat each word twice.

1.	me	/miy/	me
2.	mad	/mæd/	mad
3.	CAMera	/kæmərə/	CAMera
4.	COMic	/kamɪk/	COMic
5.	time	/taym/	time
6.	home	/howm/	home

3. CHECK YOUR LISTENING

In the following pairs of words, one word ends with the sound /m/. You will hear one word from each pair. Circle the word that you hear.

1.	say	same	5.	blue	bloom
2.	see	seem	6.	nay	name
3.	gay	game	7.	"A"	aim
4.	cry	crime	8.	glue	gloom

4. PRACTICE THE CONTRAST: WORDS WITH FINAL /m/ AS IN "ME" AND WORDS WITHOUT FINAL /m/

Some students may leave out the sound /m/ when it occurs at the end of a word.

A. Listen and repeat each word pair.

	Without /m/	/m/		Without /m/	/m/
1.	rye	rhyme	6.	Ma	Mom
2.	due	doom	7.	tie	time
3.	dough	dome	8.	who	whom
4.	dye	dime	9.	tea	team
5.	day	dame	10.	row	roam

B. The second sentence of each pair has the final /m/ sound. Listen and repeat. Notice the change in meaning. Visual clues can help. Make a simple drawing in each blank box.

1a. rye   I like that rye.

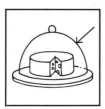

b. rhy<u>me</u>   I like that rhy<u>me</u>.

2a. due   It's his due.

b. doo<u>m</u>   It's his doo<u>m</u>.

3a. dough   It's a good dough.

b. do<u>me</u>   It's a good do<u>me</u>.

4a. dye   Did you see the dye?

b. di<u>me</u>   Did you see the di<u>me</u>?

5a. day   What a day!

b. da<u>me</u>   What a da<u>me</u>!

6a. Ma   Let's call Ma.

  b. Mo<u>m</u>   Let's call Mo<u>m</u>.

7a. tie   It's not the tie.

  b. ti<u>me</u>   It's not the ti<u>me</u>.

8a. who   Did you say "Who?"

  b. who<u>m</u>   Did you say "Who<u>m</u>?"

9a. tea   Look at the tea.

  b. tea<u>m</u>   Look at the tea<u>m</u>.

10a. row   Did you row there?

b. roa<u>m</u>   Did you roa<u>m</u> there?

↻ 5. CHECK YOUR LISTENING

Work with a partner. Read a sentence from 4B to your partner. Can your partner define the sentence? He or she must be truthful.

Your partner will: • Say: I know what _____ means.
                       It means _____. (definition or paraphrase)
                       or
                  • Act out what the word means.
                       or
                  • Make a simple drawing.

Or your partner will ask: What does _____ mean? Then you must define the sentence, act it out, or make a drawing. You may do two or three sentences each.

6. CONTRACTION "I'm"

The function word "am" is usually not stressed. In conversation, native speakers use the contraction "I'm." Listen and repeat the following pairs of sentences. The first sentence has the stressed form of "am." The second sentence has the contraction. Notice the change in meaning.

	Stressed Form	Contraction
1.	I am GOing to school.	I'm GOing to school.
2.	I am BUSy.	I'm BUSy.
3.	I am sure I did it.	I'm sure I did it.
4.	I am SORRy.	I'm SORRy.
5.	I am READing a book.	I'm READing a book.

7. STRESS AND INTONATION

Each of these sentences contains the sound /m/ as in "me." You will hear each sentence four times:

1. Listen for the sound /m/. (The letters for this sound are underlined.)
2. Listen for syllable stress and word stress. *Capital letters indicate syllable stress.* Mark the word stress that you hear. Put a stress mark (´) over the stressed word or words.
3. Listen for rising or falling intonation at the end of the sentence. Mark intonation with the symbol "⤴" or "⤵."
4. Listen to the sentence again and repeat it. Pay attention to pauses and linking of words.

The first sentence is marked for you.

1. My name is on the ALbum.
2. We went to MILTie's for a HAMburger.
3. I can hum the MELody.
4. Is it VERy warm DURing the SUMMer months?
5. Can you go SWIMMing in SepTEMber?
6. My arm ALmost hit the UMpire.
7. Don't put MUStard on my ham.

8. Must you make that noise?

9. Buy some ice cream for toMORRow.

10. When did she come home from the MARket?

8. HOME ASSIGNMENT

Read the "family tree" and the following sentences aloud. Then underline all words in the sentences that have the sound /m/. Mark the sentences for stress and intonation. Finally, read the sentences aloud one more time.

My FAMily Tree

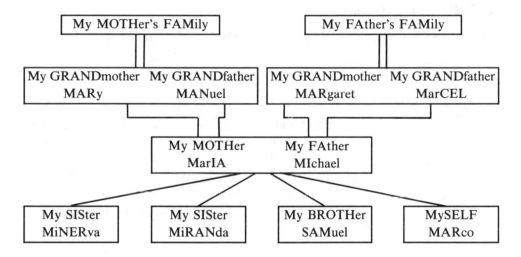

1. My GRANDmothers' names are MARy and MARgaret.

2. My GRANDfathers' names are MANuel and MarCEL.

3. My MOTHer's name is MarIA.

4. My FAther's name is MIchael.

5. My SISters' names are MiNERva and MiRANda.

6. My BROTHer's name is SAMuel.

7. My name is MARco.

UNIT
34

/n/ as in no

1. PRODUCING /n/

Examples: nice, nose, inVITE, aNNOUNCE, can, nine, man

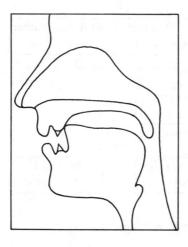

- Place the tip of your tongue on your upper gum ridge. This stops the air from flowing out of the mouth.
- Produce the sound by letting air flow out through your nose.
- Your vocal cords should vibrate.

2. PRACTICE THE SOUND

A. Practice the /n/ sound, first normally, then with exaggeration, then normally. Listen and repeat.

/n/   /n. . . . ./   /n/

B. Now practice the sound in words. Notice the phonetic spelling. Listen
and repeat each word twice.

1. <u>n</u>o	/now/	<u>n</u>o
2. <u>n</u>ot	/nat/	<u>n</u>ot
3. DIN<u>N</u>er	/dɪnər/	DIN<u>N</u>er
4. FUN<u>N</u>y	/fəniy/	FUN<u>N</u>y
5. brai<u>n</u>	/breyn/	brai<u>n</u>
6. lear<u>n</u>	/lərn/	lear<u>n</u>

3. CHECK YOUR LISTENING

A. In the following pairs of words, one word ends with the sound /n/. You
will hear one word from each pair. Circle the word that you hear.

1.	gay	gai<u>n</u>		5.	sue	soo<u>n</u>
2.	bee	bea<u>n</u>		6.	low	loa<u>n</u>
3.	lie	li<u>n</u>e		7.	sigh	sig<u>n</u>
4.	bow	bo<u>n</u>e		8.	pay	pai<u>n</u>

B. In the following pairs of words, one word has a final /n/. The other word
has a final /l/. You will hear one word from each pair. Circle the word
that you hear.

1.	di<u>n</u>e	DIa<u>l</u>		5.	sa<u>n</u>e	sa<u>l</u>e
2.	mai<u>n</u>	mai<u>l</u>		6.	see<u>n</u>	sea<u>l</u>
3.	mea<u>n</u>	mea<u>l</u>		7.	sto<u>n</u>e	sto<u>l</u>e
4.	mi<u>n</u>e	mi<u>l</u>e		8.	te<u>n</u>	te<u>ll</u>

C. In the following pairs of words, one word has a final /n/. The other has a final /m/. Circle the word that you hear.

1.	bun	bum	5.	ran	ram
2.	cone	comb¹	6.	sane	same
3.	dine	dime	7.	seen	seem
4.	gain	game	8.	warn	warm

🔔 4. PRACTICE THE CONTRAST: WORDS WITH FINAL /n/ AS IN "NO" AND WORDS WITHOUT FINAL /n/

Some students may leave out the sound /n/ when it occurs at the end of a word.

A. Listen and repeat each word pair.

1.	me	mean
2.	play	plane
3.	tray	train
4.	Joe	Joan
5.	ray	rain

B. The second sentence of each pair has the final /n/ sound. Listen and repeat. Notice the change in meaning. Visual clues can help. Make a simple drawing in each blank box.

1a. me   Is it me?

b. mean   Is it mean?

¹Note: the "b" in "comb" is silent.

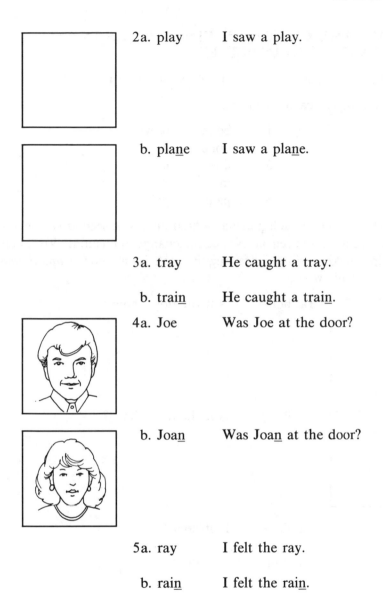

2a. play   I saw a play.

b. pla<u>ne</u>   I saw a pla<u>ne</u>.

3a. tray   He caught a tray.

b. trai<u>n</u>   He caught a trai<u>n</u>.

4a. Joe   Was Joe at the door?

b. Joa<u>n</u>   Was Joa<u>n</u> at the door?

5a. ray   I felt the ray.

b. rai<u>n</u>   I felt the rai<u>n</u>.

🔦 5. PRACTICE THE CONTRAST: FINAL /n/ AS IN "N̲O" WITH FINAL /l/ AS IN "L̲IKE"

Some students may confuse the final /n/ sound with the final /l/ sound.

A. Listen and repeat each word pair.

1.	bone	bowl
2.	done	dull
3.	fine	file
4.	in	ill
5.	pain	pail

B. The first sentence of each pair has a final /n/. The second sentence has a final /l/. Listen and repeat. Notice the change in meaning. Visual clues can help. Make a simple drawing in each blank box. *Capital letters indicate syllable stress.*

1a. bone   Is it the dog's bone?

b. bowl   Is it the dog's bowl?

2a. done   Is it done?

b. dull   Is it dull?

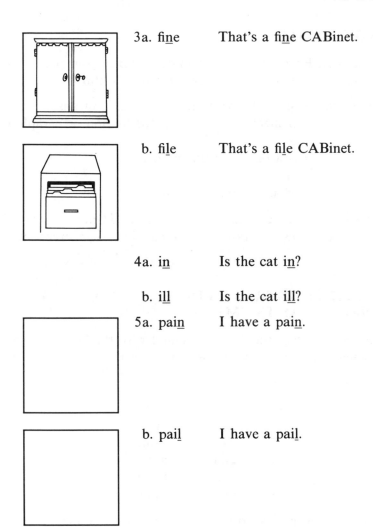

3a. fi<u>n</u>e   That's a fi<u>n</u>e CABinet.

b. fi<u>l</u>e   That's a fi<u>l</u>e CABinet.

4a. i<u>n</u>   Is the cat i<u>n</u>?

b. i<u>ll</u>   Is the cat i<u>ll</u>?

5a. pai<u>n</u>   I have a pai<u>n</u>.

b. pai<u>l</u>   I have a pai<u>l</u>.

↻ 6. CHECK YOUR LISTENING

Work with a partner. Read a sentence from 4B or 5B to your partner. Can your partner define the sentence? He or she must be truthful.

Your partner will say: • Say: I know what _____ means.
                             It means _____. (definition or paraphrase)
                             or
                           • Act out what the word means.
                             or
                           • Make a simple drawing.

Or your partner will ask: What does _____ mean? Then you must define the sentence, act it out, or make a drawing. You may do two or three sentences each.

♥ 7. PRACTICE THE CONTRAST: FINAL /n/ AS IN "<u>NO</u>" WITH FINAL /m/ AS IN "<u>ME</u>"

Some students may confuse the final /n/ sound with the final /m/ sound. When you pronounce /m/, press your lips firmly together.

A. Listen and repeat each word pair.

	/n/	/m/
1.	a<u>n</u>	a<u>m</u>
2.	ca<u>n</u>e	ca<u>m</u>e
3.	gu<u>n</u>	gu<u>m</u>
4.	pho<u>n</u>e	foa<u>m</u>
5.	pa<u>n</u>	Pa<u>m</u>

B. Each of these sentences has words with a final /m/ or a final /n/. Listen and repeat. *Capital letters indicate syllable stress.*

1. I'<u>m</u> EATing a<u>n</u> APPle.
2. She ca<u>m</u>e with her ca<u>n</u>e.
3. The gu<u>m</u> is o<u>n</u> the gu<u>n</u>.
4. Foa<u>m</u> is o<u>n</u> the pho<u>n</u>e.
5. Pa<u>m</u> fried eggs i<u>n</u> the pa<u>n</u>.

8. SYLLABIC /n̩/

A. When /n/ is in an unstressed syllable, following /t/ or /d/, no vowel sound is produced. This occurs even when a vowel letter appears between /t/ and /n/ or /d/ and /n/. For example,

RO<u>TT</u>en	/ratn̩/
SU<u>DD</u>en	/sədn̩/

This syllabic /n/ is similar to the syllabic /l/ (practiced in Unit 23). It is indicated by the symbol /n̩/.

B. Remember that /t/, /d/, /l/, and /n/ are all made with the tongue tip pressed against the upper gum ridge.

- To produce /t/ or /d/, press your tongue tip against the upper gum ridge. This action stops the flow of air
- Instead of releasing the tongue tip, keep it in place. Produce the /n̩/ sound by letting air escape through your nose.

C. Listen and repeat these words and sentences.

1.	EA<u>T</u>en	/iytn̩/	I have alREADy EA<u>T</u>en.
2.	WRI<u>TT</u>en	/rɪtn̩/	Have you WRI<u>TT</u>en to your friend?
3.	KI<u>TT</u>ens	/kɪtn̩z/	The cat had six KI<u>TT</u>ens.
4.	BI<u>TT</u>en	/bɪtn̩/	He was BI<u>TT</u>en by the mad dog.
5.	FA<u>TT</u>en	/fætn̩/	The FARmer will FA<u>TT</u>en up his TURkeys bcFORE SELLing them.
6.	GO<u>TT</u>en	/gatn̩/	If I knew, I would have GO<u>TT</u>en it for you.
7.	RO<u>TT</u>en	/ratn̩/	The fruit was RO<u>TT</u>en when we bought it.
8.	STRAIGH<u>T</u>en	/streytn̩/	Let's STRAIGH<u>T</u>en up the house beFORE my RELatives come.
9.	CO<u>TT</u>on	/katn̩/	I bought a CO<u>TT</u>on blouse, not a silk one.
10.	BU<u>TT</u>on	/bətn̩/	I lost the BU<u>TT</u>on from my coat.
11.	SU<u>DD</u>en	/sədn̩/	All of a SU<u>DD</u>en he ran out of the house.
12.	HI<u>DD</u>en	/hɪdn̩/	The toys were HI<u>DD</u>en in the CLOSet.
13.	GAR<u>d</u>en	/gardn̩/	She grows VEGetables in her GAR<u>d</u>en.

14. WI<u>D</u>en	/waydn̩/	The CITy wants to WI<u>D</u>en the street.
15. PAR<u>d</u>on	/pardn̩/	Be poLITE; say "PAR<u>d</u>on me."
16. DEA<u>D</u>en	/dɛdn̩/	Can you give me SOMEthing to DEA<u>D</u>en the pain?
17. DI<u>Dn't</u>[2]	/dɪdn̩t/	He DI<u>Dn't</u> want to see the play.
18. COUL<u>Dn't</u>[2]	/kʊdn̩t/	He COUL<u>Dn't</u> go Even if he WANTed to.
19. HA<u>Dn't</u>[2]	/hædn̩t/	We HA<u>Dn't</u> thought of it.
20. WOUL<u>Dn't</u>[2]	/wʊdn̩t/	Why WOUL<u>Dn't</u> he tell us the truth?

9. STRESS AND INTONATION

Each of these sentences contains the sound /n/ as in "<u>n</u>o." You will hear each sentence four times:

1. Listen for the sound /n/. (Letters for this sound are underlined.)
2. Listen for syllable stress and word stress. *Capital letters indicate syllable stress.* Mark the word stress that you hear. Put a stress mark (´) over the stressed word or words.
3. Listen for rising or falling intonation at the end of the sentence. Mark intonation with the symbol "⤴" or "⤵."
4. Listen to the sentence again and repeat it. Pay attention to pauses and linking of words.

The first sentence is marked for you.

1. <u>N</u>ew York Sta̍te is i<u>n</u> the <u>n</u>orthEAStern part of the U<u>N</u>ITed Sta̍tes.⤵

2. The popuLAtio<u>n</u> of <u>N</u>ew York State is Over seve<u>n</u>TEE<u>N</u> MILLio<u>n</u> PEOple.

3. The popuLAtio<u>n</u> of <u>N</u>ew York CITy is Over SEVe<u>n</u> MILLio<u>n</u>.

4. The CAPital of <u>N</u>ew York State is called ALba<u>n</u>y.

5. <u>N</u>ew York CITy is the LARGest CITy i<u>n</u> <u>N</u>ew York State.

[2]Be sure to make the /d/ sound. Follow it with /n̩/. Then drop your tongue tip to complete the /t/ sound.

6. There are five BORoughs i<u>n</u> <u>N</u>ew York CITy: The Bronx, BROOKly<u>n</u>, Ma<u>n</u>HATTa<u>n</u>, Quee<u>ns</u>, a<u>nd</u> RICHmo<u>nd</u> (or STATe<u>n</u> ISla<u>nd</u>).

7. <u>N</u>ew York CITy has two AIRports, Joh<u>n</u> F. KEN<u>N</u>edy a<u>nd</u> La GUARdia; both are i<u>n</u> Quee<u>ns</u>.

8. Gra<u>nd</u> CE<u>N</u>tral a<u>nd</u> Pe<u>nn</u>sylVA<u>N</u>ia are the two mai<u>n</u> trai<u>n</u> STAtio<u>ns</u> i<u>n</u> Ma<u>n</u>HATTa<u>n</u>.

9. PASSe<u>n</u>ger ships leave from the piers aLONG the HUDso<u>n</u> RIVer.

10. The <u>N</u>ew York PUBlic LIbrary is at Fifth AVe<u>n</u>ue and FORty-SECo<u>nd</u> Street.

🐎 10. HOME ASSIGNMENT

A. Write a paragraph about an experience you have had during the past week. Use as many words with the letter "n" as in "<u>n</u>o" as you can. Try to make your story amusing.

B. Bring your work to class. Ask a partner to read your paragraph aloud. Have fun with it. Be dramatic.

UNIT 35

/ŋ/ as in "king"

1. PRODUCING /ŋ/

Examples: A<u>N</u>ger, SI<u>N</u>gle, i<u>n</u>k, BA<u>N</u>Ker, SI<u>NG</u>ing, si<u>ng</u>, ri<u>ng</u>

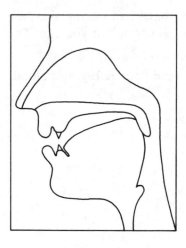

- Note that, in English, this sound does not occur at the beginning of words.
- Place the tip of your tongue against your lower gum ridge.
- Raise the back of your tongue so that it presses against the roof of your mouth (soft palate). This stops the air from flowing out of the mouth.
- Produce the sound by letting air flow out through your nose.
- Your vocal cords should vibrate.

2. PRACTICE THE SOUND

A. Practice the sound /ŋ/, first normally, then with exaggeration, then normally. Listen and repeat.

/ŋ/   /ŋ. . . . ./   /ŋ/

312

B. Now practice the sound in words. Notice the phonetic spelling. Listen and repeat each word twice.

1.	i<u>n</u>k	/ɪŋk/	i<u>n</u>k
2.	tha<u>n</u>k	/θæŋk/	tha<u>n</u>k
3.	SI<u>N</u>gle	/sɪŋgl̩/	SI<u>N</u>gle
4.	SI<u>N</u>Ger	/sɪŋər/	SI<u>N</u>Ger
5.	si<u>ng</u>	/sɪŋ/	si<u>ng</u>
6.	ki<u>ng</u>	/kɪŋ/	ki<u>ng</u>

🔋 3. CHECK YOUR LISTENING

A. In the following pairs of words, one word has the sound /m/ and the other word has the sound /ŋ/. You will hear one word from each pair. Circle the word that you hear.

1.	ha<u>m</u>	ha<u>ng</u>	6.	swi<u>m</u>	swi<u>ng</u>
2.	ra<u>m</u>	ra<u>ng</u>	7.	Sa<u>m</u>	sa<u>ng</u>
3.	ru<u>m</u>	ru<u>ng</u>	8.	sli<u>m</u>	sli<u>ng</u>
4.	ri<u>m</u>	ri<u>ng</u>	9.	cla<u>m</u>	cla<u>ng</u>
5.	hu<u>m</u>	hu<u>ng</u>	10.	bo<u>m</u>bed	bo<u>ng</u>ed

B. In the following pairs of words, one word has a final /n/ and the other word has a final /ŋ/. You will hear one word from each pair. Circle the word that you hear.

1.	si<u>n</u>	si<u>ng</u>	6.	thi<u>n</u>	thi<u>ng</u>
2.	ta<u>n</u>	ta<u>ng</u>	7.	ba<u>n</u>	ba<u>ng</u>
3.	wi<u>n</u>	wi<u>ng</u>	8.	law<u>n</u>	lo<u>ng</u>
4.	ra<u>n</u>	ra<u>ng</u>	9.	go<u>ne</u>	go<u>ng</u>
5.	su<u>n</u>	su<u>ng</u>	10.	to<u>n</u>	to<u>ngue</u>

C. In the following pairs of words, one word ends in the sounds /ŋk/ and the other word ends in the sound /ŋ/. You will hear one word from each pair. Circle the word that you hear.

1.	clink	cling	6.	sunk	sung
2.	think	thing	7.	brink	bring
3.	bank	bang	8.	rink	ring
4.	sink	sing	9.	wink	wing
5.	rank	rang	10.	zinc	zing

4. PRACTICE THE CONTRAST: /n/ AS IN "NO," /ŋk/ AS IN "BANK," AND /ŋ/ AS IN "KING"

Some students may confuse the sounds /n/, /ŋk/, and /ŋ/ when they occur in the final position.

A. Listen and repeat each group of words.

	/n/	/ŋk/	/ŋ/
1.	ban	bank	bang
2.	sin	sink	sing
3.	Min	mink	Ming
4.	tan	tank	tang
5.	win	wink	wing
6.	ran	rank	rang

B. The first sentence of each group has a final /n/ sound. The second sentence has a final /ŋk/, and the third has a final /ŋ/. Listen and repeat. Notice the change in meaning. Visual clues can help. Make a simple drawing in each blank box.

   1a. ba<u>n</u>   I heard aBOUT the ba<u>n</u>.

   b. ba<u>nk</u>   I heard aBOUT the ba<u>nk</u>.

   c. ba<u>ng</u>   I heard aBOUT the ba<u>ng</u>.

2a. Mi<u>n</u>   I thought it was Mi<u>n</u>.

b. mi<u>nk</u>   I thought it was mi<u>nk</u>.

c. Mi<u>ng</u>   I thought it was Mi<u>ng</u>.

3a. ta<u>n</u>   I like that ta<u>n</u>.

b. ta<u>nk</u>   I like that ta<u>nk</u>.

c. ta<u>ng</u>   I like that ta<u>ng</u>.

4a. wi<u>n</u>   It's a wi<u>n</u>!

b. wi<u>nk</u>   It's a wi<u>nk</u>!

c. wi<u>ng</u>   It's a wi<u>ng</u>!

5a. ra<u>n</u>   Is it "ra<u>n</u>"?

  b. ra<u>nk</u>   Is it "ra<u>nk</u>"?

  c. ra<u>ng</u>   Is it "ra<u>ng</u>"?

5. CHECK YOUR LISTENING

Work with a partner. Read a sentence from 4B to your partner. Can your partner define the sentence? He or she must be truthful.

Your partner will say: • Say: I know what _____ means.
It means _____. (definition or paraphrase)
or
• Act out what the word means.
or
• Make a simple drawing.

Or your partner will ask: What does _____ mean? Then you must define the sentence, act it out, or make a drawing. You may do two or three sentences each.

6. STRESS AND INTONATION

Each of these sentences contains the sound /ŋ/ as in "ki<u>ng</u>." You will hear each sentence four times:

1. Listen for the sound /ŋ/. (The letters for this sound are underlined.)
2. Listen for syllable stress and word stress. *Capital letters indicate syllable stress.* Mark the word stress that you hear. Put a stress mark (´) over the stressed word or words.
3. Listen for rising or falling intonation at the end of the sentence. Mark intonation with the symbol "↗" or "↘."
4. Listen to the sentence again and repeat it. Pay attention to pauses and linking of words.

The first sentence is marked for you.

1. She was WÁLKi<u>ng</u> home, SÍNGi<u>ng</u> a sóng.↘

2. We were TALKi<u>ng</u> aBOUT FALLi<u>ng</u> in love.

3. Are you GOi<u>ng</u> RIDi<u>ng</u> or JOGGi<u>ng</u>?

4. The girls were JUMping rope, and the boys were PLAYing ball.

5. Are you COMing up or STAYing down?

6. Are you WRAPPing gifts and ANswering the phone at the same time?

7. "LAUGHing on the OUTside, CRYing on the INside" is a line from a song.

8. COOKing and CLEANing are two things she hates to do.

9. My NEIGHbor is MOVing to WASHington, but I'm MOVing to Long ISland.

10. I'm FINDing new words and LOOKing them up in the DICtionary.

7. NG RULES

There may be some confusion about the sounds the letters "ng" represent. The following rules may help to make it clear. Listen and repeat.

Rule No. 1

When a word ends in the spelling "ng" or "ngue," the sound represented is always *one* sound, /ŋ/ as in "king."

Examples:
a. strong /strɔŋ/ b. sing /sɪŋ/
c. bring /brɪŋ/ d. tongue /təŋ/

Rule No. 2

When a suffix (for example, -s, -er, -ly, -ed, -ing, -ster, -ish) is added to a word ending in the sound /ŋ/ as in "king," the letters ng are pronounced /ŋ/, with a few exceptions.

Examples:
a. sings /sɪŋs/ b. SINGing /sɪŋɪŋ/
c. SINGer /sɪŋər/ d. YOUNGster /yəŋstər/
e. KINGly /kɪŋliy/ f. YOUNGish /yəŋɪʃ/
g. banged /bæŋd/

Exceptions to this rule: In comparative and superlative forms of the following adjectives, "ng" represents *two* sounds, /ŋ/ + /g/, /ŋg/.

		COMPARATIVE		SUPERLATIVE	
long	/lɔŋ/	LONGer	/lɔŋgər/	LONGest	/lɔŋgɪst/
young	/yəŋ/	YOUNGer	/yəŋgər/	YOUNGest	/yəŋgɪst/
strong	/strɔŋ/	STRONGer	/strɔŋgər/	STRONGest	/strɔŋgɪst/

Rule No. 3

When the spelling "ng" occurs in the middle of the stem or root of a word, it is represented by the <u>two</u> sounds, /ŋg/, with a few exceptions.

Examples:

FINGer	/fɪŋgər/	SINGle	/sɪŋgl/
MINGle	/mɪŋgl/	ANger	/æŋgər/

Exceptions to this rule:

Proper Names:	WASHington	/waʃɪŋtən/
	FARMingdale	/farmɪŋdeyl/
	SPRINGfield	/sprɪŋfiyld/
Words:	GINGham[1]	/gɪŋəm/
	strength	/strɛŋkθ/ or /strɛŋθ/ (alternate pronunciations)
	length	/lɛŋkθ/ or /lɛŋθ/ (alternate pronunciations)

Rule No. 4

When "n" is immediately followed by "c," "x," or "k," it is usually pronounced /ŋk/, *two* sounds.

Examples:	ANchor	/æŋkər/
	ANXious	/æŋkʃəs/
	link	/lɪŋk/

---

[1]Gingham is a cotton material that has a pattern of squares.

Rule No. 5

The spelling "nge" in final position usually represents two sounds /n/ + /dʒ/, /ndʒ/.

Examples: strange   /streyndʒ/   aRRA**NGE**   /əreyndʒ/
change   /tʃeyndʒ/

🏃 8. HOME ASSIGNMENT

A. In the following words, the underlined letters represent the sounds /ŋ/, /ŋk/, /ŋg/, /m/, or /n/. Say the word aloud, then write the correct phonetic symbol or symbols in the blank. Refer to the rules in 7.

Example: a. ri**ng**   /ŋ/   d. ti**m**e   /m/
b. su**n**   /n/   e. A**N**kle   /ŋk/
c. A**N**gry /ŋg/   f. spo**nge** /ndʒ/

1. JU**N**gle   ____   9. ra**nge**   ____

2. SI**NG**er   ____   10. you**ng**   ____

3. I**N**sti**n**ct   ____   11. E**N**gland ____

4. ALbu**m**   ____   12. HA**MM**er ____

5. DURi**ng**   ____   13. zi**nc**   ____

6. LI**N**coln ____   14. law**n**   ____

7. SAVi**ng**   ____   15. WEDDi**ng** ____

8. LO**NG**er   ____

B. 1. Make up a short sentence with each of the above words and underline the word. Practice saying the sentences aloud.

      Example: We found the <u>ring</u> on the shelf.
                    I like to watch the <u>sun</u> rise.
                    Are you <u>angry</u> with me?
                    What <u>time</u> is it, please?
                    I twisted my <u>ankle</u> when I fell.
                    Use a <u>sponge</u> to clean the car.

2. Work with a partner. Your partner may read your sentences. Are the sounds clear?